D1564771

Spanish, Catalan, and Galician Literary Authors of the Twentieth Century:

an annotated guide to bibliographies

by
DAVID S. ZUBATSKY

The Scarecrow Press, Inc.
Metuchen, N.J., & London
1992

Portions of this bibliography first appeared as "An Annotated Bibliography of Twentieth-Century Catalan and Spanish Author Bibliographies," *Hispania*, 61 (1978), 654–79.

British Library Cataloguing-in-Publication data available

Library of Congress Cataloging-in-Publication Data

Zubatsky, David S., 1939–
Spanish, Catalan, and Galician literary authors of the twentieth century : an annotated guide to bibliographies / by David S. Zubatsky.
p. cm.
Includes bibliographical references.
ISBN 0-8108-2518-X (alk. paper)
1. Bibliography—Bibliography—Catalan literature. 2. Bibliography—Bibliography—Gallegan literature. 3. Bibliography—Bibliography—Spanish literature. 4. Catalan literature—20th century—Bibliography. 5. Gallegan literature—20th century—Bibliography. 6. Spanish literature—20th century—Bibliography. 7. Authors, Catalan—20th Century—Bibliography. 8. Authors, Gallegan—20th century—Bibliography. 9. Authors, Spanish—20th century—Bibliography. I. Title.
Z2691.A1Z83 1992
[PC3911]
016.016849'509—dc20 92-4041

Manufactured in the United States of America

Printed on acid-free paper

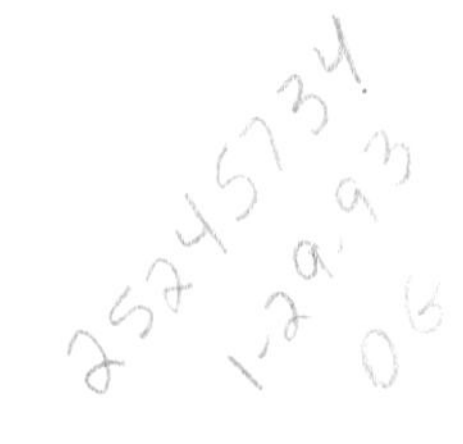

CONTENTS

PREFACE

The purpose of this compilation is to present, through an author arrangement, an annotated bibliography of personal bibliographies of twentieth-century Catalan, Galician, and Spanish writers of novels, drama, poetry, and short stories, as well as essayists, journalists, linguists, and literary critics. Personal bibliographies are defined as bibliographies of a writer's works and/or those written about the writer and the writer's works.

This guide includes citations that appear in periodicals, dissertations, and *festschrift* volumes. Because of the limited distribution in the United States of the works by and about the authors in short-lived magazines, pamphlets, *festschrift* volumes, or anthologies, the compiler has been inclusive rather than exclusive in the choice of bibliographies to be included. In most instances, the annotations will indicate the difference to the user by noting the bibliography's contents, coverage, number of entries, and any other pertinent information.

As noted above, the arrangement of the bibliography is alphabetical by author. Whenever an author is better known by a pseudonym, he or she is so listed with appropriate cross-references provided. A listing of the general bibliographies and biobibliographies that should be consulted further by researchers appears after the author section.

I wish to thank the staff, especially Mrs. Catherine Foutz, of the Interlibrary Loan Section of Millersville University of Pennsylvania's Ganser Library for providing most valuable assistance in my research.

David S. Zubatsky
Millersville University
Millersville, PA

ABBREVIATIONS FOR BIBLIOGRAPHIES INDEXED

Alarcón	Alarcón, Norma and Kossna, Sylvia. *Bibliography of Hispanic Writers (From the "MLA International Bibliography," 1922--1978).* Bloomington, Ind.: Chicano-Riqueño Studies, 1980. 86p.
Alonso	Alonso, Santos. *Literatura leonesa actual: Estudio y antología de 17 escritores.* Valladolid: Junta de Castilla y León, Consejería de Educación y Cultura, 1986. 390p. (Colección de Estudios de Lengua y Literatura, 4).
CILH	*Cuadernos de Investigación de la Literatura Hispánica* (Madrid), No. 7 (1986).
Correa	Correa, Gustavo. *Antología de la poesía española (1900–1980).* Madrid: Editorial Gredos, 1980. 2vs. (Biblioteca Románica Hispánica, VI. Antología Hispánica, 35).
Galerstein	Galerstein, Carolyn L., ed. *Women Writers of Spain: An Annotated Bio-Bibliographical Guide. Non-Castilian Materials Edited by Kathleen McNerney.* Westport, Conn.: Greenwood Press, 1986. 389p. (Bibliographies and Indexes in Women Studies, No. 2).
González Muela	González Muela, Joaquín, and Rozas, Juan Manuel. *La generación poética de 1927.* 3rd ed. Madrid: Istmo, P. L., 1987. 373p.

Mantero	Mantero, Manuel. *Poetas españoles de posguerra.* Madrid: Espasa-Calpe, 1986. 580p.
O'Connor	O'Connor, Patrica W. *Dramaturgas españolas de hoy (una introducción).* Madrid: Fundamentos, 1988. 176p.
Pariente	Pariente, Angel, ed. *Antología de la poesía surrealista en lengua española.* Madrid: Júcar, 1985. 1985. 466p. (Los Poetas, 64/65).
Pérez-Stansfield	Pérez-Stansfield, María Pilar. *Direcciones del teatro español de posguerra: Ruptura con el teatro burgués y radicalismo contestatario.* Madrid: José Porrúa Turanzas, 1983. 367p.
Resnick	Resnick, Margery, and Courtiuron, Isabelle de. *Women Writers in Translation: An Annotated Bibliography, 1945–1982.* New York: Garland, 1984. 272p.

THE GUIDE

ABELLO I SOLER, MONTSERRAT (1918–)
Galerstein, pp. 3–4.

AGUIRRE, FRANCISCA (1930–)
Galerstein, pp. 7–8.

ALARCOS LLORACH, EMILIO (1922–)
Torres, José Carlos de. "Nuestros filólogos: El Prof. E. Alarcos Llorach," *Boletín de Filología Española*, Nos. 42/45 (enero/diciembre de 1972), 3–12. "Bibliografía," pp. 5–12. Contents: I. Libros. II. Artículos. III. Traducción. IV. Prólogos. V. Conferencias. VI. Reseñas (Selected).

ALBALA, ALFONSO (1924–1973)
Albalá Hernández, Paloma. *Bibliografía de Alfonso Albalá*. Madrid: Universidad Complutense, 1982. 22p. (Trabajos del Departamento de Bibliografía, Serie A: Escritores Contemporáneos, 5). Contents: I. Obra inédita. II. Ediciones, poemas sueltos, obra crítica (por orden cronológico, 1943–1980; includes reviews). III. Secciones fijas en la prensa diaria (por orden cronológico, 1957–1970). IV. Entrevistas (por orden cronológico, 1966–1972). V. Obra sobre Alfonso Albalá (por orden cronológico, 1966–1981).

ALBANELL, PEP. *See* SENNELL, JOLES.

ALBERCA LORENTE, LUISA (1920–)
Galerstein, pp. 8–12.

ALBERT I PARADIS, CATERINA (1873–1966)
Galerstein, pp. 13–15.

ALBERTI, RAFAEL (1902–)

Alberti, Rafael. *Obras completas: Poesía.* Edición, introducción, bibliografía y notas de Luis García Montero. Madrid: Aguilar, 1988. 3 vs. "Bibliografía de la obra poética," v. 1, pp. clxv-clxxi. Contents: I. Primeras ediciones. II. Antologías y ediciones de poesías completas. "Bibliografía sobre la obra de Rafael Alberti (selective)," pp. clxxii–clxxvi.

______. *Poesías completas de Rafael Alberti.* Buenos Aires: Losada, 1961. 1190p. "Bibliografía de Rafael Alberti," pp. 1111–1127. Partially annotated entries are chronologically arranged under the following headings: I. Poesía (1924–1960). II. Ediciones privada (1941–1959). III. Prosa (1933–1959). IV. Teatro (1930–1959). V. Antologías, selecciones, prólogos (1937–1959). VI. Adaptaciones teatrales (1937–1944). VII. Traducciones (1932–1959). VIII. Obra de Rafael Alberti (traducida). IX. Discografía. X. Música con letra de Rafael Alberti. XI. Exposiciones de pinturas y dibujos.

______. *Sobre los ángeles. Yo era un tonto y lo que he visto me ha hecho dos tontos.* Madrid: Cátedra, 1981. 207p. "Algunos estudios sobre *Sobre los ángeles* y algunos estudios sobre *Yo era un tonto* y *Lo que he visto me ha hecho dos tontos*," pp. 57–58.

Correa, v. 1, pp. 298–99, 541–43. Works by and about the author.

Diego, Fernando de. *El teatro de Alberti.* Madrid: Fundamentos, 1988. 237p. "Bibliografía," pp. 221–32. Contents: I. Obra dramática de Rafael Alberti (orden cronológico de escritura). II. Estudios sobre el teatro de Rafael Alberti. III. Artículos de periódicos y revistas de los estrenos de las obras de Rafael Alberti.

García Montero, Luis. "Introducción a la bibliografía fundamental de la poesía de Rafael Alberti," *El Libro Español*, No. 305 (noviembre de 1983), 54–58. Contents: I. Indices bibliográficos. II. Ediciones (arranged chronologically). III. Antologías. Ediciones de poesías completas.

______. "Introducción bibliográfica al teatro y a la prosa de Rafael Alberti," *El Libro Español*, No. 307 (enero de 1984), 51–56. Entries are arranged chronologically.

González Martín, Jerónimo. *Rafael Alberti: Estudio.* Madrid: Ediciones Júcar, 1978. 259p. "Bibliografía selecta," pp. 236–57. Contents: I. Primeras fuentes. A. Libros en verso. B. Prosa. C. Teatro. D. Traducciones. E. Artículos, prefacios, antologías. II. Fuentes secundarias. A. Bibliografía y biografía. B. Estudios críticos. 1. Libros. 2. Artículos (by language). 3. Tesis doctorales. 4. Traducciones de la obra de Alberti.

González Muela, pp. 49–53. Works by and about Alberti arranged chronologically.

"Homenaje a Rafael Alberti," *Galeradas: Boletín de Información Bibliográfica*, No. 10 (marzo de 1977), 2–11 and No. 11 (abril de 1977), 2–11. Contents: I. Poesía. II. Teatro. III. Prosa y ediciones privadas. IV. Estudios críticos. V. Testimonios, semblanzas, biografías. VI. Estudios bibliográficos.

Jiménez-Fajardo, Salvador. *Multiple Spaces: The Poetry of Rafael Alberti*. London: Támesis, 1985. 166p. (Colección Támesis, Serie A-Monografías, 106). "Selected Bibliography," pp. 163–66. Contents: I. Primary Sources. A. Poetry (By year, 1925–1978). B. Prose (By year, 1947–1976). C. Drama (By year, 1931–1964). II. Selected Secondary Sources (few sources published after 1979).

Lobrera Gil, Jesús. "Breve apunte biográfico sobre Rafael Alberti," *Arbor*, No. 461/464 (1984), 107–13. Includes a chronology, a list of first editions of Alberti, and an "estudios sobre Rafael Alberti" section.

Marrast, Robert. "Essai de bibliographie de Rafael Alberti," *Bulletin Hispanique*, tome 57, Nos. 1/2 (1955), 147–77. 379 items. Contents: I. Oeuvres. A. Poésie. B. Théâtre. C. Prose (autobiographie, conférences, comptes-rendus, articles divers). D. Adaptations d'oeuvres espagnoles. E. Traductions d'oeuvres étrangères. F. Éditions d'oeuvres, préfaces, éditions d'anthologies. G. Oeuvres traductes, Traductions inédites. H. Oeuvres publiées dans les anthologies espagnoles ou étrangères. II. Directions de revues.

______. ______: Addenda et corrigenda," *Bulletin Hispanique*, tome 59, No. 4 (octubre/decembre 1957), 429–35.

Nantell, Judith. *Rafael Alberti's Poetry of the Thirties: The Poet's Public Voice*. Athens: The University of Georgia Press, 1986. 243p. "Selected Bibliography," pp. 225–34. Includes works by and about Alberti arranged alphabetically.

Salinas de Marichal, Solita. *El mundo poético de Rafael Alberti*. Madrid: Gredos, 1968. 269p. "Textos de Alberti y sobre Alberti," pp. 261–69.

Torres Nebrera, Gregorio. *El teatro de Rafael Alberti*. Madrid: Sociedad General Español de Librería, S.A., 1982. 373p. "Ediciones de las obras teatrales de Rafael Alberti (se sigue el orden en el que se han analizado en este estudio), pp. 369–71. "Estudios sobre el teatro de Rafael Alberti," pp. 371–73.

ALBO, NURIA (1930–)

Galerstein, pp. 15–16.

ALBORNOZ, AURORA DE (1926–)
Galerstein, pp. 16–17.

ALDECOA, IGNACIO (1925–1969)
Aldecoa, Ignacio. Cuentos. Edición de Josefina Rodríguez de Aldecoa. Octava edición. Madrid: Cátedra, 1982. 252p. "Bibliografía," pp. 51–53. Contents: I. Poesía. II. Novela. III. Relatos. IV. Viajes. V. Traducciones. VI. Bibliografía sobre Ignacio Aldecoa.
Andrés-Suárez, Irene. *Los cuentos de Ignacio Aldecoa: Consideraciones teóricas en torno al cuento literario*. Madrid: Editorial Gredos, 1986. 267p. "Bibliografía," pp. 247–60. Contents: I. Obras de Ignacio Aldecoa. A. Poesía. B. Novela. C. Relatos. 1. Libros. 2. Indice cronológico de los relatos. C. Cuentos publicados por primera vez como parte de un libro. 1. Cuentos póstumos. 2. Indice de los relatos que componen los libros. D. Relatos de viajes. E. Ensayos. F. Textos inéditos. II. Sobre la obra de Ignacio Aldecoa. A. Monografías. B. Artículos. C. Obras generales. D. Reseñas y entrevistas.
Aproximación crítica a Ignacio Aldecoa. Compilación e introducción por Drosoula Lytra. Madrid: Espasa-Calpe, 1984. 233p. "Bibliografía selecta," pp. 221–33. Contents: I. Obras de Ignacio Aldecoa. A. Poesía. B. Novela. C. Relato. D. Otros textos. II. Sobre Ignacaio Aldecoa. A. Libros. B. Artículos y otros escritos.
Goicoechea Tabar, María Jesús. "Bibliografía crítica de Ignacio Aldecoa," *Boletín de la Institución "Sancho El Sabio,"* año 17, tomo 17 (1973), 333–47. Contents: I. Obra escrita por Ignacio Aldecoa. A. Poesía. B. Novela. C. Relatos. D. Cuentos en antologías. E. Viajes. F. Ensayo. G. Guiones cinematográficos. H. Traducciones. II. Crítica de Ignacio Aldecoa. A. Entrevista. B. Estudios, notas, reseñas. C. Obras generales.
Ignacio Aldecoa: A Collection of Critical Essays. Laramie: University of Wyoming, Department of Modern and Classical Languages, 1977. 142p. "Selección bibliográfica," pp. 133–42. Contents: I. Obras de Ignacio Aldecoa. I. Estudios sobre Ignacio Aldecoa y su obra.
Lasagabáster Madinabeitia, Jesús María. *La novela de Ignacio Aldecoa: De la Mímesis al símbolo*. Madrid: Sociedad General Española de Librería, 1978. 452p. "Bibliografía," pp. 447–52. Contents: I. Obras de Ignacio Aldecoa. A. Poesía. B. Novela. C. Relato. D. Otros textos. II. Sobre la obra de Ignacio Aldecoa. A. Monografías. B. Obras generales. C. Artículos. D. Entrevistas, reseñas, notas (includes only reviews of the novels).
Lytra, Drosoula. *Soledad y convivencia en la obra de Aldecoa*. Madrid: Fundación Universitaria Española, 1979. 183p. "Obras

de Aldecoa," pp. 167–68. "Bibliografía selecta" (includes works about Aldecoa), pp. 169–83. Incomplete bibliographic information for some of the citations.

Martín Negales, José Luis. *Los cuentos de Ignacio Aldecoa.* Madrid: Ediciones Cátedra, 1984. 287p. "Bibliografía," pp. 279–84. Contents: I. Obras de Ignacio Aldecoa. A. Poesía. B. Novela. C. Relatos. D. Otros textos. II. Estudios sobre Ignacio Aldecoa. A. Monografías. B. Artículos, entrevistas, reseñas.

Martínez Domene, Pedro G. "Bibliografía de Ignacio Aldecoa," *Letras de Duesto* (Bilboa), 12 (1982), 191–207. Contents: I. Bibliografía de Ignacio Aldecoa. A. Poesía (By year, 1947–49). B. Novela (By year, 1954–1973). C. Relatos y cuentos (By year, 1955–1977). D. Viajes (By year, 1961–62). E. Textos inéditos. F. Ensayos, cuentos, críticas y artículos no recogidos en libro (By year, 1944–1969). G. Traducciones (By year, 1963–69). H. Antologías (By year, 1958–1974). II. Bibliografía sobre la obra y persona de Ignacio Aldecoa. A. Obras generales y manuales. B. Monografías. C. Artículos, entrevistas, reseñas. 368 items. Many entries are from newspapers.

ALEGRE CUDOS, JOSE LUIS (1951–)

CILH, p. 237.

ALEIXANDRE, VICENTE (1898–1984)

Aleixandre, Vicente. *Antología poética.* Madrid: Alianza Editorial, 1977. 190p. "Referencias bibliográficas de los volúmenes a los cuales pertenecen los poemas," pp. 175–79. A very complete description of all books of poetry published by Aleixandre. All editions are included.

______. *Historia del corazón.* Prólogo de José Luis Cano. Madrid: Espasa-Calpe, 1983. 143p. (Selecciones Austral, 110). "Bibliografía de Vicente Aleixandre (primeras ediciones)," pp. 31–32. Contents: I. Poesía (1928–1974). II. Prosa (1950–1958). III. Antologías y obras completas (1956–1977).

______. *Nuevos poemas varios.* Recopilación de Alejandro Duque Amusco. Edición de Irma Emiliozzi y Alejandro Duque Amusco. Esplugues de Llobregat: Plaza & Janés, 1987. 153p. "Tabla de procedencias (apéndice de la recopilación)," pp. 141–154. Index to the poems included in the compilation. Includes bibliographical information.

______. *Pasión de la tierra.* Edición de Gabriele Morelli. Madrid: Cátedra, 1987. 198p. "Bibliografía crítica de *Pasión de la tierra,*" pp. 89–90. "Tabla sinóptica de las ediciones de *Pasión de la tierra,*" pp. 81–84.

"Bibliografía sobre Vincente Aleixandre," *Papeles de Son Armadans*, Año 3, tomo 11, Nos. 32/33 (1958), 443–63. Items are alphabetically arranged. Bibliography includes books, essays, articles and newspaper *notas* published concerning the work or the personality of Vicente Aleixandre.

Blas Vega, José. "Bibliografía de Vicente Aleixandre," *Poesía Hispánica*, Segunda época, Nos. 299/300 (noviembre/diciembre de 1977), 56–61. Contents: I. Obra poética. II. Obras en prosa. III. Antologías y obras completas. IV. Traducciones. V. Estudios: libros. VI. Estudios: ensayos y artículos (selección). VII. Homenajes.

Colinas, Antonio. *Aleixandre*. Barcelona: Editorial Barcanova, 1982. 127p. "Bibliografía," pp. 119–26. Contents: I. Bibliografía de Vincente Aleixandre. A. Primeras ediciones. 1. Poesía. 2. Prosa. 3. Antologías y obras completas. 4. Ediciones críticas de algunos libros. 5. Traducciones de sus obras. II. Bibliografía sobre Vicente Aleixandre. A. Libros. B. Artículos y ensayos. III. Números homenaje en revistas y periódicos.

Correa, v. 1, pp. 368, 547–550. Works by and about the author.

Daydí-Tolson, Santiago, ed. *Vicente Aleixandre: A Critical Appraisal*. Ypsilanti, Michigan: Bilingual Press/Editorial Bilingüe, 1981. 330p. "Bibliography," pp. 282–323. Partially annotated entries. Contents: I. Aleixandre's Works. A. Poetry Books. B. Prose Books. C. Translations. 1. English. 2. Other Languages. II. Books on Aleixandre. III. Special Journal Issues on Aleixandre. IV. Selected Articles. V. Other Critical Works. VI. Bibliographies.

González Muela, pp. 53–56. Works by and about Aleixandre arranged chronologically.

Granados, Vicente. *La poesía de Vicente Aleixandre: formación y evolución*. Madrid: CUPSA Editorial, 1977. 292p. "Bibliografía," pp. 287–92. Contents: I. Obras de Vicente Aleixandre (includes various editions; books only). II. Revistas dedicadas a Vicente Aleixandre. III. Antologías de Vicente Aleixandre. IV. Obras sobre Vicente Aleixandre (mainly published from 1973–1976).

Jiménez, José Olivio. *Vicente Aleixandre: Una aventura hacia el conocimiento*. Madrid: Ediciones Júcar, 1982. 238p. (Los poetas, 33). "Bibliografía," pp. 231–34. Contents: I. Libros originales del autor (1928–1974). II. Bibliografía mínima sobre el autor. A. Libros. B. Algunos ensayos y artículos.

Novo Villaverde, Yolanda. *Vicente Aleixandre: Poeta surrealista*. Santiago de Compostela: Universidad de Santiago de Compostela, 1980. 183p. (*Its* Monografías, 58). "Vicente Aleixandre," pp. 171–78 (Critical studies and list of *homenajes*).

Schwartz, Kessel. *Vicente Aleixandre*. New York: Twayne Publishers, 1970. 188p. "Selected Bibliography," pp. 171–84. Contents: I. Primary Sources. A. Books by Vicente Aleixandre. B. Pamphlets, Articles, Letters, Essays, Scattered Poetry. II. Secondary Sources. A. Books. B. Articles.

ALFARO, MARIA (1900–)
Galerstein, p. 17.

ALONSO, AMADO (1896–1952)
"Bibliografía de Amado Alonso," *Nueva Revista de Filología Hispánica*, tomo 8 (1953), 3–15. 200 items, by year, 1922–52.

ALONSO, DAMASO (1898–1990)
Alonso, Dámaso. *Antología de nuestro monstruoso mundo. Duda y amor sobre el Ser Supremo*. Edición del autor. Madrid: Cátedra, 1985. 212p. (Letras Hispánicas, 228). "Bibliografía selecta," pp. 59–60. Criticism only.
______. *Hijos de la ira*. Edición, introducción y notas de Miguel J. Flys. Madrid: Castalia, 1986. 176p. (Clásicos Castellanos, 152). "Noticia bibliográfica," pp. 59–61. Contents: I. Libros de poesía. II. Antologías. III. Traducciones. "Bibliografía selecta sobre el autor," pp. 63–64. Contents: I. Libros. II. Colecciones de artículos y homenajes.
Alvarado de Ricord, Elsie. *La obra poética de Dámaso Alonso*. Madrid: Editorial Gredos, 1968. 179p. "Bibliografía poética de Dámaso Alonso," pp. 165–74. Contents: I. Libros. II. Poesías sueltas. III. Traducciones hechas por Dámaso Alonso. IV. Poesía de Dámaso Alonso traducida a otras lenguas. V. Sobre Dámaso Alonso.
"Bibliografía de y sobre Dámaso Alonso," *Anthropos* (Barcelona), No. 106/107 (1990), 48–52. Contents: I. Obra crítica y filológica. A. Contenido de las *Obras completas*. B. Bibliografía selecta. II. Obra de creación. III. Bibliografía sobre Dámaso Alonso (descriptive annotations).
Correa, v. 1, pp. 256–57, 536–38. Works by and about the author.
Debicki, Andrew P. *Dámaso Alonso*. New York: Twayne Publishers, 1970. 167p. "Selected Bibliography," pp. 149–60. Contents: I. Primary Sources. A. Books of Verse. B. Uncollected Poems. C. Creative Prose. D. Plays. E. Selected Translations. F. Selected Editions and Critical Studies. II. Secondary Sources. A. Bibliography and Biography. B. Critical Studies. C. Doctoral Dissertations and Theses.

Díez de Revenga, Francisco Javier. "En torno a la bibliografía de Dámaso Alonso," pp. 113–20, in *Damaso Alonso: Premio de Literatura en lengua castellana "Miguel de Cervantes" 1978* (Barcelona: Anthropos, 1988). A bibliographic essay of books by and about Dámaso Alonso. Also see "Cronología de Dámaso Alonso (1898–1978), pp. 120–23 in the same volume.

González Muela, pp. 56–57. Works by and about Dámaso Alonso are arranged chronologically.

Huarte Morton, Fernando. "Bibliografía de Dámaso Alonso," *Papeles de Son Armadans*, Año 3, tomo 11, Nos. 32/33 (nov./dic. 1958), 465–518. 322 entries. Contents: I. Obra literaria. A. Verso. 1. Traducciones. B. Prosa. 1. Traducciones. II. Obra científica. A. Lingüística. B. Literatura. 1. Teoría. Método. 2. Estilística. 3. Historia de la literatura (todas las épocas). 4. Grupos de autores. 5. Edad Media. 6. Siglos XVI-XVIII (by author). 7. Siglos XIX-XX (by author). 8. Contemporáneos (by author). III. Sobre Dámaso Alonso (by year, 1921–58).

______. "Bibliografía de Dámaso Alonso," in *Homenaje universitario a Dámaso Alonso* (Madrid: Editorial Gredos, 1970), pp. 295–347. Up-dates his 1958 bibliography. Works are listed by year, 1917–70 (pp. 295–332), 332 items. An "índice de los títulos y de los nombres citados en la bibliografía" appears on pp. 333–43, and a list of criticism "sobre la poesía de Dámaso Alonso (borrador)," appears on pp. 344–47.

"Selected Bibliography, 1921–1973," *Books Abroad*, 48 (2), Spring 1974, 318–20. Contents: I. Poetry; Prose; Varia (all by year, books only). II. Dámaso Alonso in *Books Abroad*, 1929–74.

ALONSO, MARIA ROSA (n.d.)

Galerstein, p. 18.

ALONSO I MANANT, CECILIA (1905–1974)

Galerstein, p. 19.

ALOS, CONCHA (1922–)

Galerstein, pp. 19–21.

Rodríguez, Fermín. *Mujer y sociedad: La novelística de Concha Alós*. Madrid: Editorial Orígenes, 1985. 195p. "Lista de obras citadas," pp. 189–93. Includes works by and about Concha Alós.

ALTOLAGUIRRE, MANUEL (1905–1959)

Altolaguirre, Manuel. *Poesías completas*. Edición de Margarita Smerdou y Milagros Arizmendi. Madrid: Ediciones Cátedra, 1982. 391p. "Bibliografía del autor," pp. 83–88. Contents: I.

Poesía. II. Prosa. A. Novela. B. Biografía. III. Antologías. IV. Traducciones. V. Ensayos, conferencias y artículos. C. Teatro. D. Cine. E. Revistas. F. Colecciones poéticas. "Bibliografía crítica," pp. 89–93. Contents: I. Estudios generales y antologías. II. Revistas y prensa periódica.

Correa, v. 1, pp. 447–48, 551. Works by and about the author.

Crispin, John. *Quest for Wholeness: The Personality and Works of Manuel Altolaguirre*. Valencia: Albatros Hispanófila Ediciones, 1983. 123p. "Bibliography," pp. 118–23. Contents: I. Works by Altolaguirre. A. Books of Verse. II. Other Published Books. III. Works Published in Periodicals or Preserved in the Altolaguirre Archives. A. Autobiography. B. Theatre. C. Creative Prose. D. Critical Prose (Selection of Main Essays in Periodicals). IV. Translations. V. English Translations of Poems by Altolaguirre. VI. The Generation of 1927 and Its Times. VII. Biographical and Critical Studies on Altolaguirre. VIII. Periodicals Edited or Printed by Altolaguirre Available in Facsimile Reprints.

González Muela, pp. 57–59. Works by and about Altolaguirre are arranged chronologically.

ALVAR, MANUEL (1923–)

Alvar, Manuel. *Análisis de Ciudad del paraíso*. Roma: Instituto Español de Lengua y Literatura, 1974. 46p. "Bibliografía de Manuel Alvar," pp. 35–46. Contents: I. Libros (By year, 1945–1975). II. Artículos (By year, 1942–1974).

"Bio-bibliografía de Manuel Alvar," v. 1, pp. 23–47; v. 4, pp. 569–76 in *Philologica Hispaniensia in Honorem Manuel Alvar* (Madrid: Gredos, 198?–87). Alvar's works are listed by year through 1986. There is also a "trabajos en prensa o concluidos" section in volume 4.

Quilis, Antonio. "Nuestros filólogos: Manuel Alvar," *Boletín de Filología Española*, No. 13 (oct./dic. 1964), 3–14. "Publicaciones," pp. 7–14. Contents: I. Libros. II. Artículos. Reviews are not included.

ALVAREZ DE TOLEDO, LUISA ISABEL, DUQUESA DE MEDINA SIDONIA (1930–)

Galerstein, pp. 21–22.

ALVAREZ QUINTERO, SERAFIN (1871–1938) and JOAQUIN (1873–1944)

Romo Arregui, J. "Serafín y Joaquín Álvarez Quintero: Bibliografía," *Cuadernos de Literatura Contemporánea*, Nos. 13/14 (1944), 65–83. Contents: I. Ediciones. A. Teatro completo. B.

Comedias y dramas. C. Género lírico. D. Entremeses y pasos. E. Sainetes, pasillos. F. Jugetes cómicos. G. Obras diversas. II. Ediciones escolares de algunas obras. III. Traducciones. IV. Escritos no escritos en colaboración. V. Obras estrenadas sin editar. VI. Obras sin estrenar ni editar.

ANDRES, ELENA (1931–)
Galerstein, pp. 23–24.

ANDUJAR, MANUEL (1913–)
CILH, p. 232.

ANGLADA, MARIA ANGELES (1930–)
Galerstein, p. 24.

ANTONANA, PABLO (1927–)
"Pablo Antoñana: Bibliografía," pp. 321–23 in José Luis Martín Nogales' *Cincuenta años de novela española (1936–1986): Escritores navarros* (Barcelona: PPU, 1989). Contents: I. Novelas. II. Cuentos. III. Otros textos. IV. Artículos, entrevistas y reseñas.

APARICIO, JUAN PEDRO (1941–)
"Juan Pedro Aparicio: Bibliografía," *Alonso*, p. 267. Books are listed by year, 1975–1986.

ARCONADA, CESAR MUNOZ (1900–1964)
Santonja Gómez, Gonzalo. "Cesar M. Arconada: Bio-bibliografía," *Publicaciones de la Institución "Tello Tellez de Meneses"* (Palencia), No. 47 (1982), 5–57.

ARDERIU I VOLTAD, CLEMENTINA (1899–1976)
Galerstein, pp. 25–27.

ARENYS, TERESA D' (n.d.)
Galerstein, pp. 27–28.

ARITZETA I ABAD, MARGARIDA (1953–)
Galerstein, p. 28

ARNICHES, CARLOS (1866–1943)
Arniches, Carlos. *Del Madrid castizo: sainetes*. Edición de José Montero Padilla. Tercera edición. Madrid: Cátedra, 1981. 161p.

"Bibliografía," pp. 46–48. Contents: I. Ediciones (By year, 1917–66). II. Estudios (criticism, by year, 1931–77).

_____. *Teatro completo. Prólogo biográfico-crítico por E.M. del Portillo.* Madrid: Aguilar, editor, 1948. 4vs. "Relación de las obras de Arniches escritas en colaboración y que no figuran en estos volúmenes," v. IV, pp. 1097–1102.

Lentzen, Manfred. *Carlos Arniches: vom "género chico" zur "tragedia grotesca."* Geneva: Droz, 1966. 237p. "Bibliographie der Werke von Carlos Arniches," pp. 208–18. Chronological listing, 1888–1944. "Zeitungsartikel über Carlos Arniches und sein Werk," pp. 228–30.

McKay, Douglas R. *Carlos Arniches.* New York: Twayne Publishers, Inc., 1972. 150p. "Appendix," pp. 129–43 contains a list of 179 plays in chronological order according to the date of their première.

Ramus, Vicente. *Vida y teatro de Carlos Arniches.* Madrid-Barcelona: Alfaguara, 1966. 354p. "Bibliografía," pp. 301–26. Contents: I. Bibliografía de Carlos Arniches. A. Literatura no teatral. B. Epistolario. C. Literatura teatral (by year, 1888–1943). D. Películas realizadas con argumentos de Carlos Arniches. II. Bibliografía sobre la vida y la obra de Carlos Arniches.

Romo Arregui, Josefina. "Carlos Arniches: bibliografía," *Cuadernos de Literatura Contemporánea,* Nos. 9/10 (1943), 299–307. Contents: I. Ediciones. A. Teatro lírico y dramático. B. En colaboración. II. Artículos y reseñas críticas.

Seco, Manuel. *Arniches y el habla de Madrid.* Madrid-Barcelona: Alfaguara, 1970. 614p. "Bibliografía," pp. 561–77. Contents: I. Autoridades literarias. A. Obras de Carlos Arniches. 1. Ediciones utilizadas. 2. Obras que han servido de base al presente estudio. B. Obras de Carlos Arniches en colaboración con otros autores. C. Obras de otros autores. II. Estudios y repertorios.

ARQUIMBAU, ROSA MARIA (1910–)

Galerstein, p. 30.

ARRABAL, FERNANDO (1932–)

Arrabal, Fernando. *El cementario de automóviles. El arquitecto y el Emperador de Asiria.* Edición de Diana Taylor. Madrid: Cátedra, 1984. 234p. (Letras Hispánicas, 198). "Bibliografía," pp. 65–72. Contents: I. Obra de Arrabal. A. Teatro. 1. En español (By year, 1965–77). 2. En francés. a. Editions Julliard (By year, 1958–65). b. Christian Bourgois (By year, 1968–82). B. Novela. 1. En Español (By year, 1966–83). 2. En francés (By year, 1959–77).

C. Poesía. D. Ensayos, documentos. 1. En Español. 2. En francés. E. Entrevistas. F. Películas. II. Crítica sobre Arrabal.

______. *La hija de King Kong: novela*. Traducido por Fernando Arrabal. Barcelona: Seix Barral, 1988. 213p. "Bibliografía," pp. 209–13. Contents: I. La obra de Arrabal publicada en castellano. A. Teatro (By year, 1975–86). B. Narrativa (By year, 1983–87). C. Cartas. D. Poesía (By year, 1966–85). II. Libros consagrados a la obra de Arrabal.

______. *Pic-nic. El triciclo. El laberinto*. Edición de Angel Berenguer. Quinta edición. Madrid: Cátedra, 1983. 267p. (Letras Hispánicas, 63). "Bibliografía," pp. 123–24. Criticism only.

______. *Teatro pánico*. Edición de Francisco Torres Monreal. Madrid: Cátedra, 1986. 232p. "Bibliografía," pp. 75–84. Contents: I. La obra de Arrabal publicada en castellano. A. Teatro (By year, 1975–86). B. Narrativa (By year, 1983–85). C. Cartas. D. Poesía (By year, 1966–85). E. Conferencias, artículos . . . (By year, 1963–76). II. Críticos y comentarios sobre el teatro de Arrabal. A. Libros consagrados enteramente a la obra de Arrabal. B. Capítulos. C. Artículos. D. Tesis y memorias inéditas.

Bérenguer, Joan P. *Bibliographie d'Arrabal: entretiens avec Arrabal; Plaidoyer pour une différence*. Grenoble: Presses Universitaires de Grenoble, 1979? 54p.

Donahue, Thomas J. *The Theater of Fernando Arrabal: A Garden of Earthly Delights*. New York: New York University Press, 1980. 153p. "Bibliography," pp. 147–49. Works by and about Arrabal. "Editions of Arrabal's Plays in English," pp. 149–50.

Podol, Peter L. *Fernando Arrabal*. Boston: Twayne Publishers, 1978. 177p. "Selected Bibliography," pp. 167–73. Contents: I. Primary Sources. A. In French. 1. Editions Julliard. 2. Christian Bourgois. 3. Other Publishers. B. In Spanish. C. In English. 1. New York: Grove Press. 2. London: Calder and Boyars. 3. Others. D. Interviews. E. Essays of Arrabal. II. Secondary Sources (annotated). III. Addenda I: Unpublished Dissertations in the United States. Addenda II: Books in Preparation.

Ruyter-Tognotti, Danièle de. *De la prison à l'exil: Structures relationnelles et structures spatiales dans trois pièces d'Arrabal*. Paris: Librairie Nizet, 1986. 310p. "Bibliographie," pp. 295–301. Emphasis on French titles. Contents: I. Oeuvre de Fernando Arrabal. A. Pièces étudieés. B. Ensemble des oeuvres dramatiques par ordre chronologique (By year, 1952–80). C. Poésie. D. Romans. E. Films. F. Documents. G. Articles ou conférences d'Arrabal cités. II. Livres et articles sur Arrabal consultés.

Torres Monreal, Francisco. *Introducción al teatro de Arrabal.* Murcia: Editorial Godoy, 1981. 201p. "Cronología de la obra de Arrabal," pp. 179–82. By year, 1952–81. Includes books only.

ASENSIO, EUGENIO (1902–)

Homenaje a Eugenio Asensio. Madrid: Editorial Gredos, 1988. 502p. "Bibliografía de Eugenio Asensio," pp. 9–17. Ninety entries listed by year, 1949–1988.

AUB, MAX (1903–1972)

Aub, Max. *La calle de Valverde.* Edición de José Antonio Pérez Bowie. Madrid: Cátedra, 1985. 543p. "Bibliografía," pp. 107–13. Contents: I. Obras de Max Aub. A. Narrativa (By year, 1929–1982). II. Teatro (By year, 1928–1971). III. Poesía (By year, 1925–1971). IV. Ensayo (By year, 1936–1985; books only). V. Estudios sobre Max Aub. A. Libros. B. Artículos (selected).

Borras, Angel A. *El teatro del exilio de Max Aub.* Sevilla: Secretariado de Publicaciones de la Universidad de Sevilla, 1975. 180p. (Colección de bolsillo, 37). "Bibliografía," pp. 175–80. Contents: I. Fuentes: Obras de Max Aub. II. Artículos y libros consultados (most citations are on the life and work of Max Aub).

Moraleda, Pilar. *Max Aub: Temas y técnicas del teatro menor.* Córdoba: Universidad de Córdoba, Servicio de Publicaciones, 1989. 340p. (Monografías, 15). "Bibliografía," pp. 317–37. Contents: I. Obras de Max Aub. A. Obras dramáticos (By year, 1928–1975). B. Obras narrativa (By year, 1929–1972). C. Ensayo y crítica literaria (By year, 1935–1985). D. Obras poéticas (By year, 1925–1982). E. Varia (By year, 1966–1985). F. Obras traducidas (By year, 1962–67). II. Bibliografía sobre Max Aub. A. Estudios críticos sobre la obra dramática. B. Estudios críticos sobre la obra narrativa. C. Estudios críticos sobre la obra poética. D. Entrevistas y coloquios. E. Estudios inéditos.

Soldevilla Durante, Ignacio. *La obra narrativa de Max Aub* (1929–1969). Madrid: Editorial Gredos, 1973. 471p. (Biblioteca Rómanica Hispánica. II. Estudios y ensayos, 189). "Bibliografía," pp. 454–66. I. Fuentes: obras de Max Aub. A. Libros (novelas y relatos). B. Otros libros consultados. C. Otras obras. D. Textos en revistas. E. Correspondencia. F. Traducciones consultadas. II. Estudios y artículos sobre Aub. III. Apéndice bibliográfico (1969–72). A. Obras. B. Estudios y artículos sobre Aub.

AYALA, FRANCISCO (1906-)

Alvarez Calleja, José. *Bibliografía de Francisco Ayala.* Mieres del Camino: Instituto "Bernaldo de Quirós," 1983. 51p. (Serie bibliografías, 3).

Amorós, Andrés. *Bibliografía de Francisco Ayala.* Syracuse, N.Y.: Centro de Estudios Hispánicos, 1973. 95p. (Bibliotheca Hispana Novíssima, 4). Contents: I. Obras narrativas de Francisco Ayala (by work). II. Libros de crítica literaria. III. Artículos de crítica literaria no recogidos en libro. IV. Reseñas de libro de literatura. V. Ensayo sociológico y político (libros). VI. Artículos de sociología y política no recogidos en libro. VII. Reseñas de libros de sociología, historia, política. VIII. Traducciones. IX. Críticas sobre Francisco Ayala como narrador o en general. X. Críticas sobre Francisco Ayala como ensayista. XI. Entrevistas con Francisco Ayala. XII. Hallazgos. XIII. Índice de nombres citados. XIV. Apéndice (Supplement).

Ayala, Francisco. *Muerte de perro. El fondo de vasco.* Prólogo de Mariano Baquero Goyanes. Madrid: Espasa-Calpe, 1981. 340p. "Bibliografía selecta," pp. 39–40. Contents: I. Obras de ficción (1925–1978). II. Crítica literaria (1929–1975). III. Tratados y ensayos (1943–1972).

Bieder, Maryellen. *Narrative Perspective in the Post-Civil War Novels of Francisco Ayala: "Muertes de perro" and "El fondo del vaso".* Chapel Hill: University of North Carolina, Department of Romance Languages, 1979. 133p. (North Carolina Studies in the Romance Languages and Literatures, 207). Includes works by and about Ayala not cited in the Amorós bibliography. "Bibliography," pp. 128–33. Contents: I. Francisco Ayala: Selected Bibliography. II. Works Cited. III. Francisco Ayala: Recent Works. IV. Critical Studies of Ayala's Fiction: An Updating.

Ellis, Keith. *El arte narrativo de Francisco Ayala.* Madrid: Editorial Gredos, 1964. 259p. (Biblioteca Románica Hispánica. II. Estudios y Ensayos). "Bibliografía," pp. 238–51. Contents: I. Obras de Ayala. A. Obras narrativas. B. Obras narrativas publicadas en revistas o en antologías. C. Libros de crítica literaria. D. Libros de sociología y política. E. Artículos en revistas (by *revista*). II. Obras sobre Ayala. A. Libros que contienen ensayos u otras referencias a su obra. B. Artículos en revistas.

Escudero Martínez, Carmen. *Cervantes en la narrativa de Francisco Ayala.* Murcia: Universidad de Murcia, 1989. 109p. "Bibliografía," pp. 105–09. A listing of critical works, which updates the Amorós bibliography above.

Hiriart, Rosario. *Conversaciones con Francisco Ayala.* Madrid: Espasa-Calpe, 1982. 155p. (Colección Austral). "Cronología: vida y obra," pp. 147–55.

Irizarry, Estelle. *Teoría y creación literaria en Francisco Ayala.* Madrid: Editorial Gredos, 1971. 247p. "Bibliografía," p. 259–71. Contents: I. Obras de Francisco Ayala. A. Novelística. B. Libros discursivos (sociología, crítica literaria, política). C. Ensayos sueltos no recogidos en libros. D. Notas críticas de obras específicas (reviews not included in books). II. Estudios y artículos sobre Fraancisco Ayala. A. Bibliografías. B. Artículos y libros.

AZORIN (Pseud. of José Martínez Ruiz, 1873–1967)

Azorín. *Don Juan.* Edición, introducción, bibliografía y notas de José María Martínez Cachero. Madrid: Espasa-Calpe, 1977. 96p. "Bibliografía de Azorín," pp. xcix-ciii. Includes those works not published in Azorin's *Obras completas*, published by Editorial Aguilar (1947–1954), plus others from 1953 to 1976. "Bibliografía sobre Azorín," pp. ciii-cxxv (annotated and selected).

_____. *Obras selectas.* Madrid: Biblioteca Nueva, 1969. 1396p. "Bibliografía," pp. 1363–1381, compilado por Ángel Cruz Rueda. Includes some 1,961 entries. Contents: I: Lista completa de las obras de D. José Martínez Ruiz (Azorín). A. Primera época: la de Martínez Ruiz y seudónimos de "Candido" y "Ahriman" (by year, 1893–1901). B. Segunda época: "Azorín" como personaje literario y como seudónimo (1902–1925). C. Tercera época: teatro y nuevas obras (1926–1936). D. Cuatra época: desde el movimiento nacional (17 de julio de 1936–1938–1942). E. Quinta época: desde los setenta años de "Azorín" (1943–53). F. Sexta época: desde los ochenta años de "Azorín" (1954–61). G. En torno de publicación. H. Traducciones. II. Libros y estudios acerca de Azorín.

_____. *La ruta de Don Quijote.* Edición de José María Martínez Cachero. Madrid: Cátedra, 1984. (Letras Hispánicas, 214). "Bibliografía crítica sobre Azorín," pp. 51–71. Annotated entries.

Cruz Rueda, Ángel. "Azorín: bibliografía," *Cuadernos de Literatura Contemporánea*, Nos. 16/17 (1945), 357–67. A selected bibliography of his works only, arranged by year, 1893–1945.

Fox, Edward Inman. *Azorín as a Literary Critic.* New York: Hispanic Institute in the United States, 1962. 176p. "Appendix," pp. 163–70 is "an index of Azorín's literary criticism which is available to the general public—that is, collected and published in volumes." Most are from his *Obras completas* (Madrid, 1947–54 edition). Works are listed under author. "Bibliography," pp. 171–176.

_____. "Una bibliografía anotada del periodismo de José Martínez Ruiz (Azorín): 1894–1904," *Revista de Literatura*, Nos. 55/56 (julio/diciembre de 1965), 231–44. 256 titles. The bibliography lists Azorín's first articles from 1894 until 1904, when he assumes the pseudonym "Azorín."

Gamallo Fierros, Dionisio. *Hacia una bibliografía cronológica en torno a la letra y el espíritu de Azorín.* Madrid: Dirección General de Archivos y Bibliotecas, 1956. 69p. (Separata del *Boletín de la Dirección General de Archivos y Bibliotecas*, No. 27, 1956, with additions). Lists over 500 entries about the work of Azorín chronologically.

Glenn, Kathleen M. *Azorín (José Martínez Ruiz).* Boston: Twayne Publishers, Inc., 1981. 16p. "Selected Bibliography," pp. 156–58. Contents: I. Primary Sources (Selective listing of works, arranged chronologically, 1900–1954). II. Secondary Works (very selective).

Maass, Angelika. *Azorín oder der Mensch im Zeichen der Ebene (Eine Auseinandersetzung mit dem Werk Azoríns am Beispiel von "La ruta de Don Quijote").* Bern: Peter Lang, 1984. 306p. "Literaturverzeichnis," pp. 297–300. Contents: I. Werkausgaben. II. Sekundärliteratur. A. Monographien. Werke zu einzelnen Themen (chronologisch nach Erscheinen). B. Artikel und Essays über Azorín (Chronologisch nach Erscheinen). Very selective bibliography.

Martínez Cachero, José María. "Cincuenta referencias bibliográficas españoles sobre Azorín en la década de los 40," *Anales Azorinianos*, No. 1 (1983/84), 32–48. Contents: I. Azorín, entrevistado. II. Azorín reseñado. III. Azorín comentado (artículos). IV. Azorín comentado (libros). Bibliographic essay.

Rand, Marguerite C. *Castilla en Azorín. Prólogo de Azorín.* Madrid: Revista de Occidente, 1956. 777p. "Bibliografía," pp. 733–53. Contents: I. Obras de Azorín. A. Libros (contained in Azorín's *Obras completas*, 1947–54). B. Obras más recientes. II. Estudios sobre la vida y las obras de Azorín. A. Libros. B. Artículos y estudios más breves. III. Obras de referencia general.

Ricau, Marie-André. "Dix ans d'études azoriniennes: 1957–1967: bibliographie critique." Doctorat de 3e cycle, 1969, Univ. de Paris.

Riopérez y Milá, Santiago. *Azorín íntegro: Estudio biográfico, crítico, bibliográfico y antológico.* Madrid: Editorial Biblioteca Nueva, 1979. 755p. "Bibliografía general," pp. 709–35. Contents: I. Obras de Azorín. A. Obras completas. B. Reediciones de las obras completas. C. Obras selectas. D. Otros libros de Azorín. E. Reediciones de obras de Azorín precedidas de estudios críticos. F. Antologías extranjeras de las obras de Azorín. G. Ensayos bibliográficos de las obras de Azorín y de los estudios sobre las mismas. II. Obras específicas en torno a la vida y literatura de Azorín. III. Obras genéricas en torno a Azorín (estudios generales, enciclopedias y diccionarios). IV. Estudios críticos, sociológicos y ambientales en torno a la generación de 1898. V. Estudios complementarios de la época literaria de Azorín (biografías de escritores, obras y ensayos de movimientos estéticos). VI. Hemerografía (revistas, periódicos y diarios que contienen artículos sobre Azorín, la generación de 1898 y su época literaria)—By journal title.

Sáinz de Bujanda, Fernando. *Clausura de un centenario: Guía bibliográfica de Azorín.* Madrid: Revista de Occidente, 1974. 283p. (Selecta, 50). Contents: I. "Lista de obras," pp. 153–255. A. Lista de obras. 1. Lista completa de títulos por orden cronológico (1893–1973). 2. Descripción de las portadas de las primeras ediciones y datos adicionales (1893–1973). 3. Libros rehabilitados *versus* libros repudiados. 4. Libros anunciados y no publicados. B. Lista de traducciones. C. Lista de prólogos. D. Lista de artículos: fuentes y remisión a otro lugar. II. "Orientaciones complementarias," pp. 257–65. A. Modificaciones introducidas en los libros originarios. 1. Cambios en los textos (by work). 2. Cambios en títulos. B. Ediciones críticas. III. "Apéndice," pp. 277–80. A. Libros sobre la vida y obra de Azorín. 1. Libros y folletos. 2. Revistas (números extraordinarios) y homenajes. IV. "Indice de autores," pp. 281–83.

BADELL, ANA MARIA (1932–)

Galerstein, p. 30.

BADIA MARGARIT, ANTONIO MARIA (1920–)

Cerdá Massó, Ramón. "Nuestros filólogos: Antonio María Badia Margarit," *Boletín de Filología Española*, Nos. 20/21 (julio/diciembre de 1966), 3–26. "Bibliografía," pp. 10–26, is arranged by year, 1945–66.

BADOSA, ENRIQUE (1927–)

CILH, pp. 185–26. Contents: I. Poesía. II. Traducciones. III. Ensayo.

BALBIN, RAFAEL DE (1910–)

Garrido Gallardo, Miguel Ángel. "Nuestros filólogos: Rafael de Balbín," *Boletín de Filología Española*, Nos. 46/49 (enero/diciembre de 1973), 3–14. "Bibliografía," pp. 6–14. Contents: I. Poesía (1941–68). II. Trabajos críticos: libros (1944–71). III. Trabajos críticos: artículos (1944–71).

BALLESTEROS DE GAIBROIS, MERCEDES (1891–)
Galerstein, pp. 31–34.

BAQUERO GOYANES, MARIANO (1923–)
"Publicaciones del Profesor Mariano Baquero Goyanes," pp. 655–62 in *Estudios literarios dedicados al profesor Mariano Baquero Goyanes* (Murcia, 1974). Contents: I. Libros (1949–1972). II. Ediciones (1953–1973). III. Estudios y artículos (1944–1972).

BARBERA, CARMEN (n.d.)
Galerstein, pp. 34–35.

BARBERO SANCHEZ, TERESA (1934–)
Galerstein, p. 35.

BAROJA, PIO (1872–1956)
Baroja, Pío. *El árbol de la ciencia*. Edición de Pío Caro Baroja. Madrid: Cátedra, 1985. 303p. "Bibliografía," pp. 29–31. Contents: I. Sobre el autor. II. Sobre la obra. III. Obras colectivas y monográficos de revistas.

______. *Las inquietudes de Shanti Andía*. Edición de Julio Caro Baroja. Octava edición. Madrid: Cátedra, 1988. 376p. "Bibliografía," pp. 31–33. Contents: I. Ediciones de *Las inquietudes de Shanti Andía* (1911–1951). II. Traducciones. A. Alemán. B. Francés. C. Inglés. D. Portugués. E. Vascuence. III. Estudios (*Las inquietudes de Shanti Andía*; By year, 1911–1962).

Billick, David J. "Pío Baroja: A Checklist of Graduate Research, 1923–1980," *Bulletin of Bibliography*, 39 (1982), 4–8. The bibliography includes "senior and honor's theses for the B.A., master's theses, and doctoral dissertations. Items are arranged alphabetically by author and whenever possible, I have noted pagination and the availability of abstracts in *Dissertation Abstracts*, *Dissertation Abstracts International*, or the *Revista de la Universidad de Madrid*. For works subsequently printed in book form, publishing information along with any change in title is included in brackets."

Campos, Jorge. "Bibliografía," I, pp. 323–89, in *Baroja y su mundo* (Madrid: Ediciones Arion, 1962). Contents: I. Obras de Baroja (includes only books, arranged chronologically, 1896–1956). II. Traducciones de obras de Baroja (by language). III. Prólogos. IV. Obras sobre Baroja o con particular relación al autor. V. Tesis sobre Baroja. VI. Artículos y ensayos sobre Baroja. VII. Relación de colaboraciones periodísticas de Pío Baroja (by year, 1893–1955).

______. *Introducción a Pío Baroja*. Madrid: Alianza Editorial, 1981. 126p. "Obras de Pío Baroja," pp. 117–20. Contents: I. Cuentos y novelas cortas (By year). II. Trilogías (By year). III. Biografías (By year). IV. Artículos y ensayos (By year). V. Verso. VI. Memorias. "Estudios sobre Baroja," pp. 121–22.

Caro Baroja, Pío, ed. *Guía de Pío Baroja: El mundo barojiano*. Madrid: Ediciones Caro Raggio; Ediciones Cátedra, 1987. 316p. "Obras de Pío Baroja," pp. 33–57. Contents: I. Primeras ediciones (By year, 1896–1956). II. Sus editores. III. Colaboraciones periodísticas desde 1890 a 1905. IV. Colaboraciones periodísticas desde 1890 a 1904, por años. V. Colaboraciones periodísticas desde 1893 a 1955. "Los géneros literarios en las obras de Don Pío," pp. 59–165. Contents: I. Cuentos y novelas cortas (Se incluyen algunos ensayos). A. En obra suelta. B. En publicaciones periódicas (1911–1953). "Reediciones y traducciones," pp. 167–76. Contents: Reediciones posteriores a 1939; por editorales (1939–1954). "Obras publicadas hasta 1987 por la Editorial del Centenario," pp. 178–79. "Ediciones para bibliófilos (1972–1986), p. 181. "Traducciones," pp. 181–86. (By language). "Bibliografía," pp. 187–293. Contents: I. Escritos para la bibliografía de Pío Baroja. A. Obras generales de consulta (el 98, etc.). B. Obras generales sobre Pío Baroja. C. Artículos y ensayos en periódicos y revistas. D. Tesinas en Gaucher College (Maryland, 1924). II. Estudios sobre Baroja. III. Estudios sobre la obra. IV. Biografías e impresiones personales. V. Monografías. VI. Estudios reunidos. VII. Obras con particular relación al autor. VIII. Tesis, artículos y ensayos sobre Baroja. IX. Pio Baroja y su mundo. X. Prólogos a las obras de Baroja. XI. Breve censo de personajes. XII. Indice temático.

Cueto Pérez, Magdalena. *Aspectos sistemáticos en la narrativa de Pío Baroja: El Arbol de la ciencia*. Oviedo: Universidad de Oviedo, Servicio de Publicaciones, 1985. 236p. "Bibliografía sobre Baroja," pp. 227–36.

BAROJA, RICARDO (1871–1953)

Baroja, Ricardo. *Gente del 98. Arte, cine y ametralladora*. Edición de Pío Caro Baroja. Madrid: Cátedra, 1989. 367p. "Bibliografía," pp. 33–37. Contents: I. Obras de Ricardo Baroja (By year, 1894–1967). II. Obras sobre Ricardo Baroja.

BARTRA, AGUSTI (1908–)

"Bibliografía de Agustí Bartra," *Faig*, 18 (setiembre de 1982), 23–28.

BARTRE, LEUCIDA (1881–)
Galerstein, pp. 35–36.

BASSA, MARIA GRACIA (1883–1961)
Galerstein, p. 36.

BECKER, ANGELICKA (1942–)
Galerstein, p. 36.

BELLIDO, JOSE MARIA (1922–)
Pérez-Stansfield, p. 341.

BELLIDO CORMENZANA, JOSE (1921–)
"José Bellido Cormenzana," pp. 3–9 in L. Teresa Valdivieso's *España: Bibliografía de un teatro "silenciado"* (Lincoln, Neb.: Society of Spanish and Spanish-American Studies, 1979). Contents: I. Notas biográficas. II. Obras inéditas. III. Obras publicadas. IV. Traducciones. V. Escritos y declaraciones. VI. Estudios críticos. Critical and/or content annotations for most entries.

BENAVENTE, JACINTO (1866–1954)
Díaz, José A. *Jacinto Benavente and His Theatre*. Long Island City, N.Y.: Las Américas Publishing Col, 1972. 215p. "Bibliography," pp. 204–15. Contents: I. Studies (books). II. Articles and Periodicals. III. Index of Plays Mentioned in Work (listed alphabetically).
Peñuelas, Marcelino. *Jacinto Benavente*. New York: Twayne Publishers, Inc., 1968. 178p. "Appendix: Plays and Other Works by Jacinto Benavente," pp. 163–74. Plays are arranged in chronological order according to the date of their *première* (172 plays listed).
Romo Arregui, Josefina. "Jacinto Benavente: Bibliografía," *Cuadernos de Literatura Contemporánea*, No. 15 (1945), 251–59. Contents: I. Ediciones. A. Obras dramáticas. B. Obras diversas. II. Prólogos. III. Traducciones y adaptaciones. IV. Estudios (very few). V. Traducciones a varios idiomas. VI. Guiones y adaptaciones cinematográficas y teatrales.
Rubio Jiménez, Jesús. "Colaboraciones de Benavente en la prensa madrileña, 1890–1900," *Cuadernos Bibliográficos*, No. 44 (1982), 135–51. Arranged by year and then by date (page nos. are not given for entries).
Sánchez Estevān, I. *Jacinto Benavente y su teatro: Estudio biográfico crítico*. Barcelona: Ariel, 1954. 350p. "Catálogo alfabético del teatro de Jacinto Benavente hasta 1953," pp. 311–19.

Starkie, Walker. *Jacinto Benavente*. London: Oxford University Press, 1924. 218p. "Bibliography of Critical Works on Benavente," pp. 213–15. "List of Benavente's Plays," pp. 217–18. Plays are chronologically arranged, 1892–1924.

BENET, JUAN (1928-)

Benet, Juan. *Una tumba y otros relatos*. Introducción de Ricardo Gullón. Madrid: Taurus, 1981. 347p. "Cronología," pp. 343–44. "Bibliografía," pp. 345–46. Contents: I. Obras. Narrativa (1961–1981). II. Teatro (1953–1967). III. Ensayo (1966–1976). IV. Traducciones. V. Algunos escritos referentes a la obra de Juan Benet.

______. *Un viaje de invierno*. Edición de Diego Martínez Torrón. Madrid: Cátedra, 1980. 372p. (Letras Hispánicas, 140). "Bibliografía," pp. 103–10. Contents: I. Obras de Juan Benet (por orden cronológico). A. Narrativa (1961–1980). B. Teatro (1957–1970). C. Poesía. D. Ensayo (1966–1978). E. Artículos de revista (1953–1977). F. Entrevistas y respuestas a encuestas (1969–1977). G. Repertorios bibliográficos sobre Juan Benet. H. Recensiones de *Un viaje de invierno*. II. Estudios (selección).

Cabrera, Vicente. *Juan Benet*. Boston: Twayne Publishers, Inc., 1983. 152p. "Selected Bibliography," pp. 146–148. Contents: I. Primary Sources. II. Secondary Sources (annotated). A. Books. B. Articles. C. Bibliographic Compilations.

Compitello, Malcolm Alan. *Bibliography: Juan Benet and His Critics," Anales de la Novela de Posguerra*, 3 (1978), 123–41. 182 entries. Contents: I. Works by Juan Benet (arranged chronologically under each of the following headings): A. Narrative. B. Theater. C. Poetry. D. Essay. E. Articles and Reviews. F. Interviews and Answers to *Encuestas*. II. Works on Juan Benet (arranged alphabetically under each of the following headings): A. Reviews. B. Studies. Bibliographic essay introduces the bibliography.

______. "Bibliography," pp. 153–65 in *Critical Approaches to the Writing of Juan Benet* (Hanover, N.H.: University Press of New England, 1984). Contents: I. Works by Juan Benet (arranged chronologically under each of the following headings): A. Novels and Short Fiction. B. Theater. C. Poetry. D. Translations. E. Essays. F. Articles and Books Reviews. G. Interviews/Answers to *Encuestas*/Addresses. II. Works on Juan Benet (arranged alphabetically under each of the following headings): A. Reviews. B. Studies.

Juan Benet. Edición de Kathleen M. Vernon. Madrid: Ediciones Taurus, 1986. 296p. "Bibliografía de Juan Benet," pp. 289–90.

Contents: I. Novelas y cuentos (1961–1985). II. Teatro (1953–1970). III. Poesía (1972). IV. Traducciones. V. Ensayos y colecciones de artículos (1965–1983). "Bibliografía sobre Juan Benet," pp. 291–96. Contents: I. Libros y volúmenes especiales dedicados a Benet. II. Bibliografías. III. Artículos. IV. Entrevistas, encuestas, coloquios.

Zoetmulder, Ingrid. "Provisional bibliografía benetiana," in *Cuadernos de Norte* (Revista Hispánica de Amsterdam), 1976, p. 133–36. Contents: I. Publicaciones de Juan Benet Goitia. A. Novelas. B. Cuentos. C. Ensayos. D. Teatro. E. Artículos en revistas. II. Publicaciones sobre Juan Benet Goitia.

BENET I JORNET, JOSEP M. (1940–)

"Josep M. Benet i Jornet," pp. 10–15 in L. Teresa Valdivieso's *España: bibliografía de un teatro "silenciado"* (Lincoln, Neb.: Society of Spanish and Spanish-American Studies, 1979). Contents: I. Notas biográficas. II. Obras inéditas. III. Obras publicadas. IV. Traducciones. V. Escritos y declaraciones. VI. Estudios críticos. Critical and content annotations for most entries.

BENEYTO CUNYAT, MARIA (1925–)

Galerstein, p. 37.

BENGUEREL, XAVIER (1905–)

"Xavier Benguerel: Selected Bibliography," *Catalan Writing*, No. 3 (October 1989), 26–28. Contents: I. Fiction. II. Poetry. III. Translations. IV. Chronology.

BERGAMIN, JOSE (1897–)

Bergamín, José. *El cohete y la estrella. La cabeza a pájaros*. Edición de José Estebán. Madrid: Cátedra, 1981. 136p. (Letras Hispánicas, 138). "Bibliografía," pp. 35–40. Contents: I. Obras de José Bergamín. A. Prosa (1923–1979). B. Teatro (1925–1978). C. Poesía (1962–1980). II. Sobre su personalidad. III. Sobre su obra ensayística. IV. Estudios sobre su obra poética. V. Estudios sobre su obra aforística. VI. Estudios sobre la obra de José Bergamín (colecciones de estudios).

______. *Por debajo del sueño: antología poética*. Málaga: Litoral, 1979. 268p. "Nota bibliográfica." (no page nos.; 8 pages). Contents: I. Prosa. A. Libros (1923–1976). B. Textos publicados en revistas y reimpresos en libros (1926–1974). II. Teatro. A. Libros (1925–1953). B. Textos publicados en revistas (1944–1961). III. Poesía. A. Libros (1962–1978). B. Textos publicados en revistas (1927–1978). IV. Prólogos, estudios y traducciones (1926–1976).

V. Artículos sobre José Bergamín. A. Artículos generales. B. Sobre *Cruz y Raya*. C. Artículos críticos sobre su obra, interviews, etc. VI. Traducciones. A. En alemán. B. En francés. C. En italiano.

______. *El pozo de la angustia*. Prólogo de Carlos Gurméndez. Barcelona: Anthropos, 1985. 91p. "José Bergamín: biobibliografía," pp. 83–91. Covers 1895–1984.

"Bibliografía," *Litoral* (Valencia), Nos. 37/40 (1973), 56–61. Contents: I. La obra de José Bergamín. II. Artículos sobre José Bergamín. III. Traducciones.

Dennis, Nigel. *José Bergamín: A Critical Introduction, 1920–1936*. Toronto: University of Toronto Press, 1986. 250p. "Bibliography," pp. 225–35. Contents: I. Books by Bergamín, 1923–1936 (arranged by year). II. Articles by Bergamín in *Cruz y Raya*. A. Essays. B. Anthologies. C. Critical Commentaries. D. Special Supplements. III. Articles by Bergamín, 1921–July 1936 (arranged by year). IV. About Bergamín and *Cruz y Raya*. A. About Bergamín. B. About *Cruz y Raya*.

BERTRANA, AURORA (1899–1974)

Galerstein, pp. 37–38.

BLASCO-IBANEZ, VICENTE (1867–1928)

Betoret-París, Eduardo. *El costumbrismo regional en la obra de Blasco-Ibáñez*. Valencia: Fomento de Cultura Ediciones, 1958. 344p. "Bibliografía," pp. 335–42. Contents: I. Obras de Vicente Blasco-Ibáñez. A. Novelas. B. Cuentos y novelas cortas. C. Viajes. D. Historia, política y crítica. E. Obras no autorizadas por Blasco. F. Teatro. II. Obras consultades y utilizadas en la preparación de esta tesis.

Cascó Contell, Emilio. *Genio y figura de Vicente Blasco-Ibáñez: Agitador, aventurero y novelista*. Madrid: Afrodisio Aguado, S.A., 1957. 237p. (Colección vida y historia, 6). "Apéndice 6," pp. 219–25, contains a "lista de las obras de Blasco-Ibáñez traducidas a diferentes idiomas" (by language). Unfortunately, no dates or places of publication are noted for these translations.

Di Salvo, Thomas J. *El arte cuentístico de Vicente Blasco Ibáñez*. Madrid: Editorial Pliegos, 1988. 180p. (Pliegos de ensayo, 27). "Bibliografía," pp. 175–78. Contents: Colecciones de los cuentos de Blasco (By year, 1887–1949). II. Estudios críticos generales. A. Libros. B. Artículos.

León Roca, J. L. *Vicente Blasco-Ibáñez*. Valencia: Ediciones Prometeo, 1967. 661p. "Bibliografía," pp. 620–60. Contents: I. Publicaciones editoriales. II. Publicaciones periodísticas. Both sections are bibliographies of critical studies and biographical sketches of Blasco-Ibáñez and his work.

Medina, Jeremy T. *The Valencian Novels of Vicente Blasco Ibáñez.* Valencia: Albatros/Hispanófila Ediciones, 1984. 100p. "Selected Bibliography," pp. 99–100. Criticism only.

Smith, Paul. *Vicente Blasco Ibáñez.* London: Grant & Cutler, 1976. 127p. (Research Bibliographies and Checklists, 14). Partially annotated entries. Contents: I. Primary Material. A. Repudiated Works. B. Recognized Works. C. Correspondence. D. English Translations. E. Dramatizations and Films. F. Blasco Ibáñez's Translations from the French. II. Secondary Material. A. Books, Pamphlets, Dissertations. B. Articles, Parts of Books, and Other References. III. Index of Blasco Ibáñez's Works. IV. Index of Other Writers.

BLECUA, JOSE MANUEL (1913–)

Navarro, Rosa. "Bibliografía de Jose Manuel Blecua," pp. 7–17 in *Homenaje a José Manuel Blecua ofrecido pos sus discípulos, colegas y amigos* (Madrid: Gredos, 1983). One hundred and forty-five of Blecua's literary criticism works are listed by year, 1938–1982.

BLEIBERG, GERMAN (1915–)

Bleiberg, Germán. *Antología poética.* Selección del autor. Madrid: Alianza Editorial, 1985. 168p. (El libro de bolsillo, 1078). "Obras de Germán Bleiberg," pp. 167–68. Contents: I. Obra poética recogida in volumen (By year, 1935–73). II. Teatro (By year, 1937–76).

Correa, v. 2, pp. 163, 612. Contents: I. Libros. II. Artículos y estudios (criticism).

BOHIGAS BALAGUER, PEDRO (1901–)

Morató, Josefina, and Modesta Oñate. "Bibliografía del doctor Pedro Bohigas Balaguer," *Biblioteconomía* (Barcelona), Nos. 73/74 (1971), 3–30. Three hundred items are listed under the following categories: I. Lengua y literatura. Reseñas. II. Historia de la cultura, paleografía y ciencias del libros. Reseñas. III. Varia. IV. Índice.

BOIXADOS, MARIA DOLORES (192?–)

Galerstein, pp. 49–50.

BORBON, MARIA PAZ DE (1862–)

"María Paz de Borbón," in María del Carmen Simón Palmer's "Tres escritoras españolas en el extranjero," *Cuadernos Bibliográficos*, 47 (1987), 162–68. Contents: I. Manuscritos (1862–1908). II. Obras impresas (1883–1946). III. Traducciones. IV. Publicaciones periódicas (By journal). V. Estudios (criticism).

BORRAS, TOMAS (1891–)

Agulló y Cobo, Mercedes. "Escritores contemporáneos: Tomás Borrás," *El Libro Español*, 1 (1958), 338–341. "Bibliografía," pp. 337–42. Contents: I. Publicaciones. II. Traducciones. Books and pamphlets only are listed.

BOTELLA PASTOR, VIRGILIO (1906–)

Botella Pastor, Virgilio. *La gran ilusión*. Barcelona: Anthropos, 1988. 531p. (Memoria rota: Exilios y heterodoxias, 17). "Virgilio Botella Pastor: bio-bibliografía," pp. 529–31.

BOUSONO, CARLOS (1923–)

Bousoño, Carlos. *Selección de mis versos*. Madrid: Ediciones Cátedra, 1980. 193p. "Bibliografía," pp. 33–36. Contents: I. Libros de poesía (By year, 1943–1976). II. Libros y ensayos de teoría y crítica literarias. III. Algunos trabajos sobre Carlos Bousoño.

______. *Teoría de la cultura y de la expresión poética: Antología de textos y poemas*. Barcelona: Anthropos, 1987. 107p. (Suplemento *Anthropos*, 1987, 3). "Cronología de Carlos Bousoño," pp. 105–107. Includes biographical and bibliographical information," 1923–1987.

Correa, v. 2, pp. 269, 616–17. Contents: I. Libros. II. Artículos y estudios (criticism).

Mantero, pp. 545–46. Contents: I. Libros de poesía. II. Otras publicaciones. III. Sobre Bousoño.

BRAVO-VILLASANTE, CARMEN (1918–)

Galerstein, pp. 51–52.

Peña Muñoz, Manuel. *Bibliografía de Carmen Bravo-Villasante*. Madrid: Artes Gráficas Minerva, 1978. 55p.

BRINES, FRANCISCO (1932–)

CILH, p. 11.

Correa, v. 2, pp. 503, 623. Works by and about the author.

García Martín, J. L. "La poesía completa de Francisco Brines," *Cuadernos Hispanoamericanos*, No. 420 (1985), 194–200. A detailed survey.

BROSSA, JOAN (1919–)

Brossa, Joan. *Antologia poètica (1941–1978).* A cura de Pere Gimferrer. Barcelona: Edicions 62, 1980. 95p. "Bibliografia," p. 15. Contents: I. Estudis. II. Entrevista. "Tavles cronològiques," unpaged. Brossa's works are included under the "vida" section of the table.

______. *Teatre complet.* Barcelona: Edicions 62, 1973. 2 vols. "Relació de l'obra dramàtica de Joan Brossa" (arranged by year, 1945–1968), I, pp. 53–56. "Estudis essencials sobre l'obra de Joan Brossa," I, pp. 57–58.

BUERO VALLEJO, ANTONIO (1916–)

"Bibliografía de y sobre Antonio Buero Vallejo," *Anthropos* (Barcelona), No. 79 (1987), 15–24.

Buero Vallejo, Antonio. *El sueño de la razón: Fantasía en dos partes.* Edición de José García Templado. Madrid: Plaza y Janés, 1986. 283p. (Colección Clásicos Plaza y Janés, 56). "Noticia cronológica (1916–1984)," pp. 11–22. Includes bio-bibliographical data. "Bibliografía mínima sobre Buero Vallejo y *El sueño de la razón,*" pp. 85–86. "Ediciones de *El sueño de la razón,*" p. 87.

______. *La tejedora de sueños. Llegada de los dioes.* Edición de Luis Iglesias Feijoo. Sexta edición. Madrid: Cátedra, 1983. 342p. "Bibliografía selecta," pp. 83–100. Contents: I. Obras de Buero Vallejo (By year, 1949–77). II. Versiones de Buero Vallejo estrenadas. III. Ediciones de las obras incluidas en este volumen. A. *La tejedora de sueños* y traducciones. B. *Llegada de los dioses.* IV. Bibliografía selecta de estudios sobre Buero Vallejo. A. Libros sobre el autor. B. Libros sobre el teatro español contemporáneo (indicates pages that cover Buero Vallejo). C. Artículos. D. Sobre *La tejedora de sueños.* E. Sobre *Llegada de los dioses.*

______. *El terror inmóvil.* Edición de Mariano de Paco. Murcia: Universidad de Murcia, Cátedra de Teatro, 1979. 95p. "Bibliografía esencial," pp. 17–20. Contents: I. Obras dramáticas de Buero Vallejo, 1949–1979 (señalamos la fecha de estreno salvo cuando se indica expresamente). II. Versiones estrenadas. III. Sobre Buero Vallejo (books or excerpts from books only).

______. *El tragaluz.* Con cuadros cronológicos, introducción, bibliografía, notas y llamadas de atención, documentos y orientaciones para el estudio a cargo de José Luis García Barrientos. Madrid: Castalia, 1985, 213p. (Castalia Didática, 9). "Buero Vallejo y su tiempo," pp. 8–15. A table which is divided into the following sections: Año; acontecimientos históricos; vida cultural y artística; vida y obra de Antonio Buero Vallejo.

Estudios sobre Buero Vallejo. Edición de Mariano de Paco. Murcia: Impreso en Sucessores de Nogués, 1984. 377p. "Bibliografía," pp. 351–77. Contents: I. De Buero Vallejo. A. Obra dramáticas (chronologically arranged and includes all editions). B. Versiones estrenadas (by year). C. Otros escritos. II. Libros sobre Buero Vallejo y sobre el teatro español de postguerra.

Forys, Marsha. *Antonio Buero Vallejo and Alfonso Sastre: An Annotated Bibliography*. Metuchen, N.J.: Scarecrow Press, 1988. 209p. (The Scarecrow Author Bibliographies, 81). Descriptive annotations are included only when the main idea is not readily apparent from the title. The 1,512 entries for Buero Vallejo are included on pp. 3–147. Contents: I. Books, Theses and Dissertations. II. Journals, Magazines, and Newspapers. III. Unverified Citations (those that the compiler was unable to check personally). Author index on pp. 197–209.

Halsey, Martha T. *Antonio Buero Vallejo*. New York: Twayne Publishers, Inc., 1973. 178p. "Bibliography," pp. 165–74. Contents: I. Primary Sources. A. Plays by Buero Vallejo (in order of performance, except where play has not been performed). B. Collections of Plays by Buero Vallejo. C. Essays by Buero Vallejo. D. Interviews with Buero Vallejo. II. Secondary Sources. III. Addendum.

Kronik, John W. "Antonio Buero Vallejo: A Bibliography (1949–70)," *Hispania*, 54, No. 4 (December 1971), 856–68. 346 items. "Comprehensiveness and inclusiveness have been the guiding criterion." However, the following materials have been excluded from the bibliography: master's theses; reviews of performances of Buero's plays or of published volumes of plays of Buero; ephemeral news reports in the daily press; histories of literature, manuals, encyclopedias and general surveys. Contents: I. Plays by Buero (by work). II. Translations by Buero. III. Collections of Plays by Buero. IV. Other Writings by Buero. V. Critical Writings about Buero.

Paco, Mariano de. "Bibliografía de y sobre Antonio Buero Vallejo," pp. 101–24, in *Antonio Buero Vallejo: Premio de Literatura en Lengua Castellana "Miguel de Cervantes"* (Barcelona: Anthropos, 1987). Contents: I. De Antonio Buero Vallejo. A. Obras dramáticas (By year, includes publishing history as well as first performance information). B. Versiones estrenadas. C. Otras obras de creación. D. Otros escritos (selection). II. Sobre Antonio Buero Vallejo. A. Estudios sobre Buero Vallejo. B. Libros que incluyen a Buero Vallejo.

Ruggeri Marchetti, Magda. *Il teatro di Antonio Buero Vallejo o il processo verso la verità*. Roma: Bulzoni Editore, 1981. 184p. An annotated and very detailed bibliography. "Bibliografia," pp. 165–82. Contents: I. Raccote. II. Drammi. III. Poesia. IV. Prose critiche e polemiche. V. Critica (on Buero Vallejo, 1973–1980).

BURGOS, CARMEN (1867–1932)
Galerstein, pp. 52–54.

CABAL, FERMIN (1948–)
"Fermín Cabal: Bibliografía," *Alonso*, p. 371. Only his published plays are listed.

CABALLERO BONALD, JOSE MANUEL (1926–)
Caballero Bonald, José Manuel. *Selección natural*. Madrid: Ediciones Cátedra, 1983. 252p. (Letras Hispánicas, 173). "Bibliografía," pp. 37–43. Contents: I. Primeras ediciones de sus libros. A. Poesía. B. Novela. C. Otros obras. II. Bibliografía selecta sobre su obra poética. A. Libros. B. Algunos ensayos y reseñas críticas.
Correa, v. 2, pp. 413, 620. Works by and about the author.
"Jose Manuel Caballero Bonald," in Julia Elizabeth Cabey Riley's *Bibliografía de algunos poetas andaluces de posguerra* (Madrid: Universidad Complutense, Departamento de Bibliografía, 1984).

CABANERO, ELADIO (1930–)
Correa, v. 2, pp. 475, 622. Works by and about the author.

CABEZA DE LEON, SALVADOR FRANCISCO JAVIER (1864–)
Villamil, Enrique F. "Bio-bibliografía de Cabeza de León," *Cuadernos de Estudios Gallegos*, 3 (1948), 253–306. Contents: I. Obras impresas de Cabeza de León," pp. 285–91. II. La obra inacabada de Cabeza de León," pp. 291–306.

CAJAL, ROSA MARIA (1920–)
Galerstein, pp. 55–56.

CALVO, MIGUEL ALONSO. *See* GARCIASOL, RAMON DE.

CALVO DE AGUILAR, ISABEL (1916–)
Galerstein, pp. 56–57.

CALVO-SOTELO, JOAQUIN (1905-)

Calvo-Sotelo Ibáñez-Martín, Pedro. *Bibliografía de Joaquín Calvo-Sotelo*. Madrid: Editorial de la Universidad Complutense, 1981. 12p. (Trabajos del Departamento de Bibliografía; Serie A. Escritores Contemporáneos, 3). 112 entries. Contents: I. Manuscritos. II. Obras dramáticas (por orden cronológico, 1934–1977). III. Varia (1943–1980). IV. Traducciones. V. Estudios sobre la obra de Joaquín Calvo-Sotelo.

Rehder, Ernest C. "Plays of Joaquín Calvo-Sotelo." Unpublished Ph.D. dissertation, University of Florida, 1971. 144p. "Chronological listing and summary (1930–1970) of Plays by Joaquín Calvo-Sotelo Through 1970," pp. 133–137.

CAMINO, LEON FELIPE. *See* FELIPE, LEON.

CAMPION, ARTURO (1854–1937)

Amézaga, Elías. "Ficha bio-bibliográfica de Arturo Campión," *Letras de Deusto* (Bilbao), No. 44 (1989), 29–37.

CAMPOS, JESUS (1938-)

Pérez-Stansfield, pp. 341–42.

CAMPOS, JORGE (1916–1982)

Agulló y Cobo, Mercedes. "Escritores contemporáneos: Jorge Campos," *El Libro Español*, 1 (1958), 511–14. "Bibliografía," pp. 513–14. Books, pamphlets, and translations only.

Campos, Jorge. *Cuentos sobre Alicante y albatera*. Prólogo de Ricardo Blasco. Barcelona: Anthropos, 1985. 129p. (Memoria rota; Exilios y heterodoxias, 6). "Jorge Campos: bio-bibliografía," pp. 123–29. Contents: I. Narrativa (By year, 1940–85). II. Estudios literarios (By year, 1946–81). III. Ediciones, antologías y prólogos (By year, 1940–83).

CANAL, EVA (1857–1932)

"Eva Canal," in María del Carmen Simón Palmer's "Tres escritoras españolas en el extranjero," *Cuadernos Bibliográficos*, 47 (1987), 159–62. Contents: I. Obras impresas (1889–1921). II. Colaboración en publicaciones periódicas. III. Otras obras sin localizar.

CANALES, ALFONSO (1923-)

"Alfonso Canales," in Julia Elizabeth Cabey Riley's *Bibliografía de algunos poetas andaluces de posguerra* (Madrid: Universidad Complutense, Departamento de Bibliografía, 1984).

Correa, v. 2, pp. 375, 619. Contents: I. Libros. II. Artículos y estudios (criticism).

CANELA, MERCE (1956–)
"Mercè Canela: Selected Bibliography," *Catalan Writing*, No. 4 (March 1990), 27. Contents: I. Fiction. II. Translations. III. Awards and Citations.

CANELO, PUREZA (1946–)
CILH, p. 153.
Correa, v. 2, pp. 593, 625. Works by and about the author.
Galerstein, pp. 57–58.

CANO, JOSE LUIS (1911–)
CILH, pp. 160–61. Contents: I. Poesía. II. Antologías poéticas. III. Ediciones y antologías de poetas con prólogo y notas. IV. Crítica y ensayo.
"José Luis Cano," in Julia Elizabeth Cabey Riley's *Bibliografía de algunos poetas andaluces de posguerra* (Madrid: Universidad Complutense, Departamento de Bibliografía, 1984).

CANSINOS-ASSENS, RAFAEL (1882–)
Pera, Cristóbal. "Las novelas cortas de Rafael Cansinos-Asséns en las revistas literarias (1915–1931)," *Monographic Review/Revista Monográfica* (Odessa, Texas), 4 (1988), 163–78. "Bibliografía," p. 167. The bibliography is arranged by year, 1915–31.

CANYA I MARTI, LLUCRETA (1898–)
Galerstein, p. 58.

CAPMANY FARNES, MARIA AURELIA (1918–)
Galerstein, pp. 59–65.
"María Aurelia Capmany Farnes," *O'Connor*, pp. 147–48.

CARBO, JOAQUIM (1932–)
"Joaquim Carbó: Selected Bibliography," *Catalan Writing*, No. 4 (March 1990), 37–38. Contents: I. Fiction. II. Theatre. III. Novels in Comic Book Format. IV. Translations. V. Awards and Citations.

CARNER, JOSEP (1884–1970)
Gabernet i Macia, Ramón. "Aportació bibliográfica al centenari de Josep Carner, 1884–1984," *Revista de Lliberia Antiquaria* (Barcelona), No. 7 (1984), 22–23. Only centenary studies included.

CARNERO, GUILLERMO (1947–)
Correa, v. 2, p. 563. Works by the author.

CARNICER, RAMON (1912–)
"Ramón Carnicer," *Alonso*, p. 65. Only books are listed, 1961–1986.

CARO ROMERO, JOAQUIN (1940–)
"Joaquín Caro Romero," in Julia Elizabeth Cabey Riley's *Bibliografía de algunos poetas andaluces de posguerra* (Madrid: Universidad Complutense, Departamento de Bibliografía, 1984).

CARRANQUE DE RIOS, ANDRES (1902–1936)
Fortea, José Luis. *La obra de Andrés Carranque de Ríos*. Madrid: Editorial Gredos, 1973. 240p. (Biblioteca Románica Hispánica. II. Estudios y Ensayos, 195). "Novelas, poesías, cuentos y artículos de Carranque de Ríos," pp. 226–27. "Artículos sobre Carranque de Ríos (orden cronológico)," pp. 227–29.

CASACUBERTA, JOSEP MARIA DE (n.d.)
Soberanas i Lleó, Amadeu J. "Bibliografia essencial de J. M. Casacuberta," v. 2, pp. 416–29 in *Homenatge a Josep M. de Casacuberta* (Montserrat: Publs. de l'Abadia, 1980–81). Contents: Entries are arranged by year, 1914–1977.

CASANOVA DE LUTOSLAWSKI, SOFIA (1862–1958)
Galerstein, pp. 69–72.

CASONA, ALEJANDRO (pseud. of Alejandro Rodríguez Alvarez, 1903–1965).
Casona, Alejandro. *La dama del Alba*. Edición de José R. Rodríguez Richart. 3a ed. Madrid: Cátedra, 1984. 151p. (Letras Hispánicas, 202). "Bibliografía," pp. 51–56. Contents: I. Ediciones de *La dama del alba* (1944–1981). II. Traducciones (1945–1972). III. Estudios sobre *La dama del alba*.
_____. *Obras completas*. Prólogo de Federico Carlos Sáinz de Robles. Madrid: Aguilar, 1966. 2 vs. "Bibliografía," I, ccxxxviii-ccxliv. Contents: I. Obras de Alejandro Casona. II. Ediciones y traducciones de las obras de Casona (by work). III. Obras acerca de Casona.
_____. *Tres farsas infantiles*. Edición de Evaristo Arce. Gijón: Biblioteca de la Quintana, 1983. 204p. "Bibliografía," pp. 14–23. Contents: I. Obras de Casona. A. Teatro (Listed by year, 1929–1965; gives first performance information). B. Comedias en un

acto (Listed by year, 1935–1962). C. Teatro infantil. D. Revisiones. E. Adaptaciones de teatro extranjero. F. Opera. G. Poesía. H. Prosa. I. Charlas radiofónicas. J. Guiones de cine. II. Obras sobre Casona (books only).

Cervelló-Margolef, Juan Antonio. *Alejandro Casona: Estudios sobre su teatro con una bibliografía sobre el tema.* Köln: Stiasny, 1973. 192p. "Bibliografía casoniana," pp. 149– . Contents: I. Ediciones de las obras completas de Alejandro Casona. II. Selección de las obras de Alejandro Casona. III. Ediciones de cada una de las obras de Alejandro Casona en particular (By chronological work, 1926–1966; includes various editions). IV. Obras de Alejandro Casona que faltan en la edición preparada por F. C. Sáinz de Robles para en Editorial Aguilar de Madrid (By work and by year, 1915–1955). V. Traducciones, adaptaciones y prólogos escritos por Alejandro Casona. VI. Conferencias y artículos periodísticos de Alejandro Casona. VII. Guiones cinematográficos escritos por Alejandro Casona (By year, 1941–1964). VIII. Libretos para operas. IX. Traducciones de las obras de Alejandro Casona (By work). X. Artículos periodísticos, recensiones y estudios críticos sobre las obras de Alejandro Casona. XI. Estudio de las obras dramáticas de Alejandro Casona. XII. Adaptaciones para la televisión española de las obras dramáticas de Alejandro Casona.

Forys, Marsha. "Alejandro Casona: A Bibliography of Criticism through 1987," *Hispania*, 73 (September 1990), 577–92. Includes 504 citations of criticism of Casona's works, as well as descriptions of his life and work. "Citations have been gathered through 1987 and include such things as scholarly evaluations of Casona's work, reviews written after the openings of his plays, interviews, and eulogies written immediately after his death. Sources excluded in this bibliography are general histories of literature, dictionaries, and encyclopedias of biography, and books and articles in which Casona is mentioned but is not the central idea of the book or article. Citations are annotated only when the main idea is not easily understood from the title" (The author). Contents: I. Books, Dissertations and Theses. II. Periodicals. III. Unverified Citations.

Moon, Harold K. *Alejandro Casona.* Boston: Twayne Publishers, Inc., 1985. 157p. "Selected Bibliography," pp. 141–53. Contents: I. Primary Sources. A. Collections (by year, 1941–1967). B. Editions of Individual Plays. C. Films (arranged by year, 1940–46). D. Poetry (arranged chronologically). E. Articles and Essays (arranged by year, 1955–1965). II. Secondary Sources (briefly annotated).

Rodríguez Richart, J. *Vida y teatro de Alejandro Casona*. Oviedo: C.S.I.C., Instituto de Estudios Asturianos del Patronato "José María Quadrado," 1963. 201p. "Bibliografía," pp. 183–98. Contents: I. Obras teatrales de Casona (hasta 1961). A. Título, lugar y año de estreno. B. Ediciones de sus obras. C. Traducciones estrenadas. II. Libros. revistas y periódicos consultadas.

CASTANO, ADOLFO (1928–)
CILH, p. 143.

CASTELO, SANTIAGO (1948–)
CILH, p. 179.

CASTILLO-PUCHE, JOSE LUIS (1919–)
Cerezales, Manuel. *José Luis Castillo-Puche*. Madrid: Ministerio de Cultura, 1981. 167p. (España, escribir hoy, 6). "Cronología," pp. 163–64. "Bibliografía," pp. 165–166. Castillo–Puche's works are listed by year, 1953–1980.
González-Grano de Oro, Emilio. *El español de José L. Castillo-Puche: Estudio léxico*. Madrid: Editorial Gredos, 1983. 478p. (Biblioteca Románica Hispánica. II. Estudios y Ensayos, 334). "Bibliografía," pp. 395–99. Contents: I. Obras de ficción (novela, cuento y otras narraciones), biografía, viaje, ensayo de Castillo-Puche (by year, 1943–1982). II. Artículos de Castillo-Puche (by year 1956–1983). III. Material no publicado de Castillo-Puche. IV. Escritos sobre Castillo-Puche (very selective). "Cronología de José L. Castillo-Puche," pp. 403–07.

CASTRO, AMERICO (1885–1972)
"A Bibliography of the Writings of Américo Castro," pp. 1–36, in *Américo Castro: The Impact of His Thought* (Madison, Wisc.: Hispanic Seminary of Medieval Studies, 1988). The 479 entries are arranged by year, 1910–1983.

CASTRO, JUAN ANTONIO (1927–)
"Juan Antonio Castro," pp. 16–20 in L. Teresa Valdivieso's *España: Bibliografía de un teatro "silenciado"* (Lincoln, Neb.: Society of Spanish and Spanish-American Studies, 1979). Contents: I. Notas biográficas. II. Obras inéditas. III. Obras publicadas. IV. Traducciones. V. Escritos y declaraciones. VI. Estudios críticos.
Pérez-Stansfield, p. 342.

CASTROVIEJO, CONCHA (1915–)
Galerstein, pp. 75–76.

CELA, CAMILO JOSE (1916-)

Cela, Camilo José. *La colmena.* Edición de Raquel Asún. Madrid: Editorial Castalia, 1984. 456p. (Clásicos Castalia, 140) "Noticia bibliográfica," pp. 75–76. Contents: I. Las ediciones más importantes de *La colmena* (By year, 1951–1983). "Bibliografía selecta," pp. 77–85. Contents: I. Camilo José Cela y la novela española de posguerra. II. Camilo José Cela y *La colmena.* III. Bibliografía de Camilo José Cela (Books only by year, 1942–1983).

______. *La colmena.* Edición de Jorge Urrutia. Madrid: Ediciones Cátedra, 1988. 347p. (Letras Hispánicas, 300). "Bibliografía," pp. 35–39. Contents: I. Ediciones principales de *La colmena.* II. Bibliografía crítica.

Contreras, Pedro A. "Bibliografía de Camilo José Cela," *Insula*, No. 518/19 (Febrero/marzo de 1990), Supplement insert, pp. i-viii. Contents: I. Obras completas y escogidos. II. Obras narrativas. A. Novelas. B. Novelas cortas. C. Poesía. D. Teatro. E. Artículos y ensayos. F. Viajes. G. Varios. 1. Diccionarios. 2. Miscelánea. 3. Biografía. 4. Versiones y ediciones. Books only included in sections I and II. III. En torno a Camilo José Cela. A. Monográficos. B. Selección de estudios (articles).

Huarte Morton, Fernando. "Camilo José Cela: bibliografía," *Revista Hispánica Moderna*, 28, Nos. 2/4 (abril/octubre de 1962), 210–20. Contents: I. Ediciones. II. Poemas y artículos sueltos, folletos, prólogos (selección). III. Antologías. IV. Traducciones. V. Estudios sobre Cela (interviews and newspaper book reviews are omitted).

______. "Ensayo de una bibliografía de *La familia de Pascual Duarte*," *Papeles de Son Armadans*, Año 13, tomo 48, No. 142 (1968), 59–165. A descriptive bibliography. Includes all editions and translations, listed by year, 1942–1968.

______. "Ediciones de *La Familia de Pascual Duarte*," *Los Cuadernos del Norte* (Oviedo), No. 15 (1982), 4–9.

Lapuente, Felipe-Antonio. "La crítica norte-americana frente a Cela," *Boletín de Filología Española*, Nos. 36/37 (julio/diciembre de 1970), 11–20. Annotated entries. Contents: I. Libros. II. Artículos. III. Tesis doctorales. A. Tesis terminadas. B. Tesis sin terminar.

McPheeters, D. W. *Camilo José Cela.* New York: Twayne Publishers, Inc., 1969. 178p. "Selected Bibliography," pp. 166–72. Contents: I. The writings of Cela. A. Collections. B. Books. II. Secondary Sources. A. Books. B. Articles.

Mantero, pp. 546–47. Contents: I. Libros de poesía. II. Otras publicaciones. III. Sobre Camilo José Cela.

Urrutia, Jorge. *Cela: "La Familia de Pascual Duarte."* Madrid: Sociedad General Español de Librería, 1982. 156p. "Ediciones de *La Familia de Pascual Duarte,*" pp. 147–48. "Libros y números monográficos de revista sobre Jorge Cela," pp. 149–50. "Estudios," pp. 151–56.

CELA TRULOCK, JORGE (1932–)

Sáez Sánchez, Carmen. *Bibliografía de Jorge Cela Trulock.* Madrid: Editorial de la Universidad Complutense, 1981. 12p. (Trabajos del Departamento de Bibliografía; Serie A: Escritores Contemporáneos, 4). Contents: I. Novelas (por orden cronológico, 1958–1981). II. Cuentos, artículos y reseñas (por orden cronológico, 1953–1981). III. Estudios sobre la obra de Jorge Cela Trulock (por orden cronológico, 1954–1980).

CELAYA, GABRIEL (pseud. of Rafael Múgica Celaya, 1911–1991)

Celaya, Gabriel. *Memorias inmemoriales.* Edición de Gustavo Domínguez. 2a. edición. Madrid: Cátedra, 1982. 188p. (Letras Hispánicas, 130). "Bibliografía," pp. 43–48. Contents: I. Obras de Gabriel Celaya. A. Poesía (By year, 1935–80). B. En colaboración con Amparo Gastón (By year, 1953–58). C. Narración (by year, 1946–65). D. Teatro. E. Ensayo. F. Traducciones (By year, 1947–1954). II. Algunos estudios sobre su obra (very selective).

______. *Poesía.* Introducción y selección de Angel González. Madrid: Alianza Editorial, 1977. 160p. "Bibliografía de Gabriel Celaya," pp. 30–32. Contents: I. Poesía (By year, 1935–1976). II. Narración (By year, 1946–1965). III. Teatro. IV. Ensayo (By year, 1951–1974).

Chicharro Chamorro, Antonio. *Gabriel Celaya: Frente a la literatura española.* Sevilla: Ediciones Alfar, 1987. 100p. "Bibliografía de Gabriel Celaya (selective)," pp. 85–92. Contents: I. Publicaciones de cáracter literario. A. Poesía. 1. Libros de poesía (By year, 1935–1984). 2. Publicaciones que recogen determinados libros de poesía ya publicados y/o inéditos (By year, 1950–1984). 3. Antologías. 4. Libros de poesía escritos en colaboración con Amparo Gastón (1953–1958). B. Narrativa (By year, 1946–1980). C. Teatro. II. Publicaciones de cáracter téorico y crítico literario. A. Libros. B. Libros en colaboración. C. Otras publicaciones. "Bibliografía sobre Gabriel Celaya (selección)," p. 93.

Correa, v. 2, pp. 123–24, 610–11. Contents: I. Libros. II. Artículos y estudios (criticism).

Ugalde, Sharon Keefe. *Gabriel Celaya.* Boston: Twayne Publishers, Inc., 1978. 164p. "Selected Bibliography," pp. 151–57. Contents: I. Primary Sources. A. Poetry (by year, 1935–1976). B. Poetry in Collaboration with Amparo Gastón. C. Narratives. D. Essays. E. Drama. F. Translations. G. Selected Articles. II. Secondary Sources (annotated).

CERNUDA, LUIS (1902–)

Cárdenas, Mercedes de. "La poesía de Luis Cernuda. Temas, estilo y símbolos." Unpublished Ph.D. dissertation, Michigan State University, 1972. 318p. "Bibliografía," pp. 286–318. Contents: I. Obras de Cernuda. A. Libros de Cernuda. B. Poesías sueltas. C. Prosa. 1. Creación. 2. Ensayo y crítica. D. Traducción. E. Epistolario. F. Poemas de Cernuda traducidos a otras lenguas. II. Bibliografía sobre Luis Cernuda. A. Homenajes. B. Poemas dedicados a Cernuda. C. Estudios sobre Luis Cernuda. D. Bibliografía general.

Cernuda, Luis. *Antología.* Edición de José María Capote Benot. Madrid: Ediciones Cátedra, 1981. 383p. "Bibliografía selecta," pp. 53–56. Contents: I. Obras de Luis Cernuda. A. Poesía. B. Prosa. II. Obras sobre Luis Cernuda. A. Libros. B. Homenajes. C. Estudios y artículos.

______. *Poesía completa.* Edición a cargo de Derek Harris y Luis Maristany. 2a. ed. revisada. Barcelona: Barral, 1977. 978p. "Publicaciones poéticas de Luis Cernuda," pp. 935–44. Contents: I. Libros. A. Ediciones en vida de Cernuda. B. Otras ediciones y traducciones. II. Publicaciones hemerográficas. A. Poesía. B. Traducción. III. Textos inéditos.

______. *Prosa completa.* Barcelona: Barral, 1975. 1611p. "Bibliografía," pp. 1542–77. Contents: I. Publicaciones en prosa de Luis Cernuda. A. Libros. B. Publicaciones hemerográficas. II. Bibliografía sobre Luis Cernuda. A. Homenajes. 1. Revistas. 2. Poemas. B. Monografías. C. Estudios y artículos.

Correa, v. 1, pp. 457–58, 552–53. Works by and about the author.

Curry, Richard K. *En torno a la poesía de Luis Cernuda.* Madrid: Editorial Pliegos, 1985. 186p. "Bibliografía," pp. 153–82. Contents: 1927–36. A. Reseñas. B. Homenajes. C. Artículos, ensayos y miscelánea. II. 1937–40. A. Reseñas. B. Artículos, ensayos y miscelánea. III. 1950–62. A. Reseñas. B. Homenajes. C. Monografías. D. Artículos, ensayos y miscelánea. IV. 1963–74. A. Reseñas. B. Homenajes. C. Monografías. D. Artículos, ensayos y miscelánea. V. 1975–83. A. Reseñas. B. Homenajes. C. Monografías. D. Artículos, ensayos y miscelánea.

González Muela, pp. 59–62. Works by and about Cernuda are arranged chronologically.

Harris, Derek. *Luis Cernuda: A Study of the Poetry*. London: Támesis Books, Ltd. 1973. 188p. "Bibliography," pp. 185–88. Contents: I. Works by Cernuda (includes journal and newspaper articles). II. Works on Cernuda. III. Other Works Cited.

Jiménez-Fajardo, Salvador. *The Word and the Mirror: Critical Essays on the Poetry of Luis Cernuda*. Rutherford, N.J.: Fairleigh Dickinson University Press, 1989. 243p. "Bibliography," pp. 225–28. Contents: I. Works by Cernuda (By year, 1927–1982). II. Translations by Cernuda. III. Homage Issues. IV. Criticism. A. Books. B. Selected Articles.

Maristany, Luis. *"La Realidad y el deseo" de Luis Cernuda*. Barcelona: Editorial Caia, 1982. 105p. "Breve guía bibliográfica de *La Realidad y el deseo*," pp. 101–05. Contents: I. Ediciones de Luis Cernuda. II. Bibliografía sobre *La Realidad y el Deseo*. A. Monografías. B. Artículos.

Müller, Elisabeth. *Die Dichtung Luis Cernuda*. Genève: Librairie E. Droz; Paris: Librairie Minard, 1962. 198p. (Kölner romanistische Arbeiten. Neue Folge-Heft 25). "Bibliographie," pp. 180–91. Contents: I. Werke Cernudas. A. Gedichte. B. Prosa. C. Einzelveröffentlichungen: Gedichte. D. Einzelveröffentlichungen: Prosa. E. Übersetzungen. II. Studien über Cernuda (in chronological order, 1926–61). III. Allgemeine Literatur.

Peregrín Otero, Carlos. "Bibliografía sobre Cernuda," *La Caña Gris* (Valencia), Nos. 6/7/8 (otoño 1962), 200–14. Includes 196 items arranged chronologically, 1927–61.

Real Ramos, César. *Luis Cernuda y la generación del 27*. Salamanca: Ediciones Universidad de Salamanca, 1983. 138p. (Acta Salmanticensia, Serie Varia, Filosofía y Letras, 148). "Orientación bibliográfica" (criticism), pp. 133–38.

Silver, Philip. *Luis Cernuda: El Poeta en su leyenda*. Madrid, Barcelona: Alfaguara, 1972. 262p. "Bibliografía," pp. 255–62. Contents: I. Ediciones de obras y traducciones de Cernuda. A. Obras. B. Traducciones de Cernuda. II. Otras obras citadas (including critical studies on Cernuda). III. Estudios monográficos sobre Cernuda (includes theses).

CIGES APARICIO, MANUEL (1873–1936)

Ciges Aparicio, Manuel. *Novelas*. Edición, introducción y notas de Cecilio Alonso. Valencia: Consellería de Cultura, 1986. 3 vols. (Clàssics Valencians, 3–5). "Obras de Manuel Ciges Aparicio," v. 1, pp. 88–90. Contents: I. Originales (By year, 1903–1934). II. Traducciones (By year, 1903–1928).

CIRLOT, JUAN-EDUARDO (1916–1973)

Cirlot, Juan-Eduardo. *Obra poética.* Edición de Clara Janés. Madrid: Ediciones Cátedra, 1981. 325p. "Bibliografía," pp. 43–47. Contents: I. Obra de Juan-Eduardo Cirlot (arranged chronologically under the following headings): A. Poesía. B. Poemas en prosa y aforismos. C. Simbología. D. Libros sobre arte. E. Monografías. F. Ensayos literarios. II. Breve bibliografía sobre la obra poética de Cirlot.

Pariente, pp. 81–82. Contents: I. Libros de poesía (By year, 1943–81). II. Procedencia de los Textos.

CLAVERIA, CARLOS (1909–1974)

"Bio-bibliografía de Carlos Clavería (1909–1974)," *Archivum* (Oviedo), 25 (1975), 23–39. Contents: Nota biográfica. II. Literatura española y comparada. III. Lingüística. IV. Trabajos misceláneos. V. Traducciones. VI. Reseñas. VII. Reseñas sobre la vida y la obra de Carlos Clavería.

COLINAS, ANTONIO (1946–)

"Antonio Colinas: Bibliografía," *Alonso*, p. 347. Contents: I. Poesía (By year, 1969–1983). II. Novela (By year, 1985–1986). III. Otras obras (By year, 1974–1981). Books only.

Correa, v. 2, pp. 581, 625. Works by and about the author.

COLLANTES DE TERAN Y DELAIME, ALEJANDRO (1901–1933)

Márquez González, María del Pilar. *Alejandro Collantes de Terán, poeta de Sevilla.* Sevilla: Gráf. del Sur, 1973. 284p. (Publicaciones de la Excma. Diput. provincial de Sevilla. Sección literatura, I, 1). "Apéndice II: Noticia de la obra editada en prosa y de la obra inédita en verso y en prosa," pp. 254–264. Contents: I. Obra editada en prosa. A. Novela. B. Teatro. C. Otros trabajos. II. Obra inédita en verso y prosa. A. Verso. 1. Poesía. 2. Teatro. B. Prosa. 1. Novela. 2. Teatro. 3. Otros trabajos. "Apéndice III: Descripción de la bibliografía del autor," pp. 265–72 (by work).

CONDE, CARMEN (1907–)

CILH, pp. 125–26. Poetry books only.

Conde, Carmen. *Antología poética.* Selección y estudio preliminar de Rosario Hiriart. Madrid: Espasa-Calpe, 1985. 209p. "Bibliografía," pp. 205–09. Contents: I. Obras de Carmen Conde. A. Poesía. 1. Libros. B. Prosa. 1. Novela. 2. Estudios, ensayos, biografías y memorias. III. Antologías. IV. Libros para niños.

_____. *Brocal; Y poemas a María*. Edición de Rosario Hiriart. Madrid: Biblioteca Nueva, 1984. 151p. "Bibliografía," pp. 145–51. Contents: I. Obras de Carmen Conde. A. Poesía. 1. Libros. B. *Brocal*, ediciones. II. Prosa. A. Novela. B. Estudios, ensayos, biografías y memorias. III. Antologías. IV. Libros para niños.

_____. *Memoria puesta en olvido (antología personal)*. Madrid: Ediciones Torremozas, 1987. 317p. "Bibliografía," pp. 309–13. Contents: I. Obras de Carmen Conde. A. Poesía. 1. Libros (By year, 1934–1985). 2. *Brocal*, ediciones (1929–1980). II. Prosa. A. Novela (By year, 1944–1980). B. Estudios, ensayos, biografías y memorias (By year, 1944–1986). III. Antologías (By year, 1955–1971). IV. Libros para niños (By year, 1943–1985).

Correa, v. 2, pp. 45–46, 605. Contents: I. Libros. II. Artículos y estudios (criticism).

Galerstein, pp. 77–81.

Luis, Leopoldo de. *Carmen Conde*. Madrid: Ministerio de Cultura, Dirección General de Promoción del Libro y la Cinematografía, 1982. 158p. "Bibliografía," pp. 153–56. Contents: I. Poesía (By year, 1929–1980). II. Antologías. III. Prosa (By year, 1944–1980). IV. Ensayos literarios (By year, 1944–1979). V. Libros para niños (By year, 1943–1982).

CORPUS BARGA (Pseud. of Andrés García de la Barga Gómez de la Serna, 1887–1975)

Fuentes Moya, Rafael, and Carmen Rodríguez Santos. *Bibliografía de Corpus Barga*. Madrid: Universidad Complutense, 1982. 55p. (Trabajos del Departamento de Bibliografía, 8). Contents: Poemas, novelas, artículos (By year, 1904–1978). II. Traducciones. III. Bibliografía sobre Corpus Barga.

CREMER, VICTORIANO (1908–)

Correa, v. 2, pp. 205, 614–15. Contents: I. Libros. II. Artículos y estudios (criticism).

"Victoriano Cremer: Bibliografía," *Alonso*, p. 13. Contents: I. Poesía (By year, 1944–1986). II. Narrativa (By year, 1958–1970). III. Teatro. IV. Otras obras (By year, 1968–1983). Books only.

CRESPO, ANGEL (n.d.)

"Cronología de Angel Crespo," *Anthropos* (Barcelona), No. 97 (1989), 30–34. Includes bio-bibliographical information.

CRIADO DE VAL, MANUEL (1917–)

Ruiz Ortiz, Víctor. "Bibliografía y perfil literaria e historia de Val," pp. 681–93 in *Imago Hispaniae: Homenaje a Manuel Criado de Val* (Kassel: Reichenberger, 1989).

CRUSAT, PAULINA (1900–)

Galerstein, pp. 83–84.

CUNQUEIRO, ALVARO (1911–)

Martínez Torrón, Diego. *La fantasía lúdica de Alvaro Cunqueiro*. La Coruña: Ediciós do Castro, 1980. 179p. "Bibliografía," pp. 173–75. Contents: I. Bibliografía de Alvaro Cunqueiro (facilitada por el autor). A. En gallego (by year). B. En castellano (by year).

Odriozola, Antonio. "Lembranza de Alvaro Cunqueiro e unha bibliografia máis da sua obra," *Grial*, No. 72 (abril/maio/xunio 1981), 235+. Contents: I. Os libros de Cunqueiro e as suas ediciόns imaxinadas (by work). D. Pequenas historias (by work). E. Anaios na prensa. F. As terras galegas (by work). G. Cociña do país (by work). H. Estampas e xentes galegas. I. Obra en galego completa. II. Colaboraciόns no outros libros. III. Artigos nas publicaciόns periόdicas.

Torre, Cristina de la. *La narrativa de Alvaro Cunqueiro*. Madrid: Editorial Pliegos, 1988. 164p. "Bibliografía," pp. 155–64. Contents: I. Obras de Alvaro Cunqueiro (By year, 1939–1976). II. Obras críticas.

CHABAS, JUAN (1898–1954)

Pérez Bazo, Javier. *Juan Chabás y Martí: Vida y obra*. Alicante: Instituto de Estudios Alicantinos, 1981. 295p. (Serie 1, No. 71). Contents: "Bibliografía activa del autor," pp. 265–75. I. Artículos en publicaciones periódicas. A. Creación: verso y prosa (by year, 1922–1960). B. Crítica literaria (by year, 1919–1970). C. Crítica teatral (by year, 1927–1937). D. Noticias teatrales (by year, 1933–1934). E. Política y cultura (by year, 1937–1948). II. Libros. A. Creación: verso y prosa (by year, 1921–1956). B. Crítica literaria e historias de literatura (by year, 1929–1962). C. Varia (by year, 1929–1955). D. Traducciones (by year, 1923–1930). "Bibliografía pasiva sobre el autor," pp. 277–79.

______. "Síntesis biográfica: Anotaciones sobre la obra y bibliografía de Juan Chabás," *Dianium* (Denia, Alicante), 4 (1989), 15–35.

CHACEL, ROSA (1898–)

Galerstein, pp. 84–87.

Porlan, Alberto. *La sinrazión de Rosa Chacel*. Madrid: Anjana Ediciones, 1984. 105p. "Bibliografía de Rosa Chacel (books only)," pp. 103–104. Contents: I. Novela (By year, 1930–84). II. Ensayo (By year, 1971–81). III. Relatos (By year, 1952–71). IV. Poesía (By year, 1936–78). V. Memorias. VI. Diarios.

CHAMPOURCIN Y MORAN DE LOREDO, ERNESTINA DE (1905–)

Galerstein, pp. 89–91.

CHICHARRO, EDUARDO (1905–1964)

Pariente, pp. 82–83. Contents: I. Libros de poesía (By year, 1966–74). II. Estudios sobre su poesía. III. Procedencia de los textos.

CHORDA I REQUESIENI, MARI (1942–)

Galerstein, p.76.

DELGADO, AGUSTIN (1941–)

"Agustín Delgado: Bibliografía," *Alonso*, p. 245. Contents: I. Poesía (By year, 1967–1983). II. Ensayo. Books only.

DELIBES, MIGUEL (1920–)

Alvar, Manuel. *El mundo novelesco de Miguel Delibes*. Madrid: Gredos, 1987. 158p. (Biblioteca Románica Hispánica; Estudios y Ensayos, 354). "Bibliografía," pp. 127–45. Contents: I. Obras de Miguel Delibes (By year, 1947–1982). II. Estudios sobre la obra de Miguel Delibes (By year, 1948–1983).

Delibes, Miguel. *La mortaja*. Edición de Gonzalo Sobejano. Madrid: Cátedra, 1984. 201p. (Letras Hispánicas, 202). "Bibliografía," pp. 67–75. Contents: I. De Miguel Delibes. A. Novelas. B. Narrativa breve. C. Ensayos. D. Teatro. E. Obras completas. II. Sobre Miguel Delibes. A. Novela española contempóranea. B. Miguel Delibes y su obra. C. Cuento español contempóraneo.

Gullón, Agnes. *La novela experimental de Miguel Delibes*. Madrid: Taurus, 1980. 167p. (Persiles, 128). "Referencias: Particulares sobre Miguel Delibes," pp. 161–64.

Rey, Alfonso L. *La originalidad novelística de Delibes*. Santiago de Compostela: Universidad de Santiago de Compostela, 1974. 293p. "Bibliografía," pp. 283–93. Contents: I. Novelas de Delibes. II. Libros y artículos consultadas.

Rodríguez, Jesús. *El sentimiento del miedo en la obra de Miguel Delibes*. Madrid: Editorial Pliegos, 1989? 141p. (Pliegos de Ensayo, 38). "Bibliografía," pp. 137–41. Contents: I. De Miguel Delibes. A. Novelas (By year, 1948–1983). B. Narrativa breve (By year, 1957–1984). C. Ensayos (By year, 1956–1982). D. Teatro. II. Sobre Miguel Delibes.

DIAZ DE ESCOVAR, NARCISO (1860–1935)

Bejarano Robles, F. *Bibliografía de las obras de D. Narciso Díaz de Escovar*. Málaga: Publicaciones de la Caja de Ahorros Provincial, Imprenta Dardo, 1961. 60p.

DIAZ DE SAEZ, FRANCISCA (n.d.)

Galerstein, p. 93.

DIAZ FERNANDEZ, JOSE (1899–1941)

Boetsch, Laurent. *José Díaz Fernández y la otra generación del '27*. Madrid: Editorial Pliegos, 1985? 167p. (Pliegos de ensayo, 7). "Bibliografía," pp. 165–67. Includes works by and about José Díaz Fernández.

DIAZ-PLAJA, GUILLERMO (1909–1984)

CILH, pp. 202–03. Includes the author's poetical works only, 1941–79.

Santos, Dámaso. *Conversaciones con Guillermo Díaz-Plaja*. Madrid: Ed. Magisterio Español, 1972. 218p. "Bibliografía," pp. 207–16. Two hundred items listed chronologically, 1928–72.

DICENTA, JOAQUIN (1862–1917)

Dicenta, Joaquín. *Juan José*. Edición de Jaime Mas. Madrid: Cátedra, 1982. 159p. "Bibliografía," pp. 61–64. Contents: I. Estudios sobre la obra de Joaquín Dicenta. II. Otras obras utilizadas que contienen información.

DIEGO, GERARDO (1896–1987)

Correa, v. 1, pp. 198–99, 528–30. Works by and about the author.

Diego, Gerardo. *Alondra de verdad. Angeles de Compostela*. Edición, introducción y notas de Francisco Javier Díez de Revenga. Madrid: Castalia, 1985. (Clásicos Castalia, 145). "Noticia bibliográfica," p. 59. Contents: I. Ediciones completas de *Alondra de Verdad*. II. Ediciones completas de *Angeles de Compostela*. "Bibliografía selecta," pp. 61–66. Contents: I. Bibliografía sobre Gerardo Diego. II. Homenajes. III. Libros poéticos de Gerardo Diego (By year, 1920–1972). IV. Colecciones de obras y antologías propios (By year, 1941–1980).

_____. *Manual de espumas. Versos humanos*. Edición de Milagros Arizmendi. Madrid: Cátedra, 1986. 231p. "Bibliografía del autor (By year, 1920–1985)," pp. 67–69. "Bibliografía crítica," pp. 69–72. "Homenajes," p. 72.

_____. *Obras completas*. Edición preparada por Gerardo Diego. Edición, introducción, cronología, bibliografía y notas de Francisco Javier Díez de Revenga. Madrid: Aguilar, 1989– "Bibliografía de la obra poética," v. 1, pp. lxxxvii–xcvii.

Gallego Morell, Antonio. *Vida y poesía de Gerardo Diego*. Barcelona: Editorial Aedos, 1956. 272p. (Biblioteca biográfica, 7). "Bibliografía," pp. 221–65. Contents: I. Ediciones. A. Poesía. B. Antologías y textos. C. Tirajes apartes y folletos. II. Prosa (by year, 1918–1955). III. Algunos poemas no recogidos en libro (by year, 1919–1956). IV. Estudios. V. Traducciones. VI. Elogios y retratos literarios. VII. Libros y poemas dedicados. VIII. Iconografía.

Pérez, J. Bernardo. *Fases de la poesía creacionista de Gerardo Diego*. Valencia: Albatros, 1989. 155p. (Albatros/Hispanófila, 52). "Bibliografía," pp. 151–55. Contents: I. Obra poética, artículos, conferencias y antologías de Gerardo Diego. II. Obras y artículos de referencia (includes criticism and general works).

DIESTE, EDUARDO (1882–1954)

Dieste, Eduardo. *Obra selecta. Cuentos, teatro y teoría de estética*. Prólogos de Rafael Dieste y de Carlos Gurméndez. Barcelona: Anthropos, 1987. 259p. "Eduardo Dieste: Bio-bibliografía," pp. 255–59.

DIESTE, RAFAEL (1899–1981)

"Cronoloxia e bibliografía de Rafael Dieste," *Grial* (Vigo), No. 78 (1982), 489–500.

Dieste, Rafael. *Historias e invenciones de Félix Muriel*. Edición de Estelle Irizarry. Madrid: Cátedra, 1985. 262p. "Bibliografía," pp. 65–80. Contents: I. Obras de Rafael Dieste (en orden de publicación). A. Libros (By year, 1926–1985). B. Obras no recogidas en libros de Dieste (By year, 1934–1982). C. Traducciones y adaptaciones de otros autores (By year, 1939–1958). II. Estudios sobre Rafael Dieste. III. Sobre *Historias e invenciones de Félix Muriel*. IV. Otros artículos sobre poesía, teatro y narrativa. V. Sobre los ensayos de Rafael Dieste.

Irizarry, Estelle. *La creación literaria de Rafael Dieste*. La Coruña: Edicios do Castro, 1980. 292p. "Bibliografía," pp. 279–287. Contents: I. Obras de Rafael Dieste. A. Libros. B. Obras varias (hasta 1939). 1. Colaboraciones en *Hora de España*. 2. Colaboraciones en *Nova Galiza* (Selecció). C. Obras varias (desde 1939). D. Traducciones de otros autores, adaptaciones. II. Estudios sobre la obra de Rafael Dieste. A. Artículos generales (por orden alfabético). B. Sobre *Historias e invenciones de Félix Muriel.* C. Otros escritos artículos sobre poesía, teatro y narrativa. D. Sobre los libros de ensayos de Rafael Dieste.

DIEZ, LUIS MATEO (1942-)
"Luis Mateo Díez; Bibliografía," *Alonso*, p. 305. Contents: I. Poesía (By year, 1972–1986). II. Ensayo. Books only.

DIEZ-CANEDO, ENRIQUE (1879–1944)
Fernández Gutiérrez, José María. *Enrique Díez-Canedo: Su tiempo y su obra.* Badajoz: Departamento de Publicaciones de la Excma. Diputación, 1984. 215p. "Bibliografía," pp. 210–15. Contents: I. Libros. II. Folletos y libros o colaboraciones breves. III. Artículos no recogidos en volumen. IV. Traducciones. V. Prólogos, introducciones o epílogos.

DIOSDADO, ANA (1938-)
Galerstein, pp. 93–95.
"Ana Diosdado," *O'Connor*, pp. 151–52.

DOMENCHINA, JUAN JOSE (1898–1959)
Rosenbaum, Sidonia C. *Juan José Domenchina: bibliografía," Revista Hispánica Moderna*, 3 (1937), 216–17. Contents: I. Ediciones. II. Estudios.

DOMENECH I ESCATE DE CANELLAS, MARIA (1877–1952)
Galerstein, p. 95.

DONA JIMENEZ, JUANA (1919-)
Galerstein, pp. 95–96.

DUQUE, AQUILINO (1931-)
"Aquilino Duque," in Julia Elizabeth Cabey Riley's *Bibliografía de algunos poetas andaluces de posguerra* (Madrid: Universidad Complutense, Departamento de Bibliografía, 1984).

DURAN, MANUEL (1925-)
Correa, v. 2, pp. 391, 620. Works by and about the author.

ECHEVARRIA, MARIA JESUS (n.d.)
Galerstein, p. 97.

ENCISO, PILAR (1926-)
"Pilar Enciso," *O'Connor*, p. 152

ENSENYAT, FRANXESA (1952-)
Galerstein, p. 98.

ENTRAMBASAGUAS, JOAQUIN DE (1904-)
Morales, Francisco, and Victor Ruiz Ortiz. "Nuestros filólogos: Joaquín de Entrambasaguas," *Boletín de Filología Española*, Nos. 15/17 (mayo/diciembre de 1965), 3–33. Contents: I. Historia y crítica de la literatura. II. Varios. III. Creación. IV. Reseñas de libros.

ESCOBEDO, JOANA (1942-)
Galerstein, p. 98.

ESPINA, CONCHA (1879–1955)
Bretz, Mary Lee. *Concha Espina*. Boston: Twayne Publishers, Inc., 1980. 156p. "Selected Bibliography," pp. 152–53. Contents: I. Primary Sources. II. Secondary Sources.
Galerstein, pp. 99–104.
Lavergne, Gérard. *Vida y obra de Concha Espina*. Traducción de Irene Gambra. Madrid: Fundación Universitaria Española, 1986. 661p. (Biblioteca de Hispanismo, 10). "Contribución a la bibliografía cronológica de las obras de Concha Espina y de las críticas," pp. 582–642. Contents: I. Obras (By year, 1888–1978; includes books, reeditions, journal and newspaper articles). II. Traducciones (By language). III. Críticas (By year, 1888–1983).
Romo Arregui, Josefina. "Concha Espina: bibliografía," *Cuadernos de Literatura Contemporánea*, No. 1 (1942), 19–22. Contents: I. Ediciones. II. Ediciones escolares. III. Traducciones. IV. Estudios.

ESPINOSA, AGUSTIN (1897–1939)
Pariente, pp. 85–86. Contents: I. Obras (By year, 1930–82). II. Procedencia de los textos.

ESPRIU, SALVADOR (1913-)
Espriu, Salvador. *Antología lírica*. Edición bilingüe de José Batlló. Madrid: Ediciones Cátedra, 1977. 327p. "Bibliografía," pp. 53–

54. Contents: I. Obra poética de Salvador Espriu (1946–1973). II. Estudios sobre la obra de Salvador Espriu.

Pijoan Picas, María Isabel. "Selección bibliográfica de Salvador Espriu," *Nuevo Hispanismo* (Madrid), No. 2 (primera 1982), 233, 235, 237–49. Contents: I. Obras de Salvador Espriu. A. Prosa. B. Teatro. C. Crítica. D. Poesía. II. Obras sobre Salvador Espriu. A. Semblanzas y entrevistas en torno a su personalidad. B. Estudios sobre la obra de Salvador Espriu. 1. Aportaciones en obras de diversa índole. 2. No exclusivas sobre el autor. a. Enciclopedias y diccionarios. b. Estudios sobre literatura en general. c. Ensayos sobre determinados géneros literarios. d. Ensayos con especial dedicación al autor. 3. Obras exclusivas sobre el citado autor. a. Monografías. b. Introducciones y apéndices. c. Tesis sobre el autor. 4. Colaboraciones en publicaciones periódicas. a. En lengua castellana. b. En lengua catalana. c. En otras lenguas. C. Volúmenes de homenaje.

Süss, Kurt. *Untersuchungen zum Gedichtwerk Salvador Esprius.* Nürnberg: Verlag Hans Carl, 1978. 210p. (Erlanger Beiträge zur Sprach- und Kunstwissenschaft, 59). "Schriften des autors," pp. 186–91. Contents: I. Sammelbände. II. Literarische Prosa. III. Theater. D. Gedichtwerk. E. Ubersetzungen, anthologien. "Arbeiter über Espriu," pp. 191–95. Contents: I. Untersuchungen, besprechungen, prologe. II. Interviews. III. Notizen, Kritik der Kritik.

ESQUER TORRES, RAMON (1932–1969)

Diez Taboada, Juan María. "Necrología: El profesor Ramón Esquer Torres," *Boletín de Filología Española*, Nos. 32/33 (julio/diciembre de 1969), 79–83. "Bibliografía," pp. 80–83. Contents: I. Libros. II. Artículos. III. Artículos en el *Boletín de Filología Española.*

ESTELLES, VICENT ANDRES (1924–)

A biobibliography of the author, including translations, appears in David Herschel Rosenthal's "Modern Catalan Poetry: A Critical Introduction with Translations" (Unpublished doctoral dissertation, City University of New York, 1977).

Pérez Montaner, Jaume, and Vicent Salvador. *Una aproximació a Vicent Andrés Estèlles.* València: Eliseu Climent, Editor, 1981. 99p. (Quaderns Tres i Quatre, 21). "Bibliografía," pp. 89–99. Contents: I. Llibres de poesia de Vicent Andrés Estèlles (By year, 1953–1980). II. Poemes publicats en antologies o revistes (By year, 1956–1980). III. Traduccions. IV. Bibliografía sobre Vicent

Andrés Estèlles V. Materials per a una ordenació cronològica de la producció d'Estèlles (1953–1980).

FABREGAS, XAVIER (1931–)

Badiou, Maryse. "Xavier Fàbregas, dades bibliogràfiques," *Estudis Escènics* (Barcelona), No. 30 (desembre de 1988), 223–32. Chronology of life and work, 1931–1987.

FABREGAT I ARMENGOL, ROSA (n.d.)

Galerstein, p. 105.

FAGUNDO, ANA MARIA (1938–)

Galerstein, pp. 105–06.

FALCON O'NEILL, LIDIA (1935–)

Galerstein, pp. 107–10.

"Lidia Falcón O'Neill," *O'Connor*, p. 153.

FARINA E COBIAN, HERMINIA (1904–1964)

Galerstein, p. 110.

FELIPE, LEON (pseud. of León Felipe Camino, 1884–1968)

Arenal de Rodríguez, Electa. "Bibliografía de León Felipe," *Cuadernos Americanos*, año 22, tomo 131, no. 6 (noviembre/diciembre de 1963), 274–91. Contents: I. Poesía. A. Ediciones. B. Poemas sueltos. C. Antologías. D. Traducciones a otras lenguas. E. Prólogos en verso. F. Discos. II. Teatro. III. Prosa. IV. Traducciones. V. Artículos, poemas y ensayos sobre León Felipe.

Ascunce Arrieta, José Angel. *La poesía profética de León Felipe*. San Sebastián: Universidad de Deusto, Facultad de Filosofía y Letras, 1987. 471p. (Cuadernos Universitarios, Departamento de Literatura, No. 5). "Bibliografía," pp. 449–64. Contents: I. Monografías (critical studies only). II. Ediciones, prólogos y apólogos (to Felipe's works). III. Notas, artículos y entrevistas (critical studies mainly).

Ayuso, José Cipriano Paulino. "Aportaciones para la bibliografía reciente de León Felipe," *Anuario de Letras* (México), 21 (1983), 297–317. Contents: I. Obras de León Felipe. II. Obras sobre León Felipe. A. Libros. B. Artículos. C. Estudios inéditos (dissertations). Updates Arenal's bibliography, emphasizing 1960s through early 1980s.

_____. *La obra literatura de León Felipe (constitución simbólico de un universo poético).* Madrid: Universidad Complutense de Madrid, Departamento de Literatura Española, Facultad de Filología, 1980. 674p. "Bibliografía," pp. 650–74. Contents: I. Obras de León Felipe. A. Poemas sueltos. B. Otros textos: carta, discursos . . . , etc. C. Otros ediciones empleados y citadas. II. Antologías. II. Diccionarios. IV. Obras y artículos sobre León Felipe. A. Libros. B. Estudios inéditos. C. Artículos.

Correa, v. 1, pp. 182, 526–28. Works by and about the author.

Couland-Maganuco, Anne-Marie. "León Felipe: Bibliografía," pp. 143–60 in *Censo de escritores al servicio de los Austrias y otros estudios bibliográficos* (Madrid: C.S.I.C., Instituto "Miguel de Cervantes," 1983). Contents: I. Bibliografías. II. Libros de poemas (By year, 1920–1980). III. Publicaciones de poemas aislados (By year, 1919–1963). IV. Antologías. V. Poemas traducidos (By year, 1939–1969). VI. Prólogos en verso (By year, 1941–1952). VII. Discos. VIII. Teatro (By year, 1946–1963). IX. Prosa (By year, 1920–1968). X. Traducciones hechas por León Felipe. XI. Poemas consagrados a León Felipe. XII. Estudios: artículos y ensayos críticos.

Felipe, León. *Ganarás la luz.* Edición de José Cipriano Paulino Ayuso. Madrid: Ediciones Cátedra, 1982. 270p. "Bibliografía," pp. 83–86. Contents: I. Ediciones de *Ganarás la luz* (1943–1981). II. Estudios generales (criticism). A. Libros. B. Artículos. C. Estudios y comentarios sobre *Ganarás la luz.*

_____. *Versos y oraciones de caminante [I y II]. Drop a Star.* Edición, estudio y notas de José Paulino Ayuso. Madrid: Editorial Alhambra, 1979. 245p. "Ediciones de *Versos y oraciones de caminante [I y II]* y *Drop a Star,*" pp. 70–71. "Bibliografía (criticism)," pp. 73–77. Contents: I. Libros. II. Artículos sobre la obra en general. III. Artículos sobre *Versos y oraciones de caminante.* IV. Artículos sobre *Drop a Star.*

FERNAN-GOMEZ, FERNANDO (n.d.)

Roura, Pierre. "Fernando Fernán-Gómez: approche bibliographique," pp. 137–51 in *Fernando Fernán-Gómez: Acteur, réalisateur et écrivain espagnol; Actes du Colloque International sur Fernando Fernán-Gómez, Bordeaux, 8 Février, 1985* (Bordeaux: Presses Universitaires de Bordeaux, 1985). Contents: I. Textes concernant Fernando Fernán-Gómez. A. Articles généraux. B. Ouvrages. C. Articles concernant les films réalisés par Fernán-Gómez. D. La place de Fernán-Gómez dans les ouvrages consacrés a l'histoire du cinéma espagnol. II. Entretiens avec Fernán-Gómez. III. Textes de Fernando Fernán-Gómez. A.

Poèmes. B. Romans et nouvelles. C. Pièces de théâtre. D. Textes divers. E. A propos du cinéma. F. A propos du métier d'acteur. G. Scénarios. Eighty-two partially annotated entries.

FERNANDEZ, MIGUEL (1931–)
CILH, pp. 87–88.

FERNANDEZ CUBAS, CRISTINA (1945–)
Galerstein, p. 110.

FERNANDEZ FLOREZ, WENCESLAO (1879?–1964)
Fernández Flórez, Wenceslao. *Volvoreta*. Edición de José-Carlos Mainer. Madrid: Cátedra, 1980. 227p. (Letras Hispánicas, 129). "Bibliografía (criticism)," p. 55.
Mature, Albert Phillip. *Wenceslao Fernández Flórez y su novela*. México: Ediciones De Andrea, 1968. 160p. "Bibliografía," pp. 152–60. Contents: Lista de obras citadas. II. Lista de trabajos sobre Fernández Flórez. III. Obras de Fernández Flórez (no periodical or newspaper material)
Romo Arregui, Josefina. Wenceslao Fernández Florez: bibliografía," *Cuadernos de Literatura Contemporánea*, No. 7 (enero/febrero de 1948), 71–74. Contents: I. Ediciones. II. Traducciones. III. Prólogos. IV. Traducciones al portugués de sus obras.

FERNANDEZ NICOLAS, SEVERIANO (1919–)
"Severiano Fernández Nicolás," *Alonso*, p. 85. Only books are listed, 1950–1973.

FERNANDEZ SANTOS, JESUS (1926–1988)
Alborg, Concha. *Temas y técnica en la narrativa de Jesús Fernández Santos*. Madrid: Editorial Gredos, 1984. 208p. (Biblioteca Románica Hispánica, II. Estudios y ensayos, 336). "Bibliografía," pp. 199–208. Includes general works as well as works by and about Fernández Santos.
Herzberger, David K. *Jesús Fernández Santos*. Boston: Twayne Publishers, Inc., 1983. 131p. "Bibliography," pp. 126–28. Contents: I. Primary Sources (1954–1981). II. Secondary Sources (annotated).
"Jesús Fernández Santos: Bibliografía," *Alonso*, p. 157. Contents: I. Novela (By year, 1954–1985). II. Libros de cuentos y cortas (By year, 1958–1982). Books only.

FERRATER, GABRIEL (1922–1972)

Bonet, Laureano. *Gabriel Ferrater: Entre el arte y la literatura; Historia de una aventura juvenil.* Barcelona: Publicacions i Edicions de la Universitat de Barcelona, 1983. 136p. "Noticia bibliográfica de los artículos, reseñas y traducciones de Gabriel Ferrater publicados en *Laye,*" pp. 135–36. Arranged by year, 1951–54.

A biobibliography of the author, including translations, appears in David Herschel Rosenthal's "Modern Catalan Poetry: A Critical Introduction with Translations" (Unpublished doctoral dissertation, City University of New York, 1977).

FERREIRO, CELSO EMILIO (1914–1979)

Alonso Montero, Xesús. *Celso Emilio Ferreiro: Estudio.* Madrid: Ediciones Júcar, 1982. 224p. "Bibliografía," pp. 215–20. Contents: I. Bibliografía de títulos (by year, 1936–1981). II. Obra completa. III. Antologías. IV. Traducciones. V. Poesía cantada: discos. VI. Bibliografía sobre Ferreiro (By year, 1964–1981).

Ferreiro, Celso Emilio. *Obras completas.* Vol. 1: Estudo e bibliografía de Xesús Alonso Montero. 2a edició. Madrid: Akal Editor, 1978. "Bibliografía," pp. 17–20. Contents: I. Poesía en galego. II. Poesía en castelán. III. Escolmas. A. Individuales. B. Con outros. IV. Poemas cantados en discos. V. Traducciós. (By language). VI. Narrativa en galego. VII. Prosa en castelán. VIII. Estudos sobor da súa poesía.

FIGUERA AYMERICH, ANGELA (1902–1984)

Figuera Aymerich, Angela. *Obras completas.* Introducción y bibliografía de Roberta Quance. Madrid: Ediciones Hiperión, 1986. 461p. (Poesía Hiperión, 102). "Bibliografía selecta sobre la vida y la obra de Angela Figuera Aymerich," pp. 447–52.

Galerstein, pp. 111–13.

FIGUEROA GAMBOA, NATALIA (1939–)

Galerstein, pp. 113–14.

FOIX, JOSEP V. (1893–1987)

Boehne, Patricia. *J. V. Foix.* Boston: Twayne Publishers, Inc., 1980. 158p. "Selected Bibliography," pp. 147–53. Contents: I. Primary Sources. A. Poetry (by year, 1927–1970). B. Prose and Prose Poetry (by year, 1956–1974). C. Collected Works. D. Anthologies. E. Translations. F. Poems in Anthologies or Collections. G. Some Individual Poems in Translations. H. Translations in Prose. II. Secondary Sources (annotated).

A biobibliography of the author, including translations, appears in David Herschel Rosenthal's "Modern Catalan Poetry: A Critical Introduction with Translations" (Unpublished doctoral dissertation, City University of New York, 1977).

Sobrevila i Masvidal, Carme. "Bio-bibliografía de J. V. Foix," pp. 11–15 in Jaime Ferrán's *J. V. Foix* (Madrid: Ediciones Júcar, 1986). Contents: I. Nota biográfica. II. Obras poéticas (Arranged by year, 1927–1985). III. Otras obras (By year, 1934–1979).

FOLCH I TORRES, JOSEPH MARIA (1880–1950)

Fàbregas, Xavier. *J. M. Folch i Torres i el teatre fantàstic*. Barcelona: Millà, 1980. 239p. (Catalunya Teatral, Estudis, 3). "Appendices," pp. 159–238. Contents: I. Cronología del teatre de Joseph M. Folch i Torres. II. La obra. III. Entrevista amb Elvira Jofre.

FOREST, EVA (1928–)

Galerstein, pp. 114–15.

FORMICA, MERCEDES (1918–)

Galerstein, pp. 115–17.

FORRELLAD, LUISA (1925–)

Galerstein, p. 117.

FRANCO, DOLORES (1912–1977)

Galerstein, pp. 117–18.

FUENTES BLANCO, MARIA DE LOS REYES (1927–)

Galerstein, pp. 118–19.

FUERTES, GLORIA (1918–)

Correa, v. 2, pp. 361, 619. Contents: I. Libros. II. Artículos y estudios (criticism).

Fuertes, Gloria. *Obras incompletas. Edición de la autora*. Madrid: Ediciones Cátedra, S.A., 1975. 367p. "Bibliografía: publicaciones, discos y otros escritos," pp. 35–38. Contents: I. Obra poética. II. Literatura infantil. III. Teatro. IV. Discos. V. Estudios (criticism).

Galerstein, pp. 119–21.

GALA, ANTONIO (1936–)

Gala, Antonio. *Los buenos días perdidos. Anillos para una dama.* Edición de A. Amorós. Madrid: Castalia, 1988. 255p. (Clásicos Castalia, 163). "Bibliografía selecta," pp. 109–16. Contents: I. Repertorios bibliográficos. II. Obras dramáticas de Antonio Gala. A. Ediciones sueltas (primeras ediciones, 1964–1987). B. Otras ediciones con prólogo o notas (By year, 1965–1983). C. Recopilaciones. III. Recopilaciones de artículos periodísticos de Antonio Gala. IV. Crítica sobre el teatro de Antonio Gala.

______. *Noviembre y un poco de yerba. Petra regalada.* Edición de Phyllis Zatlin Boring. Madrid: Ediciones Cátedra, 1981. 254p. "Bibliografía," pp. 101–09. Contents: I. Obras publicadas de Antonio Gala. A. Teatro. B. Guiones de televisión. C. Periodismo. D. Poesía. E. Conferencias. F. Relatos. G. Miscelánea. H. Guiones de cine. II. Obras teatrales inéditas. III. Crítica. IV. Selección de entrevistas.

______. *Los verdes campos del Edén.* Introducción, edición y notas de Hazel Cazorla. Salamanca: Almar, 1983. 103p. (Colección Almar-Teatro, 8). "Bibliografía," pp. 37–38. Contents: I. Ediciones principales. II. Selección de estudios críticos.

Labandeira Fernández, Amancio. "Bibliografía teatral de Antonio Gala," *Boletín "Millares Carlo"* (Las Palmas), 2 (1981), 301–45. Contents: I. *Los verdes campos del Edén.* A. Estreno. B. Representaciones. C. Premios. D. Reparto del estreno. E. Ediciones de la obra. F. Críticas sobre la obra (annotated). II. *El sol en el hormiguero.* A. Estreno. B. Representaciones. C. Premios. D. Reparto del estreno. E. Ediciones. F. Críticas sobre la obra (annotated). III. *Noviembre y un poco de Yerba.* A. Estreno. B. Representaciones. C. Premios. D. Reparto del estreno. E. Ediciones. F. Críticas sobre la obra (annotated). IV. *Spain's Strip-Tease.* A. Estreno. B. Representaciones. C. Premios. D. Reparto del estreno. E. Ediciones. F. Críticas sobre la obra (annotated). V. *Los buenos días perdidos.* A. Estreno. B. Representaciones. C. Premios. D. Reparto del estreno. E. Ediciones. F. Críticas sobre la obra (annotated). VI. *Anillos para una dama.* A. Estreno. B. Representaciones. C. Premios. D. Reparto del estreno. E. Ediciones. F. Críticas sobre la obra (annotated). VII. *Las cítaras colgadas de los árboles.* A. Estreno. B. Representaciones. C. Premios. D. Reparto del estreno. E. Ediciones. F. Críticas sobre la obra (annotated). VIII. *¿Por qué corres, Ulises?* A. Estreno. B. Representaciones. C. Premios. D. Reparto del estreno. E. Ediciones. F. Críticas sobre la obra (annotated).

Pérez-Stansfield, p. 342.

GALLARDO, JOSE CARLOS (1925-)
CILH, pp. 226–27.

GALMES DE FUENTES, ALVARO (n.d.)
"Bibliografía crítica del Prof. Alvaro Galmés de Fuentes," v. 1, pp. 19–39 in *Homenaje a Alvaro Galmés de Fuentes* (Madrid: Editorial Gredos, 1985). Contents: I. Romanística general. II. Dialectología hispánica. III. Arabismo y romanismo. IV. Estudios sobre la épica románica. V. Romancero. VI. Lengua y literatura aljamiado-morisca. VII. Otros trabajos. Bibliography includes reviews.

GALMES I SANXO, SALVADOR (1876–1951)
Rosselló Bouer, Pere. *L'obra de Salvador Galmés i Sanxo (1876–1951)*. Montserrat: Publicaciones de l'Abadia de Montserrat, 1988. 341p. (Scripta et Documenta, 34). "Bibliografia," pp. 325–37. Contents: I. Obres de Salvador Galmés. A. L'obra literària (By year, 1899–1957). B. L'obra lul•lística. C. Altres treballs. 1. Traduccions. 2. Articles i treballs diversos. II. Bibliografia sobre Salvador Galmes.

GALVARRIATU, EULALIA (1905-)
Galerstein, pp. 123–25.

GAMONEDA, ANTONIO (1931-)
"Antonio Gamoneda: Bibliografía," *Alonso*, p. 199. Poetry books only.
Gamoneda, Antonio. *Edad (poesía, 1947–1980)*. Edición de Miguel Casado. Madrid: Cátedra, 1988. 385p. (Letras Hispánicas, 271). "Bibliografía," p. 65. Contents: I. Obra poética publicada (By year, 1960–1987). II. Estudios sobre Antonio Gamoneda.

GAOS, VICENTE (1919–1980)
Correa, v. 2, pp. 221, 615. Contents: I. Libros. II. Artículos y estudios (criticism)
Mantero, pp. 547–48. Contents: Libros de poesía. II. Otras publicaciones. II. Sobre Vicente Gaos.

GARCIA BAENA, PABLO (1923-)
Correa, v. 2, pp. 301, 617. Contents: I. Libros. II. Artículos y estudios (criticism).

GARCIA BLANCO, MANUEL (1902–1966)

"Adición a la bibliografía del profesor D. Manuel García Blanco (trabajos publicados entre 1961 y 1965)," *Cuadernos de la Cátedra Miguel de Unamuno* (Salamanca), 16/17 (1966/1967), 7–8. 31 items. This bibliography up-dates the bibliography which appeared in *Streane: Estudios de filología e historia dedicados al Profesor Manuel García Blanco* (Salamanca: Universidad de Salamanca, 1962, 492p. Acta Salmanticensia, Filosofía y letras, 16), pp. 473–87.

GARCIA CABRERA, PEDRO (1905–1981)

Amado Santana, E. *Pedro García Cabrera: En torno a una existencia poética.* Santa Cruz de Tenerife: Aula de Cultura, 1985. 156p. Includes a full bibliography of magazine publications of this Canarian poet.

Pariente, pp. 86–87. Contents: I. Libros de poesía. II. Estudios sobre su poesía. III. Procedencia de los textos.

GARCIA DE DIEGO, VICENTE (1878–)

Casado, María Concepción. "Nuestros filológos: D. Vicente García de Diego," *Boletín de Filología Española*, No. 6 (abril de 1960), 1–5. A selected bibliography appears on pp. 2–5. Contents: I. Latin. II. Trabajos etimológicos. III. Lingüística general. IV. Filología hispánica. V. Dialectología hispánica. VI. Leyendas y tradiciones populares. VII. Ediciones y textos. VIII. Conferencias y discursos. IX. Obra poética.

GARCIA DE LA BARGA GOMEZ DE LA SERNA, ANDRES. *See* CORPUS BARGA.

GARCIA DIEGO, BEGONA (1926–)

Galerstein, p. 127.

GARCIA HORTELANO, JUAN (1928–)

García Hortelano, Juan. *Tormenta de verano*. Edición, introducción y notas de Antonio A. Gómez Yebra. Madrid: Castalia, 1989. 431p. (Clásicos Castalia, 174). "Noticia bibliográfica," pp. 59–60. Contents: I. Novelas (By year, 1961–82). II. Cuentos (By year, 1967–88). III. Poesía. IV. Ensayo. V. Traducciones. "Bibliografía selecta sobre Juan García Hortelano," pp. 61–62.

Troncoso Durán, Dolores. *La narrativa de Juan García Hortelano.* Santiago de Compostela: Universidad de Santiago de Compostela, 1985. 281p. (Monografías, 112). "Bibliografía," pp. 273–76. Contents: I. Obras de Juan García Hortelano. A. Novela.

B. Relato. C. Poesía. D. Otros. II. Artículos sobre de Juan García Hortelano.

GARCIA LOPEZ, ANGEL (1935-)
CILH, pp. 113–14.

GARCIA LORCA, FEDERICO (1898–1936)
Allen, Rupert. "Criticism of Lorca's Poetry Prior to 1960: A Partial and Annotated Bibliography," *Garcia Lorca Review*, 3, No. 1 (Spring 1975), 36–42.
Anderson, Andrew A. "Bibliografía lorquiana reciente." *Boletín de la Fundación Federico García Lorca*. Works by and about García Lorca, 1984- . Part I: 1 (junio de 1987), 96–112. Part II. 1 (diciembre de 1987), 107–31. Part III: 2 (junio de 1988), 107–15. Part IV: 2 (diciembre de 1988), 127–42. Part V: 3 (junio de 1989), 129–34. Part VI: 3 (diciembre de 1989), 161–78.
Bardi, Ubaldo. "Federico García Lorca Musician: Equipment for a Bibliography," *García Lorca Review*, 9 (1981), 30–42. Contents: I. Works Printed in Spain. II. Works Printed in Italy. III. Works Printed in France. IV. Works Printed in England and the United States. V. Records. VI. Pieces of Music Inspired to Lorca's Work. VII. Books of Musical History.
______. "The Fortune of García Lorca's Theater in Italy," *García Lorca Review*, 6 (1978), 1–17; 7 (1979), 1–10. Contents: I. Works Broadcast by Radio. II. Works Broadcast on Television. III. Dramatic Works and Comedies by F. G. Lorca Performed in the Italian Theatres from 1946 to 1978 (by work). IV. Works Performed by Foreign Theatre Companies (by title). V. Other Performances of Lorca's Work in Italy. VI. Works Set to Music. Annotated entries.
______. "Materiaux pour une bibliographie italienne de Federico García Lorca," *Bulletin Hispanique*, 63 (janvier/juin 1961), 88–97. Contents: I. Critiques. II. Traductions et textes. A selected bibliography of 123 partially annotated titles.
______. "The Translations of García Lorca's Works in Italy (Essay for a Bibliography)," *García Lorca Review*, 5 (1977), 1–13. Arranged by translator. Includes his poems and plays.
Braginskaja, E. V. *Federiko Garsia Lorka: Bibliogr. Ukaz.* Moscow: Kniga, 1971. 87p. Contents: I. Life of Lorca, pp. 4–13. II. Chronology of His Life and Work, pp. 14–15. III. Bibliography, pp. 16–66. IV. Indexes of Titles and Names, pp. 67–87.
Colecchia, Francesca. "English Translations of the Poetry of Federico García Lorca: A Partial Bibliography," *García Lorca Review*, 2, No. 1 (Spring 1974), 15pp. 190 items arranged under the

following categories: I. Complete Works of Poetry. II. Collections of Poetry. III. Individual Poems.

______. *García Lorca: A Selectively Annotated Bibliography of Criticism.* New York: Garland Publishing, 1979. 313p. Contents: I. Bibliography. A. Books, Book-Length Manuscripts, Dissertations. B. Articles in Journals, Chapters in Books, Collections. II. Biography. A. Lorca's Life. B. Personal Recollections and Evocations of Lorca. C. Lorca's Death. III. Elegies and Homages. IV. General Criticism. V. Lorca's Theater. A. General Criticism. B. Criticism by Work (16 plays listed). VI. Lorca's Poetry. A. General Criticism. B. By Work (12 titles). VII. Lorca's Prose, Music and Art. VIII. Appendices. A. No Location. B. Not Lorca. IX. Author Index. 1,882 entries.

______, ed. *García Lorca: An Annotated Primary Bibliography.* New York: Garland, 1982. 281p. The bibliography includes about 1,300 references to García Lorca's creative works, including writings, drawings, correspondence, interviews, and translations. Partial descriptive annotations are included for many entries, along with complete bibliographic information and listing of various editions.

______. "Selected Translations in French and English of the Theater of García Lorca: A Bibliographic Note," *García Lorca Review*, 3, No. 1 (Spring 1975), 21–28. Contents commentaries. Contents: I. English Translations. A. Collections of Plays. B. Individual Plays. II. French Translations. A. Collections of Plays. B. Individual Plays.

Comincioli, Jacques. "En torno a García Lorca: Sugerencias, documentos, bibliografía," *Cuadernos Hispanoamericanos*, No. 139 (julio 1961), 37–76. "Bibliografía," pp. 61–76. First editions are listed chronologically within each of the following categories: I. Poesía (73 items). II. Teatro (15 items). III. Textos en prosa (9). IV. Conferencias (15). V. Artículos (2). VI. Declaraciones y entrevistas (58 items). VII. Epistolario (23 items, includes all editions published in Spanish).

Correa, v. 1, pp. 228–29, 530–35. Works by and about the author.

______. "Cronología y estreno de *Yerma, poema trágico*, de García Lorca," *Revista de Archivos, Bibliotecas y Museos*, 82 (1979), 289–315.

Crow, John A. "Bibliografía hispano-americana de Federico García Lorca," *Revista Iberoamericana*, 1, No. 2 (noviembre de 1939), 469–73. This bibliography contains a list of the literary contributions of García Lorca, along with references to "revistas hispanoamericanas que han ofrecido números de homenaje a García Lorca," as well as "estudios y homenajes aparecidos en libros."

Eisenberg, Daniel. "Musical Settings," *García Lorca Review*, 3, No. 1 (Spring 1975), 29–35. A selected list of 51 items of operas and ballets based on Lorca's plays, and of settings of his poetry; it also includes orchestral and instrumental works inspired by him. Excluded are simple recitations of his works against a musical background. It does not include his arrangements of Spanish folksongs published in several versions by the Unión Musical Española, nor arrangements of songs from his theater, available from the same publisher.

García Lorca, Federico. *Amor de Don Perlimplín con Bellisa en su jardín*. Edición de Margarita Ucelay. Madrid: Cátedra, 1990. 296p. (Letras Hispánicas, 313). "Bibliografía," pp. 235–48. Contents: I. Ediciones de *Amor de Don Perlimplín con Belisa en su jardín* (Annotated by year, 1938–1987). II. Estudios de *Amor de Don Perlimplín* . . . A. Libros. B. Artículos.

______. *Bodas de sangre*. Edición de Allen Josephs y Juan Caballero. Madrid: Cátedra, 1985. 167p. "Bibliografía," pp. 83–90. Contents: I. Libros. II. Artículos. The bibliography emphasizes works on *Bodas de sangre*.

______. *Bodas de sangre: Tragedia en tres actos y siete cuadros*. Edición, introducción y notas de Mario Hernández. Madrid: Alianza Editorial, 1984. 226p. (Obras de García Lorca, 13). "Cronología de *Bodas de sangre*," pp. 17–22.

______. *Canciones, 1921–1924*. Edición, introducción y notas de Mario Hernández. Madrid: Alianza Editorial, 1982. 193p. (Obras de García Lorca, 6). "Epistolario [García Lorca's] sobre *Canciones*," pp. 171–81. Covers 1926–29.

______. *Diván del Tamarit [1931–1935]. Llanto por Ignacio Sánchez Mejías [1934]. Sonetos [1924–1936]*. Edición, introducción y notas de Mario Hernández. Madrid: Alianza Editorial, 1981. 199p. (Obras de Federico García Lorca, 3). "Cronología del *Diván del Tamarit (1931–1936)*," pp. 189–99.

______. *Diván del Tamarit; Seis poemas gallegos; Llanto por Ignacio Sánchez Mejías; Poemas sueltos*. Edición crítica de Andrew A. Anderson. Madrid: Espasa-Calpe, 1988. 317p. "Estudio textual y bibliográfico," pp. 50–146. Contents: I. *Diván del Tamarit*. II. *Seis poemas gallegos*. III. *Llanto por Ignacio Sánchez Mejías*. IV. *Poesías sueltas*. "Bibliografía," pp. 149–72. Contents: I. Obras de Federico García Lorca. II. Otras obras (criticism).

______. *Obras completas*. Edición del Cincuentenario. Recopilación, cronología, bibliografía y notas de Arturo del Hoyo. Madrid: Aguilar, 1986. 3 vols. "Cronología de la vida y de la obra de Federico García Lorca," v. 3, pp. 1091–1104. "Bibliografía," v. 3, pp. 1105–90. Contents: I. Ediciones. A. Verso (By work). B.

Teatro (By work). C. Cine. D. Prosa. 1. Impresiones y paisajes. 2. Poemas en prosa. 3. Conferencias. 4. Lecturas. 5. Artículos. 6. Autocrítica. 7. Alocuciones. 8. Homenajes. 9. Textos olvidados: conferencias, declaraciones, etc. 10. Entrevistas. 11. Cartas. E. Dibujos. F. Música. G. Obras completas. H. Adaptaciones. II. Algunas traducciones. A. Sobre las traducciones. B. By language. III. Biografía, estudios y homenajes. A. General. B. By Work, Theme, or Genre. IV. Sobre nuestra edición. "Addenda a la bibliografía (1986)," v. 3, pp. 1191–1216.

_____. *Poema del cante jondo*. Edición crítica de Christian de Paepe. Madrid: Espasa-Calpe, 1986. 326p. "Historia redaccional y editorial del *Poema del cante jondo*: De los autográfos a la edición príncipe," pp. 7–41. "Bibliografía," pp. 317–26. This bibliography emphasizes titles with some connection to the *Poema del cante jondo*.

_____. *Poeta en Nueva York*. Edición de María Clementa Millán. Madrid: Cátedra, 1987. 278p. "Bibliografía," pp. 101–05. Contents: I. Problema textual (expuesto en orden cronológico, 1972–1987). II. Análisis literario. III. Ediciones de *Poeta en Nueva York*. A. Primeras ediciones. B. Ediciones actuales (ordenadas cronológicamente, 1981–1987).

_____. *Primer romancero gitano. Llanto por Ignacio Sánchez Mejías: Romance de la corrida de toros en ronda y otros textos taurinos*. Edición, introducción y notas de Miguel García-Posada. Madrid: Castalia, 1988. 292p. "Noticia bibliográfica," pp. 75–81. Contents: I. *Primer romancero gitano*. A. Fuentes impresas. B. Manuscritos. II. *Llanto por Ignacio Sánchez Mejías*. A. Fuentes impresas. B. Fuentes escritas. C. Ediciones modernas. "Bibliografía selecta (mainly criticism)," pp. 83–88. The critical studies listed center on the *Primer romancero gitano* and the *Llanto por Ignacio Sánchez Mejías*.

_____. *Primer romancero gitano [1924–1927]. Otros romances del teatro, [1924–1935]*. Edición de Mario Hernández. Madrid: Alianza Editorial, 1981. 196p. (Obras de García Lorca, 1). "Cronología crítica del *Romancero gitano*," pp. 157–84. Covers through 1936.

_____. *El público*. Edición de María Clementa Millán. Madrid: Cátedra, 1987. 189p. "Bibliografía," pp. 113–16. The bibliography centers on critical studies and editions of *El público*.

_____. *Romancero Gitano*. Edited with Introduction and Notes by H. Ramsden. Manchester: Manchester University Press, 1988. 165p. "Select Bibliography," pp. 79–84. Contents: I. Basic Texts. II. Annotated Editions of *Romancero Gitano*. III. Critical Studies (In chronological order of first publication).

González Muela, pp. 65–69. Works by and about García Lorca are arranged chronologically.

Halman, Talat S. "Lorca in Turkish," *García Lorca Review*, 2, No. 1 (Spring 1974), 3p. Contents: I. Translations of Lorca's Theater. II. Translations of Lorca's Poetry. A. Collections of Poetry. B. Individual Poems. III. Special Lorca Issue (*Yeni Dergi*). IV. Turkish Productions of Lorca's Plays. V. Miscellaneous.

Hernández, Mario. "Cronología de *Bodas de sangre* (1928–1938), ilustrada con la palabra de Federico García Lorca," pp. 43–63 in *Lorca 1986* (Bologna: Atesa Editrice, 1987).

Higgenbotham, Virginia. "Towards an Annotated Bibliography of the Theater of García Lorca," *García Lorca Review*, 2, No. 1 (Spring 1974), 6p. Contents: I. General Studies. II. Articles on *Bodas de sangre*. III. Articles on *La casa de Bernarda Alba*.

Klein, Dennis A. "A Critical Bibliography of the Theatre of Federico García Lorca: 1940 through 1970." Unpublished Ph.D. dissertation, University of Massachusetts (Amherst), 1973. 130p. "The dissertation is a critical bibliography of the books and articles published on the theatre of Federico García Lorca between 1940 and 1970 in English, Spanish, French, and Italian, and accessible in the United States." The first part of the bibliography lists books on the life and works of García Lorca; books upon his theatre; and chapters in books upon the Spanish and European theatre scene in general. The second part is divided into ten sections which treat the articles dealing with Lorca's dramatic works: I. Lorca's Theater in General. II. The Insect Fantasy and the Puppet Farces. III. The Serious Farces. IV. The Romantic Dramas. V. The Rural Tragedies (as a unit). VI. The Rural Tragedies (on each). VII. The Surrealist Plays.

Laffranque, Marie. *Federico García Lorca*. 2e édition. Paris: Editions Seghers, 1966. 191p. "Chronologie: vie et oeuvres de Federico García Lorca"; "Vie littérairie et artistique en Espagne, hors d'Espagne," and "Evénements politiques et sociaux," pp. 131–165. "Bibliographie," pp. 167–186. Contents: I. Oeuvres de Lorca. A. Poésies. 1. Recueils. 2. Poèmes détachés. B. Oeuvres théâtrales. C. Proses. D. Conférences. E. Correspondance. F. Déclarations et articles. G. Ecrits inédits. 1. Poèmes. 2. Oeuvres théâtrales. 3. Prose. H. Dessins. I. Musique. 1. Chansons détachées. 2. Airs pour le théâtre. J. Disques. K. Oeuvres complétes. L. Traductions en français. II. Bibliographies. III. Etudes critiques. A. Livres sur Lorca. B. Articles, hommages et études breves.

______. "Pour l'étude de Federico García Lorca: Bases chronologiques," *Bulletin Hispanique* 65 (juillet/decembre 1963), 333–77.

By year, includes biographical and bibliographical information, 1898–1936; but the bibliography is not a strict bibliographical listing of works.

Larson, Everette E. *García Lorca: A Bibliography.* Washington, D.C.: Library of Congress, Hispanic Division, 1987. 44p. This work is a selected bibliography of the Library of Congress's holdings by and about García Lorca (books and phonodiscs). Call numbers are included.

Laurenti, Joseph L., and Siracusa, Joseph. *Federico García Lorca y su mundo: Ensayo de una bibliografía general. The World of Federico García Lorca: A General Bibliography Survey.* Metuchen, N.J.: The Scarecrow Press, 1975. 282p. Includes 2,247 entries. Contents: I. Cronología. II. Bibliografías. III. Ediciones. IV. Traducciones. V. Estudios. A. Generalidades. B. Poesía. C. Prosa. D. Teatro. E. Relaciones literarias (all entries under these subjects are arranged by year). VI. Biografías. VII. Elegías. VIII. Homenajes. IX. Miscelánea. X. Apéndice. XI. Indice onomástico. Many of the entries are incomplete and bibliographically inaccurate. German language coverage is only fair.

Lichtman, Celia S. "Myth and Symbolism in the Work of Federico García Lorca: Partial and Annotated Bibliography," *García Lorca Review*, 5 (1977), 19–26. Contents: I. Works in General. II. Works on the Theatre. A. Works in General. B. By Work.

Lima, Robert. *The Theatre of García Lorca.* New York: Las Américas Publishing Co., 1963. 338p. "Bibliography," pp. 303–31. Contents: I. Editions. A. Plays. B. Interviews, Lectures, Prose. C. Complete Works. II. Adaptations. III. Translations. A. Plays. B. Interviews, Lectures. C. Complete Works. IV. Studies. A. Books. B. Articles (General). C. Articles (specific, by play).

MacCurdy, G. Grant. "Bibliografía cronológica comentada de Federico García Lorca," *Hispania*, 69 (1986), 757–760. Entries are listed chronologically under the following headings: Prosa, poesía, teatro, *obras completas*, and bibliografías.

Martín, Eutimio. "La pujanate vitalidad del lorquismo: bibliografía de y sobre Federico García Lorca," *Cahiers d'Etudes Romanes*, 11 (1986), 175–90.

Meux, Richard P. "In Praise of Lorca: A Brief Bibliography," *García Lorca Review*, 2, No. 1 (Spring 1974), 2p. Contents: I. Poems Dedicated to García Lorca. II. Eulogies. III. Verified tributes.

Naudin, Marie. "French Translations of the Poetry of Federico García Lorca," *García Lorca Review*, 5 (1977), 14–18. Annotated bibliography. Contents: I. Complete Works of Poetry. II. Anthologies of Poetry. III. Individual Poems and Collections of Poetry.

IV. Works on the Poetry. A. Works in General. B. By Work. V. Prose Works.

O'Nan, Martha. "Albert Camus: Director of García Lorca's Translations," *García Lorca Review*, 6 (1978), 19–31. A listing of various translations from García Lorca's works into French prior to 1947, arranged in chronological order, appears on pp. 26–29.

Ortega, José. "Bibliografía anotada de *Poeta en Nueva York* de García Lorca," *García Lorca Review*, 8 (1980), 36–46. Contents: I. Libros. II. Artículos. III. Selecciones en libros. IV. Notas e introducciones. V. Reseñas. VI. Tesis doctorales.

Ramsden, H. *Lorca's "Romancero Gitano": Eighteen Commentaries*. Manchester: Manchester University Press, 1988. 126p. "Select Bibliography (*Romancero Gitano*)," pp. 123–26. Contents: I. Basic Texts. II. Translations into English. III. Commentary-Based Studies (with or without translation; in chronological order of first publication; content annotations).

Sibbald, Katherine. "Federico García Lorca's Original Contributions to the Literary Magazines in the Years 1917–1937," *García Lorca Review*, 2, No. 1 (Spring 1974), 14p. The bibliography "is in chronological order of publication and contains García Lorca's original contributions to the literary magazines of the nineteen twenties and thirties in both Spain and Hispanoamérica from the years 1917–1937. Not included here, however, are notices of Lorca's public lectures or details of the various interviews he gave to many magazines and newspapers before his death."

Sucharzewska, M. Jadwiga, Barbara Czopek, and Francesca Colecchia. "A Partially Annotated Bibliography of Homages to Federico García Lorca in Polish," *García Lorca Review*, 10 (1982), 1–8. Thirty-two items arranged chronologically, 1947–1977. Mainly poems and odes.

______. "Performances of Lorca's Plays in Poland: On Stage, on Radio, and on Television," *García Lorca Review*, 9 (1981), 1–29.

______. "Translations of Lorca's Works into Polish," *García Lorca Review*, 8 (Spring 1980), 1–35. Includes 133 items listed by year of translation, 1947–1978.

"Textos sobre García Lorca publicados en *Cuadernos Hispanoamericanos*," No. 435/436 (septiembre/octubre 1986), 835–836.

Tinnell, Roger D. *Federico García Lorca: Catálogo-Discografía de las "Canciones populares antiguas"* y de música basada en textos lorquianos. Plymouth: Plymouth State College of the University of New Hampshire, 1986. 122p. Contents: I. *Canciones populares antiguas* (listing by record company). II. Recordings of music, including films and videocassettes, based on Garcia Lorca's works, ranging from single songs to entire operas and ballets (arranged alphabetically by composer or recording artist). III. Grabaciones de música flamenca y popular based on Lorca's works. IV. Homenajes to Lorca (partial listing). V. Title Index. VI. Onamastic Index.

_____. "A Listing of Recordings of García Lorca's *Canciones populares antiguas* and of Recordings of Music Based on García Lorca's texts," *García Lorca Review*, 11 (1983), 1–23. Contents: I. *Canciones populares antiguas* (listing by record company). II. Recording of Music on García Lorca's Texts (arranged by composer or recording artist).

Velasco, Joseph. "Lorca en français," *Iris*, No. 1 (1987), 173–227.

Weiss, Beno. "Federico García Lorca in Italy: A. Selected Bibliography of Criticism," *García Lorca Review*, 3, No. 1 (Spring 1975), 1–20. Bibliography includes books, articles, general studies, as well as studies of individual works published in Italy.

GARCIA MARQUINA, FRANCISCO (1937–)

CILH, p. 147. Contents: I. Poesía. II. Prosa.

GARCIA NIETO, JOSE (1914–)

Mantero, pp. 548–50. Contents: I. Libros de poesía. II. Otras publicaciones. III. Sobre José García Nieto.

GARCIA PAVON, FRANCISCO (1919–1989)

Bernadach, Moïse. "Les multiples passions de F. García Pavón: Préambule à une bibliographie de l'auteur," pp. 457–77 in *Mélanges à la mémoire d'André Joucla-Ruau* (Aix-en-Provence: Université de Provence, 1978). "Contribution à une bibliographie de Francisco García Pavón (1919–)," pp. 467–77. Contents: I. Oeuvres d'imagination (By year, 1946–1970). II. Travaux sur F. García Pavón. A. Etudes et articles spécialisés (By year, 1947–1972). B. Etudes moins spécialisées (By year, 1958–1972).

King, Charles L. "Francisco García Pavón: Una reseña biobibliográfica," *Crítica Hispánica*, 8 (1986), 153–58.

Pérez-Stansfield, p. 342.

Rubio Tebas, Milagros. "Estudio bio-bibliográfico crítico de Francisco García Pavon." Memoria de Licenciatura, Departamento de Bibliografía de la Universidad Complutense de Madrid, 1976.

GARCIA PINTADO, ANGEL (1940–)

"Angel García Pintado," pp. 21–26 in L. Teresa Valdivieso's *España: Bibliografía de un teatro "silenciado"* (Lincoln, Neb.: Society of Spanish and Spanish-American Studies, 1979). Contents: I. Notas biográficas. II. Obras inéditas. III. Obras publicadas. IV. Escritos y declaraciones. V. Estudios críticos.

GARCIA RATA, FELISA (1921–)
Galerstein, p. 128.

GARCIA SERRANO, RAFAEL (1917–1988)
"Rafael García Serrano: bibliografía," pp. 317–21 in José Luis Martín Nogales' *Cincuenta años de novela española (1936–1986): Escritores navarros* (Barcelona: PPU, 1989). Contents: I. Poesía. II. Novelas. III. Cuentos. IV. Artículos. V. Otros libros. VI. Guiones de cine. VII. Estudios, entrevistas, reseñas.

GARCIA SOLALINDE, ANTONIO (1892–1937)
Seniff, Dennis P. "Antonio García Solalinde, 1892–1937: A Commemorative Bibliography," *La Corónica*, 17 (1988), 109–15.

GARCIASOL, RAMON DE (pseud. of Miguel Alonso Calvo, 1913–)
"Bibliografía de y sobre Ramón de Garciasol," *Anthropos*, No. 103 (1989), 41–45. Contents: I. Libros: Poesía (By year, 1936–1985). II. Ensayos (By year, 1944–1980). III. Prosa. IV. Otras publicaciones. A. Poemas sueltos (By year, 1955–1985). B. Antologías. C. Homenajes (By year, 1952–1989). D. Revistas (By year, 1943–1989). E. Artículos y reseñas (By year, 1945–1989). F. Entrevistas (By year, 1966–1988). G. Prólogos. V. Bibliografía sobre Ramón de Garciasol.
Garciasol, Ramón de. *Notaría del tiempo*. Barcelona: Anthropos, 1985. 144p. (Memoria rota; Exilios y heterodoxias, 5). "Ramón de Garciasol: Nota biográfica y bibliografía," pp. 141–44. The bibliography of his works is arranged by year, 1936–1985.
Mantero, pp. 550–52. Contents: I. Libros de poesía. II. Otras publicaciones. III. Sobre Garciasol.

GARFIAS, FRANCISCO (1921–)
CILH, p. 173. Contents: I. Poesía. II. Biografías. III. Antología.

GARFIAS, PEDRO (1894–1967)
"Bibliografía y antologías que incluyen poemas de Pedro Garfías," *Litoral* (Málaga), No. 115/17 (1982), 131–35. The bibliography section includes only critical studies on Garfías.
Sánchez Pascual, Angel. *Pedro Garfías, vida y obra*. Barcelona: Víctor Pozanco, 1980. 160p. (Ambito Literario; 88. Ensayo). "La obra de Pedro Garfías," pp. 88–107. Contents: I. Colaboraciones

de Pedro Garfías en revistas. A. Poemas publicados en revistas ante de 1936 (By journal). B. Poemas publicados en revistas durante la guerra civil (By journal). II. Poemas publicados en revistas de México (By journal).

GATELL, ANGELINA (1926–)
CILH, p. 213. Contents: I. Poesía. II. Prosa. III. Libros para niños.
Galerstein, pp. 129–30.

GIL, ILDEFONSO-MANUEL (1912–)
CILH, p. 254. Contents: I. Obras en verso. II. Ensayos. III. Estudios sobre poesía y poetas. Books only.
Hiriart, Rosario. *Un poeta en el tiempo: Ildefonso-Manuel Gil.* Zaragoza: Diputación Provincial, Institución Fernando El Católico, 1981. 255p. "Bibliografía," pp. 249–54. Contents: I. Obras de Ildefonso-Manuel Gil. A. Libros de poesía. B. Libros de ficción. C. Ensayos, crítica y biografías. D. Colaboraciones en revistas y periódicos (only lists titles of journals). II. Selección de estudios críticos sobre la poesía de Ildefonso-Manuel Gil.

GIL-ALBERT, JUAN (1911–)
Gil-Albert, Juan. *Fuentes de la constancia.* Edición de José Carlos Rovira. Madrid: Cátedra, 1984. 226p. (Letras Hispánicas, 205). "Bibliografía," pp. 61–65. Contents: I. Obras de Juan Gil-Albert. A. Poesía (By year, 1936–1981). B. Prosa (By year, 1927–1984). II. Estudios sobre su obra.
Peña, Pedro J. de la. *Juan Gil-Albert.* Madrid: Ediciones Júcar, 1982. 394p. (Los Poetas, 41–42). "Bibliografía," pp. 389–94. Contents: I. Obras generales (By year, 1927–1981). II. Sobre Gil-Albert.
Simón, César. *Juan Gil-Albert, su vida y obra.* Alicante: Instituto de Estudios Alicantinos, Excma. Diputación Provincial de Alicante, 1984. 139p. (*Its* Publicaciones, Ser. I., No. 95). "Bibliografía," pp. 117–35. Contents: I. Obras de Juan Gil-Albert (By year, 1927–82). II. Addenda: Artículos publicados en diarios y revistas (By year, 1939–80). III. Obra completa. IV. Publicaciones sobre Juan Gil-Albert. A. Hasta 1975. B. Desde 1976. C. Homenajes.

GIL DE BIEDMA, JAIME (1929–1990)
Correa, v. 2, pp. 495, 623. Works by and about the author.
Gil de Biedma, Jaime. *Antología poética.* Madrid: Alianza Editorial, 1981. 134p. Contents: I. "Bibliografía sobre Gil de Biedma," pp. 23–24. II. "Obras de Jaime Gil de Biedma," p. 24.
______. *Volver.* Edición de Dionisio Cañas. Madrid: Cátedra, 1989. 151p. (Letras Hispánicas, 310). "Bibliografía," pp. 41–48.

González, Shirley Mangini. *Jaime Gil de Biedma*. Madrid: Ediciones Júcar, 1979. 225p. Contents: I. "Bibliografía del autor," pp. 183–84. A. Poesía. B. Prosa. III. Crítica literaria. IV. Traducciones. II. "Bibliografía sobre el autor," pp. 184–85.

GILI I GAYA, SAMUEL (1892–1976)

"Bibliografía de Samuel Gili i Gaya," pp. 15–19 in *Vox: Homenaje a Samuel Gili i Gaya (In Memoriam)* (Barcelona: Biblograf, 1979). HIs works are listed by year, 1918–1973.

Sistac i Sanuiesen, Dolors, Maria Dolors Milà i Mallafré, and Lluís Rubio i Garcia. *Samuel Gili i Gaya: Notes per a una biobibliografia, 1892–1976*. Llerda: Cátedra de Cultura Catalana "Samuel Gili i Gaya," Instituto de Estudios Illerdenses de la Excma. Diputación Provincial de Llerida, C.S.I.C., 1976. 107p. "Bibliografia: obres publicades per Samuel Gili i Gaya," pp. 55–61 (By year, 1918–1972).

GIMENEZ CABALLERO, ERNESTO (1899–1988)

Foard, Douglas W. *Ernesto Giménez Caballero (o la revolución del poeta): Estudio sobre el nacionalismo cultura hispánico en el siglo XX*. Madrid: Instituto de Estudios Políticos, 1975. 241p. "Bibliografía," pp. 225–29. Contents: I. Fuentes primarias. II. Obras generales, fuentes secundarias. III. Revistas y periódicas.

______. *The Revolt of the Aesthetes: Ernesto Giménez Caballero and the Origins of Spanish Fascism*. New York: Peter Lang, 1989. 257p. (American University Studies, Series IX, History, 20). "Bibliography," pp. 235–52. Contents: I. Primary Sources. A. Correspondence. B. Books by Ernesto Giménez Caballero (By year, 1923–1985). C. Other Significant Publications by Giménez Caballero (By year, 1924–1981). II. Secondary Sources.

López-Vidriero, María Luisa. *Bibliografía de Ernesto Giménez Caballero*. Madrid: Universidad Complutense, 1982. 50p. (Trabajos del Departamento de Bibliografía, Serie A, Escritos Contemporáneos, 6). Contents: I. Libros, prólogos, traducciones, artículos (By year, 1918–1981; page nos. missing in journal and newspaper citations; 1,393 items). II. Entrevistas (By year, 1936–1981; 11 items). III. Estudios sobre E. Giménez Caballero (By year, 1932–1977; 18 items).

GIMFERRER, PERE (1945–)

Correa, v. 2, pp. 545, 624. Works by and about the author.

"Père Gimferrer: Selected Bibliography," *Catalan Writing*, No. 3 (October 1989), 74–76. Contents: I. Chronology. II. Poetry in

Spanish. III. Poetry in Catalan. IV. Essay, Narrative, and Other Prose. V. Translations (By language).

GINER DE LOS RIOS, FRANCISCO (1917–)

"Bibliografía: más o menos completas notas en corchetes heterodoxos," *Litoral* (Málaga), No. 172/73 (1986), 135–55. Contents: I. Libros de poesía publicados (By year, 1940–1986). II. Materiales inéditos y en preparación. A. Poesía. B. Estudios y ensayos. III. Antologías. IV. Ediciones y prólogos. V. Traducciones. VI. Antologías con poemas de Francisco Giner de los Ríos. VII. Poemas en publicaciones diversas y en revistas. VIII. Algunos ensayos y artículos. IX. Algunas notas y ensayos sobre Francisco Giner de los Ríos.

GIRONELLA, JOSE MARIA (1917–)

Salso, José Antonio. *José María Gironella*. Madrid: Ministerio de Cultura, Dirección General de Promoción del Libro y la Cinematografía, 1982. 252p. Contents: "Bibliografía," pp. 243–50. Includes works by and about Gironella.

Schwartz, Ronald. *José María Gironella*. New York: Twayne Publishers, Inc., 1972. 200p. "Selected Bibliography," pp. 190–95. Contents: I. Primary Sources. A. Original Works. B. Translations. II. Secondary Sources. A. Books. B. Articles and Periodicals.

Suárez-Torres, J. David. *Perspectiva humorística en la trilogía de Gironella*. New York: Eliseo Torres & Sons, 1975. 235p. (Torres Library of Literary Studies, 21). "Bibliografía," pp. 229–34. Contents: I. Obras de Gironella (orden cronológico). II. Obras consultadas.

GOMEZ DE BAQUERO, EDUARDO (1866–1929)

Guzmán, Catherine R. "La crítica literaria de Eduardo Gómez de Baquero y el mundo literario de su tiempo." Unpublished Ph.D. dissertation, City University of New York, 1978. "The bibliography consists of all his books and conferences and a great number of articles appearing in diverse newspapers and magazines. It is the most up to date on the works written about the author and his work."

GOMEZ DE LA SERNA, RAMON (1891–1963)

Becco, Horacio Jorge. "Bibliografía de Ramón Gómez de la Serna," *Cuadernos del Idioma* (Buenos Aires), No. 10 (1968), 145–60. A selected bibliography of basic titles. Contents: I. Ediciones. II. Crítica. III. Bibliografía.

Daus, Ronald. *Der avantgardismus Ramón Gómez de la Sernas.* Frankfurt a. M.: Klostermann, 1971. 346p. (Analecta Romanica, 29). "Bibliographie," pp. 310–37. Contents: I. Primärliteratur. A. Ramóns Werke in chronologischer Reihenfolge (1905–1964). B. Ramóns Werke in alphabetischer Reihenfolge. II. Sekundärliteratur. A. Arbeiten über Ramón. Eine auswahl. B. Andere berücksichtge Arbeiten. This bibliography updates and supplements Gaspar Gómez de la Serna's work (see below).

Gardiel, Mazzetti. "Unpublished Works of Ramón Gómez de la Serna," *Anales de la Literatura Española Contemporánea*, 7 (1982), 109–16. Description and content analysis of the unpublished works, specifically from the notebooks housed in the University of Pittsburgh's Hillman Library.

Gómez de la Serna, Gaspar. *Ramón Gómez de la Serna (obra y vida).* Madrid: Taurus, 1963. 305p. "Bibliografía," pp. 277–305. Contents: I. Ediciones (by year, 1905–62). II. Bibliografía crítica. A. Obras, estudios y ensayos. B. Artículos. C. Compendios críticos incluidos en obras de Ramón.

Gómez de la Serna, Ramón. *Aphorisms.* Translated and with an Introduction by Miguel González-Gerth. Pittsburgh: Latin American Literary Review Press, 1989. 214p. "Bibliography," pp. 209–211. Contents: I. Works by Gómez de la Serna in English Translation (By year, 1922–1980). II. Critical Works in English on Gómez de la Serna.

_____. *El secreto del acueducto.* Edición de Carolyn Richmond. Madrid: Cátedra, 1986. 291p. (Letras Hispánicas, 246). "Bibliografía," pp. 105–12. Contents: I. Ramón Gómez de la Serna y Segovia. II. Bibliografía crítica sobre Gómez de la Serna. III. Bibliografía selecta de obras de Ramón Gómez de la Serna (By year, 1905–1961).

_____. *La viuda blanca y negra.* Edición de Rodolfo Cardona. Madrid: Cátedra, 1988. 291p. (Letras Hispánicas, 298). "Bibliografía," pp. 69–74.

Granjel, Luis S. *Retrato de Ramón Gómez de la Serna.* Madrid: Ediciones Guadarrama, 1963. 260p. "Bibliografía," pp. 245–60. Contents: I. Obras de Ramón Gómez de la Serna (by year, 1904–1961). II. Bibliografía crítica.

Lafuente, F. R. "Sólo Ramón (a los cien años)," *Insula*, No. 502 (Octubre 1988), 16–17. Includes books and details of homage articles published in *ABC, El País, Diario 16*, and *El Europeo.*

López-Criado, Fidel. *El erotismo en la novelística ramoniana.* Madrid: Fundamentos, 1988. 210p. (Espiral hispanoamericana, 9). "Novelas de Gómez de la Serna," pp. 203–205. Arranged by year, 1913–1950, and includes novels published in books and journals.

"Bibliografía crítica selecta sobre la obra de Gómez de la Serna," pp. 207–09.

Ponce, Fernando. *Ramón Gómez de la Serna*. Madrid: Unión Editorial, 1968. 193p. "Bibliografía," pp. 155–169. Contents: I. Obras de Ramón Gómez de la Serna (by year, 1905–61). II. Escritos sobre Ramón Gómez de la Serna.

Studies on Ramón Gómez de la Serna. Edited by Nigel Dennis. Ottawa, Ont.: Dovehouse Editions, 1988. 220p. (Ottawa Hispanic Studies, 2). "Bibliography," pp. 207–18. Includes an extensive bibliography of critical studies devoted to Gómez de la Serna since the author's death.

Ynduráin, Francisco. "Ramón en la *Revista de Occidente*," *Revista de Occidente*, 80 (enero de 1988), 70–81. Critical essay.

GOMEZ OJLA, CARMEN (1945–)

Galerstein, pp. 132–33.

GONZALEZ, ANGEL (1925–)

Debicki, Andrew Peter. *Angel González*. Madrid: Júcar, 1989. (Los Poetas, 74). "Bibliografía," pp. 203–07. Contents: I. Libros de Angel González. A. Poesía (By year, 1956–1985). B. Prosa. Crítica literaria y antologías (By year, 1973–1986). C. Selección de artículos y ensayos (By year, 1963–1985). D. Traducciones de la poesía de Angel González (Selección; by year, 1963–1983). II. Estudios acerca de Angel González (Selección).

González, Angel. *Poemas*. 2a. ed. Madrid: Cátedra, 1980. 191p. (Letras Hispánicas, 121). "Bibliografía," pp. 27–30. Contents: I. Libros de Angel González. A. Poesía (By year, 1956–1977). B. Prosa: crítica literaria y prólogos, antologías (By year, 1973–1979). II. Bibliografía selecta sobre el autor. A. Libros. B. Generales. III. Algunos ensayos y reseñas críticas aprarecidas en periódicos y revistas.

Rivera, Susana. "Bibliografía," pp. 296–303 in *Angel González, verso a verso*. Oviedo: Caja de Ahorros de Asturias, 1987. 303p. (Libro homenaje, 5, Serie Ciencias y Humanidades). Contents: I. Obras de Angel González. A. Poesía. 1. Libros (By year, 1956–1985). 2. Poesía en revistas y periódicos (By year, 1953–1984). 3. Traducciones. B. Crítica literaria y ensayo, prólogos e introducciones. 1. Crítica literaria y ensayos (By year, 1952–1986). 2. Prólogos e introducciones (By year, 1968–1975). II. Obras acerca de Angel González. A. Estudios críticos. 1. Monográficos. 2. Generales. 3. Particulares. 4. Tesis. 5. Trabajos leídos en reuniones eruditos. B. Ensayos y reseñas críticas. Entrevistas. 1. Ensayos y reseñas críticas. 2. Entrevistas. C. Antologías.

Simposio-Homenaje a Angel González. Edición de Susana Rivera y Tomás Ruiz Fábrega. Madrid: José Estebán Editor, 1985. 151p. "Bibliografía," pp. 136–50. Contents: I. Obras de Angel González. A. Poesía. 1. Libros. 2. Poesía en revistas y periódicos. 3. Traducciones. B. Crítica literaria y ensayo, prólogos e introducciones. 1. Crítica literaria y ensayo. 2. Prólogos e introducciones. II. Obras acerca de Angel González. A. Estudios críticos. 1. Monográficos. 2. Generales. 3. Particulares. 4. Tesis. 5. Trabajos leídos en reuniones eruditos. B. Ensayos y reseñas críticas. Entrevistas. 1. Ensayos y reseñas críticas. 2. Entrevistas. C. Antologías.

GONZALEZ-BLANCO, ANDRES (1886–1924)

Martínez Cachero, José María. *Andrés González-Blanco: Una vida para la literatura.* Oviedo: Instituto de Estudios Asturianos, 1963. 195p. "Bibliografía," pp. 169–80. Contents: I. Bibliografía de Andrés González-Blanco. A. El poeta. B. El crítico literario. C. El narrador. D. Otros títulos. II. Bibliografía sobre Andrés González-Blanco.

GONZALEZ DE AMEZUA, AGUSTIN (1881–1956)

Prades, Juan de José. "Don Agustín González de Amezúa," *Anales del Instituto de Estudios Madrileños*, 1 (1966), 41–58. "Bibliografía, pp. 46–58. 181 citings. Contents: I. Estudios de tema madrileño. II. Escritores nacidos en Madrid y su provincia. III. Otras estudios literarios. IV. Estudios históricos. V. Periodismo. VI. Viaje a Méjico. VII. Bibliotecario.

GONZALEZ LLUBERA, IGNACIO (1893–1962)

Tate, R. B. "Ignacio González Llubera: Necrology and Bibliography," *Hispanic Review*, 30 (October 1962), 322–25. Contents: I. Books. II. Articles. III. In Preparation.

GONZALEZ PALENCIA, ANGEL (1889–1949)

"Publicaciones de Angel González Palencia," pp. 429–42 *in* Angel Palencia González's *Eruditos y libreros del siglo XVIII, estudios histórico-literarios*, quinta serie. Madrid: C.S.I.C., "Instituto Antonio de Nebrija," 1948. Entries are arranged chronologically, 1912–1947. Newspaper and review articles are excluded. 192 entries.

GOYTISOLO, JUAN (1931–)

Carenas, Francisco. "Bibliographical Inventory of Juan Goytisolo's Archive, Mungar Library, Special Collections, Boston University,

Boston," *Norte* (Amsterdam), 13 (julio/diciembre de 1972), 142–95. Contents: I. Reseñas de libros. 1. *Juegos de manos*. 2. *Duelo en el paraíso*. 3. *El circo*. 4. *Fiestas*. 5. *La resaca*. 6. *Problemas de la novela*. 7. *Campos de Níjar*. 8. *Para vivir aquí*. 9. *La isla*. 10. *La charca*. 11. *Fin de fiesta*. 12. *Pueblo en marcha*. 13. *Señas de identidad*. 14. *El furgón de cola*. 15. *Reivindicación del Conde Julián*. II. Entrevistas. III. Estudios generales. IV. Tesis doctorales.

Gordon, Robert Alan. "An Analysis of the Narrative Techniques of Juan Goytisolo." Unpublished Ph.D. dissertation, University of Colorado, 1971. 187p. "Bibliography," pp. 181–87. Contents: I. Primary Sources. A. Books. B. Periodical Articles. II. Secondary Sources. A. Books. B. Periodical Articles. C. Book Reviews. D. Theses.

Goytisolo, Juan. *Reivindicación del conde don Julián*. Edición de Linda Gould Levine. Madrid: Cátedra, 1985. 352p. "Bibliografía selecta sobre Juan Goytisolo y *Don Julián*," pp. 71–75.

Juan Goytisolo. Madrid: Espiral/Fundamentos, 1975. 267p. (Espiral/Figuras, 8). "Bibliografía," pp. 205–266. Bibliography is reprinted from *Norte*.

Kitching-Schulman, Aline. "Juan Goytisolo: bibliografía," pp. 107–11 in *Juan Goytisolo* (Montpellier: Centre d'Etudes et Recherches Sociocritiques, 1983; Co-textes, 5).

Navajas-Navarro, Gonzalo. "Juan Goytisolo: La novela como crítica de España." Unpublished Ph.D. dissertation, University of California, Los Angeles, 1975. 294p. "Bibliografía," pp. 284–94. Contents: I. Obra literaria y crítica. II. Bibliografía utilizada. A. General. B. Sobre Juan Goytisolo.

Ortega, José. *Juan Goytisolo: Alienación y agresión en "Señas de identidad" y "Reivindicación del Conde don Julián*." New York: Eliseo Torres and Sons, 1972. 174p. (Torres Library of Literary Studies, 12). "Bibliografía," pp. 163–69. Contents: I. General (Criticism on Goytisolo, etc.). II. La obra narrativa de Juan Goytisolo. III. Otros escritos de Juan Goytisolo.

Schwartz, Kessel. *Juan Goytisolo*. New York: Twayne Publishers, Inc., 1970. 155p. "Selected Bibliography," pp. 144–52. Contents: I. Primary Sources. A. Works. B. Translations. II. Secondary Works. A. Books. B. Articles.

Ugarte, Michael. *Trilogy of Treason: An Intertextual Study of Juan Goytisolo*. Columbia: University of Missouri Press, 1982. 171p. "Bibliography," pp. 162–67. Contents: I. Fiction and Essays by Juan Goytisolo (in chronological order). II. Other Sources (critical studies).

GRANDE, FELIX (1937-)

CILH, pp. 75–76. Contents: I. Poesía. II. Relatos. III. Ensayos. IV. Otras ediciones.

Correra, v. 2, pp. 519, 623–24. Works by and about the author.

GRANELL, EUGENIO FERNANDEZ (1912-)

Irizarry, Estelle. *La inventiva surrealista de E. F. Granell.* Madrid: Insula, 1976. 203p. "Bibliografía," pp. 197–201. Contents: I. Obras de Granell. A. Libros. B. Textos para catálogos de exposiciones. C. Artículos y comentarios literarios no recogidos en libro. D. Periodismo en *La Nación* (República Dominicana). II. Escritos sobre la obra literaria de Granell. III. Bibliografía selecta de escritos acerca de la pintura de Granell.

GROSSO, ALFONSO (1928-)

Grosso, Alfonso. *La Zanja*. Edición de José Antonio Fortes. Madrid: Ediciones Cátedra, 1981. 324p. Contents: I. "Obras de Alfonso Grosso," pp. 129–31. A. Relatos. B. Libros de viajes, reportajes y misceláneo. C. Novela. II. "Referencias bibliográficas," pp. 134–38 (critical studies are listed under Grosso's individual works).

GUARNER, LUIS (1902–1986)

Aguirre, José Luis. "Luis Guarner (1902–1986): Nota biográfico y bibliográfica," *Boletín de la Sociedad Castellonense de Cultura* (Castellón), 63 (1987), 109–25. Contents: I. Obras valencianas. A. Obras poéticas. B. Narrativa. C. Temas valencianos. D. Temas catalanes. E. Ediciones críticas. F. Descripción y viajes. II. Obras castellanas. A. Obras poéticas. B. Antologías. C. Traducciones de poetas extranjeros. D. Biografías. E. Ediciones críticas. F. Ediciones de *Poema de Cid.* G. Ensayos críticos. H. Didáctica.

GUILLEN, JORGE (1893–1984)

Bardi, Ubaldo. "Materiale per una bibliografia italiana de Jorge Guillén," *Arte e Poesia*, 8 (1970), 75–80. Includes 33 items. Contents: I. Opere di Jorge Guillén. II. Traduzioni. A. Parte prima: critica. B. Parte seconda: traduzioni e testi.

Cano, José Luis. "Jorge Guillén: Bibliografía," *El Libro Español*, No. 309 (marzo de 1984), 77–82. Contents: I. Libros. Poesía. II. Antologías. III. Libros. Prosa. IV. Ediciones. V. Algunos artículos de J. G. dispersos en revistas y libros. VI. Traducciones. VII. Homenajes y libros colectivos. VIII. Bibliografía sobre Jorge Guillén. A. Libros (critical annotations). B. Ensayos en libros.

Correa, v. 1, pp. 320, 544–47. Works by and about the author.

Debicki, Andrew P. *La poesía de Jorge Guillén*. Madrid: Editorial Gredos, 1973. 360p. (Biblioteca Románica Hispánica. II. Estudios y Ensayos, 197). I. "Bibliografía activa," pp. 333–36. Contents: Obras poéticas. Obras en prosa. II. "Bibliografía pasiva," pp. 336–50. Contents: Trabajos acerca de la época y "Generación de 1924–1925." Biografía y bibliografía. Estudios y ensayos críticos.

Díaz de Castro, Francisco J. *La poesía de Jorge Guillén: Tres ensayos*. Palma de Mallorca: Prensa Universitaria, 1987. 195p. "Principales obras de Jorge Guillén," pp. 161–165. Contents: I. Poesía (By year, 1928–1983). II. Prosa (By year, 1928–1985). "Bibliografía selecta," pp. 166–93 (Criticism; emphasis on late 1970s and 1980s). "Homenajes," p. 194.

Gómez Yerba, A. "Análisis de la bibliografía guilleniana," pp. 90–124 in *Jorge Guillén* (Barcelona: Anthropos/Ministerio de Cultura, Dirección General del Libro y Bibliotecas, Centro de las Letras Españolas, 1987).

González Muela, pp. 69–73. Works by and about Guillén are arranged chronologically.

Guillén, Jorge. *Final*. Edición, introducción y notas de Antonio Piedra. Madrid: Castalia, 1987. 351p. (Clásicos Castalia, 176). "Noticia bibliográfica," pp. 57–61. Contents: I. Obra poética (By year, 1928–1987). Anthologies, translations, and single poems are excluded. II. Publicaciones en prosa (By year, 1923–1984). "Bibliografía selecta sobre el autor," pp. 63–77.

Guillén, Rafael. "Bibliografía sobre Jorge Guillén," *Litoral* (Málaga), No. 87 (1979), 97–99.

Ivask, Ivan, and Juan Marichal. *Luminous Reality: The Poetry of Jorge Guillén*. Norman: University of Oklahoma Press, 1969. 217p. "A Jorge Guillén Bibliography," pp. 212–17. 63 items. Contents: I. Poetry. II. Prose. III. Translations into Other Languages. IV. Jorge Guillén in *Books Abroad*, 1929–68.

"Jorge Guillén in *Books Abroad/World Literature Today*, 1929–1984," *World Literature Today*, 58 (Spring 1984), 228.

MacCurdy, G. Grant. *Jorge Guillén*. Boston: Twayne, 1982. 183p. "Selected Bibliography," pp. 172–80. Contents: I. Primary Sources. A. Original Poetic Works in Spanish (listed chronologically). B. English Translations of Poetic Works. C. Selected Prose Works, including Interviews. II. Secondary Sources. A. Jorge Guillén and Contemporary Spanish Poetry. II. Miscellaneous Additional Sources. Annotated entries.

Macrí, Oreste. *La obra poética de Jorge Guillén*. Barcelona, Caracas, México: Editorial Ariel, 1976. 534p. (Letras e ideas, Maior 8). "Bibliografía," pp. 473–509. Contents: I. Perfil biográfico. II.

Fuentes bibliográficas. A. Obras. 1. Poesía. 2. Prosa. 3. Traducciones. B. Crítica. 1. Homenajes y colectivos. 2. Anónimos. 3. Nombres propios. a. Estudios. b. Estudios breves y artículos. C. Traducciones (by language).

Matthews, Elizabeth. *The Structured World of Jorge Guillén: A Study of "Cántico" and "Clamor."* Liverpool: Francis Cairns, 1985. 325p. (Liverpool Monographs in Hispanic Studies, 4). "Bibliography," pp. 322–25. Contents: I. Works by Jorge Guillén. A. Poetry. B. English Translations of Poetry. C. Selected Prose. II. Selected Secondary Sources (criticism).

Meneses, Carlos and Carretero, Silvia. *Jorge Guillén*. Madrid: Ediciones Júcar, 1981. 224p. "Bibliografía de Jorge Guillén," pp. 212–16. Contents: I. Poesía. II. Prosa. III. Crítica literaria y varios. IV. Traducciones. V. Exégesis de su propia obra. VI. Teoría poética. VII. Homenajes a Jorge Guillén. "Bibliografía general sobre Jorge Guillén," pp. 217–22. Contents: I. Antologías (citamos algunas de las más importantes). II. Estudios-artículos (selección).

Sibbald, K. M. "La producción crítica de Jorge Guillén en 1924 bajo los seudónimos de Félix de la Barca y Pedro Villa," v. 6, pp. 699–700 in *Actas del Sexto Congreso Internacional de Hispanistas* (Toronto, 1980).

GUILLEN, RAFAEL (1933-)

Guillén, Rafael. *Los alrededores del tiempo: Antología (1956–1985)*. Introducción de José Luis Cano. Granada: Ediciones Antonio Ubago, 1988. 229p. "Bibliografía," pp. 209–15.

GULLON, RICARDO (1903–1991)

Aponte Bockus, Barbara. *La obra critíca de Ricardo Gullón*. Madrid: Insula, 1975. 173p. "Bibliografía," pp. 161–171. Contents: I. Bibliografía de Ricardo Gullón. A. Libros. B. Ediciones. C. Libros prologados. D. Selección de ensayos y artículos. E. Reseñas y estudios críticos de su obra. Selección. F. Algunos escritos referentes a la persona de Gullón. II. Bibliografía general.

"Bibliografía santanderina de Ricardo Gullón, 1941–1953," pp. 16–20 in *Los años santanderinos de Ricardo Gullón (1941–1953)* (Santander, 1981). A bibliography of the articles and reviews written by Gullón in the newspaper, *Alerta* of Santander.

Estudios en honor a Ricardo Gullón. Edited by Luis T. González-del-Valle and Darío Villanueva. Lincoln, Neb.: Society of Spanish and Spanish American Studies, 1984. 387p. "Bibliografía," pp. 15–39. Contents: I. Obras (arranged by year, 1929–1980). II. Ediciones (1957–1982). III. Libros prologados (1961–1966). IV.

Traducciones (1952–1960). V. Selección de ensayos y artículos (1934–1983). VI. Selecciones de reseñas y estudios críticos de su obra (1934–1983). VII. Algunos escritos referentes a la persona de Gullón.

Ricardo Gullón: Bibliografía," *Alonso*, pp. 41–42. Contents: I. Obras originales (By year, 1934–1985). II. Ediciones críticas (By year, 1957–1981). Books only.

GUTIERREZ SOLANA, JOSE (1886–1945)

Barrio-Garay, José Luis. *José Gutiérrez Solana: Paintings and Writings*. Lewisburg, Pa.: Bucknell University Press, 1978. 182p. "Bibliography," pp. 165–73. Contents: I. General Sources. A. Books. B. Articles. II. Solana's Writings (By year). III. Interviews (By year, 1921–1944). IV. Witness Accounts. V. Biographies. VI. Books. VII. Articles and Newspaper Reviews. VIII. Medical and Psychiatric Studies.

GUTIERREZ TORRERO, CONCEPCION (1909–)

Galerstein, pp. 137–41.

HERNAN, JOSITA (1919–)

Galerstein, p. 143.

HERNANDEZ, MIGUEL (1910–1942)

Aguirre, Angel Manuel. "Bibliografía de Miguel Hernández," *Quaderni Ibero-Americana*, Nos. 35/36 (1967), 186–202. Includes 357 entries. Contents: I. Poesía. II. Poesía; sueltas y selecciones. III. Recogidas después en libros. IV. Poesías reproducidas en libros. V. Poemas inéditos. VI. Obras dramáticas. VII. Artículos y prosas sueltas. VIII. Cartas. IX. Traducciones. X. Estudios. XI. Poesías dedicadas. XII. Homenajes. XIII. Iconografía.

Balcells, José María. *Miguel Hernández: corazón desmesurado*. Barcelona: Editorial DIROSA, 1975. 229p. "Bibliografía," pp. 207–28. Contents: I. Bibliografías. II. Ediciones e inéditos. III. Traducciones (by language). IV. Estudios y artículos (Includes books, newspaper and periodical articles, and theses and dissertations). V. Números especiales de revistas. Unfortunately, page numbers are left off from journal articles.

______. "Miguel Hernández en la URSS: Notas bibliográficas," *Insula*, No. 349 (1975), 10.

Correa, v. 2, pp. 63–64, 605–07. Contents: I. Libros. II. Artículos y estudios (criticism).

Couttolenc Cortés, Gustavo. *La poesía existencial de Miguel Hernández*. México: Universidad Nacional Autónoma de México, 1979. 192p. "Bibliografía," pp. 187–92. Criticism only.

Gracia Ifach, María de. "Tabla cronológica y bibliografía de Miguel Hernández," *Revista de Occidente*, 2ª época, No. 139 (octubre de 1974), 135–39. Contents: I. Obras (orden cronológico de publicación). II. Antologías y selecciones principales. III. Traducciones más importantes.

_____. *Vida de Miguel Hernández*. Barcelona: Playa y Janés, 1982. 156p. "Bibliografía," pp. 141–56. Contents: I. Obras de Miguel Hernández (con ediciones repetidas). II. Antologías. Principales selecciones. III. En panoramas, libros de estudio, etc. IV. Biografías. Estudios. Artículos. V. Revistas monográficas o con dedicaciones parciales. VI. Traducciones. VII. Cronología de Miguel Hernández.

Hernández, Miguel. *El hombre acecha. Cancionero y romancero de ausencias*. Edición de Leopoldo de Luis y Jorge Urrutia. Madrid: Cátedra, 1984 254p. "Bibliografía," pp. 102–10. Contents: I. Obras de Miguel Hernández. II. Las principales antologías en las que pueden encontrarse poemas pertenecientes a *El hombre acecha* y a *Cancionero y romancero de ausencias*. III. Libros monográficos sobre Miguel Hernández. IV. La bibliografía que se refiere, exclusivamente a trabajos críticos dedicados, en todo en parte, a *El hombre acecha* y a *Cancionero y romancero de ausencias*.

_____. *Obra poética completa*. Introducción, estudios y notas de Leopoldo de Luis y Jorge Urrutia. Madrid: Alianza Editorial, 1982. 648p. "Bibliografía," pp. 621–27. Contents: I. Selección de ediciones (by year, 1952–1981). II. Selección de volúmenes monográficos. III. Seleccion de artículos y ensayos.

_____. *Poesías completas*. Edición, introducción y notas de Agustín Sánchez Vidal. Madrid: Aguilar, 1979. 950p. "Selección bibliográfica," pp. 912–18. Contents: I. Obras de Miguel Hernández. II. Publicaciones sobre o en relación con Miguel Hernández. A. Monografías. B. Artículos. 1. Recopilaciones de artículos. 2. Números monográficos de revistas. 3. Artículos sueltos o integrados en trabajos no monográficos.

Nichols, Geraldine Cleary. *Miguel Hernández*. Boston: Twayne Publishers, Inc., 1978. 201p. "Selected Bibliography," pp. 191–96. Contents: I. Primary Sources. A. Books of Verse (Major Editions, 1933–1977). B. Narrative Prose and Theater (1934–1968). II. Secondary Sources (annotated). A. Books and Dissertations. B. Articles and Chapters of Books. C. Special Issues of Journals Dedicated to Hernández. D. Translation of Hernández Work into English. E. Books about the Period with Special Relevance to Hernández.

Ramos, Vicente. *Miguel Hernández.* Madrid: Editorial Gredos, 1973. 378p. (Biblioteca Románica Hispánica. VII. Campo Abierto, 32). "Bibliografía," pp. 325–69. Contents: I. Teoría de Orchuela. II. Ramon Sijé. III. Miguel Hernández. A. Obra de Miguel Hernández. 1. Verso y prosa (by year, 1930–69). 2. Reproducciones de textos. 3. Traducciones. 4. Epistolario. IV. Sobre Miguel Hernández. A. Libros y folletos. B. Números monográficos de revistas. C. Artículos y poemas.

______, and Manuel Molina. *Miguel Hernández en Alicante.* Alicante: Colección "Ifach," 1976. 200p. (Colección IFACH, Número 15). "Bibliografía," pp. 185–200. Contents: I. Obra de Miguel Hernández (by year, 1930–73). II. Sobre Miguel Hernández. A. Libros (arranged by year, 1969–73). B. Artículos y poemas (by year, 1930–76; page numbers are missing).

Zardoya, Concha. "Miguel Hernández," *Revista Hispánica Moderna*, 21, Nos. 3/4 (julio/octubre de 1955), 289–93. Contents: I. Ediciones. A. Libros. B. Poesías sueltas y selecciones. 1. Recogidas después en libros. 2. No recogidas en libros. 3. Reproducida de libros. C. Obras dramáticas. 1. Recogidas después en libros. 2. No recogidas en libros. 3. Reproducidas de libros. D. Artículos y prosas sueltas. E. Traducciones. II. Estudios. III. Poesías dedicadas. IV. Iconografía.

HERRERA GARRIDO, FRANCISCA (1869–1950)

Galerstein, p. 144.

HERRERO GARCIA, MIGUEL (1895–1961)

Agulló y Cobo, Mercedes. "Don Miguel Herrero García: Bibliografía," *Revista de Literatura*, 21 (enero/junio de 1962), 171–77. Contents: I. Libros. II. Artículos en publicaciones periódicas.

HIDALGO, JOSE LUIS (1919–1947)

Correa, v. 2, pp. 197, 614. Contents: I. Libros. II. Artículos y estudios (criticism).

García Cantalapiedra, Aurelio. *Tiempo y vida de José Luis Hidalgo.* Madrid: Taurus Ediciones, 1975. 298p. "Bibliografía," pp. 283–89. Contents: I. Ediciones originales. II. Ediciones póstumas. III. Colaboraciones en diarios y revistas (by journal or newspaper). IV. Selección de escritos sobre José Luis Hidalgo.

Mantero, pp. 552–53. Contents: I. Libros de poesía. II. Otras publicaciones. III. Sobre José Luis Hidalgo.

Verso y prosa en torno a José Luis Hidalgo. Recopilación, introducción, notas y bibliografía de Aurelio García Cantalapiedra. Santander: Institución Cultural de Cantabria, 1971. 416p. "Bibliografía," pp. 363–82. Contents: I. Ediciones originales. II. Ediciones póstumas. III. Colaboraciones en diarios y revistas. IV. Poesías póstumas. V. Escritos sobre José Luis Hidalgo. VI. Referencias a su persona y a su obra. "Referencias de homenajes literarios y conferencias," pp. 383–88.

HIERRO, JOSE (1922–)

Agulló y Cobo, Mercedes. "Escritores contemporáneos: José Hierro," *El Libro Español*, 1 (1958), 173–76. "Bibliografía" pp. 174–76. Books, pamphlets, and translations only.

Cavallo, Susana. *La poética de José Hierro*. Madrid: Taurus Ediciones, 1987. 156p. "Bibliografía," pp. 149–56. Contents: I. Obras de José Hierro. A. Poesía. B. Otras obras. II. Obras adicionales consultadas. A. Obras sobre José Hierro. B. Obras generales.

Corona Marzol, Gonzalo. *Bibliografía de José Hierro Real*. Zaragoza: Universidad de Zaragoza, 1988. 63p. Contents: I. Bibliografía. A. Escritos de José Hierro (By year, 1937–1988). B. Entrevistas. Crítica e interpretación. Antologías colectivas (By year, 1947–1988). 601 items. II. Indices. A. Bibliografía de José Hierro. 1. Obras poéticas completas. 2. Poemas no incluídos en sus obras completas. 3. Libros y cuadernos de poesía (no antologías). 4. Libros y cuadernos de poesías (antológicos). 5. Poemas sueltos. 6. Narrativa: cuentos. 7. Escritos en prosa sobre tema literario (teoría, crítica, noticias, etc.). 8. Escritos en prosa sobre otras artes (teoría, crítica, noticias, etc.). 9. Páginas literarias, noticias varias. 10. Prólogos y epílogos. 11. Ediciones y adaptaciones. 12. Traducciones. 13. Dibujos. B. Bibliografía sobre José Hierro. 1. Bibliografías. 2. Entrevistas y encuestas. 3. Antologías. 4. Traducción de poemas. C. Indice alfabético de autores.

Correa, v. 2, pp. 321, 617–18. Contents: I. Libros. II. Artículos y estudios (criticism).

García Cantalapiedra, Aurelio. "Bibliografía de José Hierro," *Peña Labra* (Paris), No. 43/44 (1982), 54–55.

______. "Los primeros escritos de José Hierro sobre arte," *Peña Labra* (Paris), No. 43/44 (1982), 25–28.

Hierro, José. *Libro de las alucinaciones*. Edición de Dionisio Cañas. Madrid: Cátedra, 1986. 175p. (Letras Hispánicas, 243). "Bibliografía," pp. 79–85. Contents: I. Obra poética de José Hierro (By year, 1947–1964). A. Libros originales. B. Compilaciones parciales y antologías (By year, 1953–1982). C. Poesías completas. II. Estudios sobre su obra. A. Libros. B. Artículos.

Mantero, pp. 553–54. Contents: I. Libros de poesía. II. Otras publicaciones. III. Sobre José Hierro.

Torre, Emilio E. de. *José Hierro: Poeta de testimonio.* Madrid: Ediciones José Porrúa Turanzas, 1983. 219p. "Bibliografía," pp. 211–15. Contents: I. Obras de José Hierro. A. Poesía (by year, 1947–1978). B. Varia (By year, 1952–1982). II. Obras sobre José Hierro.

HINOJOSA, JOSE MARIA (1904–1936)

Pariente, pp. 90–91. Contents: I. Libros de poesía (By year, 1925–31). II. Estudios sobre su poesía (By year, 1928–82). III. Procedencia de los textos.

IBANEZ NOVO, MERCEDES (1946–)

Galerstein, p. 147.

ICAZA, CARMEN DE (1899–)

Galerstein, pp. 148–49.

JANER MANILA, GABRIEL (1940–)

"Gabriel Janer Manila: Selected Bibliography," *Catalan Writing*, No. 4 (March 1990), 46–47. Contents: I. Fiction. II. Theatre. III. Translations. IV. Awards and Citations.

JANES, CLARA (1940–)

CILH, p. 37. Contents: I. Poesía. II. Otros géneros.

Galerstein, pp. 151–52.

JARDIEL PONCELA, ENRIQUE (1901–1952)

Ariza Viguera, Manuel. *Enrique Jardiel Poncela: La literatura humorística española.* Madrid: Editorial Fragua, 1974. 322p. "Su obra," pp. 21–33 (by year, 1911–53). "Bibliografía," pp. 313–18. Contents: I. Estudios generales. II. Estudios particulares.

Conde Guerri, María José. *El teatro de Enrique Jardiel Poncela.* Zaragoza: Caja de Ahorros de Zaragoza, Aragón y Rioja, 1984. 149p. "Obra dramática," pp. 18–22. Entries are arranged by year, 1911–1950.

Jardiel Poncela, Enrique. *Pero . . . ¿Hubo alguna vez once mil vírgenes?* Edición de Luis Alemany. Madrid: Ediciones Cátedra, 1988. 538p. "Bibliografía," pp. 61–63. Contents: I. Ediciones (*Pero . . . ¿Hubo alguna vez once mil vírgenes*?) II. Crítica. A. Estudios generales. B. Estudios específicos (*Pero . . . ¿Hubo alguna vez once mil vírgenes*?).

______. *La Tournée de Dios. Novela casi divina.* Introducción y notas de Luis Alemany Colomé. Madrid: Biblioteca Nueva, 1989. 476p. "Bibliografía," pp. 47–49.

McKay, Douglas R. *Enrique Jardiel Poncela.* New York: Twayne Publishers, Inc., 1974. 134p. "Selected Bibliography," pp. 111–14. Contents: I. Selected Editions. II. Secondary Sources. "Appendix," pp. 115–27. Contents: I. Unpublished Plays. A. Repudiated Writings. B. Performed but Unpublished Plays. II. Published Plays. A. Collections. B. Individual Comedies. C. Monologues. III. Major Novels. A. Unpublished Writings, Repudiated by Jardiel Poncela. B. Published Works. IV. Miscellaneous Books. V. Major Lectures. A. Published Lectures. B. Radio Lectures. VI. Movie Scripts.

JARNES, BENJAMIN (1888–1949)

Bernstein, J. S. *Benjamín Jarnés.* New York: Twayne Publishers, Inc., 1972. 180p. "Selected Bibliography," pp. 160–73. Contents: I. Primary Sources. A. Novels, Short Stories, Essays, and Biographies Published in Book Form by Jarnés, and Plays of His Which Were Produced (by year, 1924–1948). B. Short Stories, Articles, Book Reviews, Prologues, Translations, and Editions by Jarnés. C. Jarnés' Fugitive Bibliography. II. Secondary Sources.

Domínguez Lasiera, Juan. *Ensayo de una bibliografía jarnesiana.* Zaragoza: Institución Fernando el Católico, 1988. 138p.

Martínez Latre, María Pilar. *La novela intelectual de Benjamín Jarnés.* Zaragoza: Institución "Fernando El Católico," 1979. 272p. (*Its* Publicación, 731). "Bibliografía," pp. 261–64. Contents: I. Obras de Jarnés. A. Artículos. B. Biografías. C. Libros de ensayo. D. Libros de género intermedio. E. Novelas. II. Escritos sobre Jarnés.

JIMENEZ, JUAN RAMON (1881–1958)

Azam, Gilbert. *L'oeuvre de Juan Ramón Jiménez: Continuité et renouveau de la poésie lyrique espagnole.* Thèse presentée devant l'Université de Toulouse II, 1978. Paris: Diffusion Librairie Honoré Champion, 1980. 741p. "Bibliographie," pp. 711–24. Contents: I. Oeuvres de Juan Ramón Jiménez. II. Projets de livres. A. Oeuvres en vers. B. Oeuvres en prose. C. Oeuvres en vers et prose. D. Oeuvre inédite de Juan Ramón Jiménez. III. Articles de journaux et de revues sur Juan Ramón Jiménez. IV. Ouvrages sur Juan Ramón Jiménez (monographs).

"Bibliografía juanramonista (Notas complementarias)," *La Torre*, Nos. 19/20 (julio/diciembre de 1957), 407–09. Additions to the 1956 Palau de Nemes work. Contents: I. Colaboración de Juan Ramón Jiménez en revistas (en orden cronológico de la primeras colaboraciones). II. Homenajes a Juan Ramón Jiménez en revistas y periódicos.

Campoamor González, Antonio. *Bibliografía general de Juan Ramón Jiménez*. Madrid: Taurus Ediciones, 1983. 725p. Contents: I. Bibliografía de Juan Ramón Jiménez. A. Libros. B. Traducciones. C. Folletos. D. Traducciones de J.R.J. E. Revistas, caudernos y hojos sueltos. F. Prólogos. G. Obra inédita de J.R.J. H. Colaboraciones de J.R.J. en revistas, periódicos y libros. I. Colecciones de poesías y poemas sueltos. J. Poemas de J.R.J. en música. K. Grabaciones. II. Bibliografía sobre Juan Ramón Jiménez. A. Estudios. B. Tesis. C. Conferencias y conmemoraciones. D. Ensayos, estudios breves, crítica miscelánea y citas mayores en libro. E. Antologías. F. Prólogos. G. Artículos, poemas, recensiones, dedicatorias, bibliografías, citas menores. H. Homenajes a J.R.J. en libros, revistas y periódicos. I. Actas en homenaje a J.R.J.. J. Iconografía. K. Emisiones por radio y televisión. L. Varios. 1. Filatelia y numismática. 2. Miscelánea. 3. Adaptaciones teatrales y cinematográficas. Includes 9,076 items, not annotated.

Cole, Leo Raymond. *The Religious Instinct in the Poetry of Juan Ramón Jiménez*. Oxford: The Dolphin Book Co., Ltd., 1967. 204p. "Bibliography," pp. 199–204. Contents: I. Bibliography on Juan Ramón. II. Recent Editions of J.R.'s Work (1959 and after). III. Principal Works on J.R.'s Poetry. IV. Other Works Consulted.

Fogelquist, Donald F. "Juan Ramón Jiménez: Bibliografía," *Revista Hispánica Moderna*, 24, No. 1 (enero de 1958), 177–95. Contents: I. Ediciones. II. Antologías. III. Traducciones. IV. Poesías sueltas. V. Artículos y conferencias. VI. Prólogos. VII. Epistolario. VIII. Traductor. IX. Estudios y homenajes.

______. "Juan Ramón Jiménez en Italia," *Cuadernos Americanos*, año 14, tomo 82, No. 4 (julio/agosto de 1955), 232–36. On p. 236 appears a "Bibliografía de estudios italianos recientes sobre Juan Ramón Jiménez y traducciones de sus obras."

Jiménez, Juan Ramón. *Antología comentada*. Selección, introducción y notas de Antonio Sánchez Barbudo. Madrid: Ediciones de la Torre, 1986. 429p. (Colección Germinal, 8). "Bibliografía (selección)," pp. 399–402. Contents: I. Obras de Juan Ramón

Jiménez. A. Principales colecciones. B. Algunas ediciones de libros de Juan Ramón Jiménez. II. Estudios sobre Juan Ramón Jiménez. A. Libros. B. Colecciones de estudios y artículos (Homenajes y congresos). "Cronología," pp. 403–18. Includes bio-bibliographical information.

______. *Antolojía poética.* Edición de Vicente Gaos. Décima edición. Madrid: Cátedra, 1984. 188p. (Letras Hispánicas, 19). "Bibliografía," pp. 57–66. Contents: I. Ediciones (de obras en verso y en verso y prosa, by year, 1900–1974). II. Antologías (By year, 1917–1974). III. Estudios (critical works, by year, 1907–1974).

______. *Diario de un poeta recién casado (1916).* Prólogo de Ricardo Gullón. Madrid: Taurus, 1982. 297p. "Nota bibliográfica," pp. 50–56. Contents: I. Ediciones del *Diario de un poeta recién casado.* II. Poemas anticipados en diarios by revistas. III. Bibliografía reciente (criticism). IV. Antologías que incluyen poemas del *Diario.*

______. *Elegías: elegías puras, elegías intermedias, elegías lamentables.* Prólogo de Francisco Garfías. Bibliografía por Antonio Compoamor. Madrid: Taurus, 1982. 124p. "Notas bibliográficas," pp. 31–40. Contents: I. Ediciones de *Elegías.* II. Poemas anticipados en revistas. III. Poemas de *Elegías.* Recogidos por Juan Ramón Jiménez en sus propias antologías y otros libros. IV. Otras antologías que incluyen poemas de *Elegías.* V. Crítica a *Elegías.*

______. *Eternidades: Verso (1916–1917).* Prólogo de Víctor García de la Concha. Madrid: Taurus, 1982. 133p. "Notas críticas," pp. 40–54. "Recojo en este apéndice las notas de los libros juanramonianos en que aparecen poemas de *Eternidades*, con indicación, en su caso, de las varientes textuales."

______. *Jardines lejanos: jardines galantes, jardines místicos, jardines dolientes.* Prólogo de Ignacio Prat. Madrid: Taurus, 1982. 250p. "Nota bibliográfica," pp. 33–40. Contents: I. Ediciones de *Jardines lejanos.* II. Poemas anticipados en revistas. III. Poemas de *Jardines lejanos* recogidos por Juan Ramón en sus propias antologías y otros libros. IV. Otras antologías que incluyen poemas de *Jardines lejanos.* V. Crítica a *Jardines lejanos.*

______. *Pastorales (1905).* Prólogo y notas bibliográficas de Antonio Campoamor y Ricardo Gullón. Madrid: Taurus, 1982. 247p. "Notas bibliográficas," pp. 44–70. Contents: I. Ediciones de *Pastorales.* II. Poemas anticipados en revistas y libros. A. En revistas. B. En libro. III. Poemas de *Pastorales* recogido por Juan Ramón Jiménez en sus propias antologías y otros libros. IV.

Variantes textuales. V. Otras antologías que incluyen poemas de *Pastorales*.

_____. *Platero y yo*. Edición de Richard A. Cardwell. Madrid: Espasa Calpe, 1988. 272p. (Colección Austral, 58). "Bibliografía," pp. 55–57. Contents: I. Biografía. II. Estudios fundamentales. III. Estudios sobre *Platero y yo*.

_____. *Poesía: en verso (1917–1923)*. Prólogo de Antonio Sánchez Romeralo. Madrid: Taurus, 1981. 127p. "Notas críticas," pp. 25–33. Contents: I. Libros o proyectos originales a que corresponden de sus textos de *Poesía*. II. Revistas en que aparecieron algunas de sus poesías: indicación bibliográfica. III. Ficha individual de los poesías, con mención en su caso, de la revista en que aparecieron y de las antologías del poeta que las recogen.

_____. *Poesías últimas escojidas (1918–1958)*. Edición, prólogo y notas de Antonio Sánchez Romeralo. Madrid: Espasa Calpe, 1982. 399p. "Indice de periódicos, revistas y publicaciones de Juan Ramón Jiménez en que fueron publicadas estas *Poesías últimas escojidas*," pp. 42–58. By title and then by journal or periodical.

_____. *Selección de poemas*. Edición, introducción y notas de Gilbert Azam. Madrid: Castalia, 1987. 227p. (Clásicos Castalia, 158). "Noticia bibliográfica," pp. 55–64. Contents: I. Obras de Juan Ramón Jiménez (By year, 1900–1986). II. Proyectos de libros. A. Obras en verso (By year, 1900–1925). B. Obra en prosa. C. Obra en verso y prosa (By year, 1907–1927). D. Obra inédita de Juan Ramón Jiménez. "Bibliografía selecta," pp. 65–71. Contents: I. Artículos de periódicos y revistas sobre Juan Ramón Jiménez. II. Publicaciones del Centenario. III. Obras sobre Juan Ramón Jiménez (books only).

_____. *Sonetos espirituales (1914–1915)*. Prólogo de Allen W. Phillips. Madrid: Taurus, 1982. 129p. "Bibliografía," pp. 45–51. Contents: I. Ediciones. II. Bibliografía sobre Juan Ramón y su obra. III. Poemas de *Sonetos espirituales* publicados antes de aparecer el libro. IV. Crítica sobre *Sonetos espirituales*. A. Libros. B. Artículos. V. Algunos libros que incluyen poemas de *Sonetos espirituales*. A. Selecciones del autor. B. Otras antologías.

Juan Ramon Jiménez Edición de Aurora de Albornoz. Madrid: Taurus Ediciones, 1980. 366p. "Bibliografía," pp. 351–362. Contents: I. Obras de Juan Ramón Jiménez. A. Ediciones del autor (1900–1957). B. Antologías y libros póstumas (1923–1979). II. Obras sobre Juan Ramón Jiménez. A. Libros. B. Estudios y artículos (selected). "Algunos artículos aparecidos en revistas y periódicos a raíz de la publicación de los principales libros de Juan

Ramón Jiménez (se excluyen las ediciones póstumas)," pp. 363–366. (entries are arranged by work of Jiménez).

"Juan Ramón Jiménez en palabras y en imágenes. Tabla cronológica, antología poética, textos en prosa, documentos gráficos," *Poesía* (Madrid), No. 13/14 (1981/82), 5–285. "Indice bibliográfico de prosas," pp. 278–83. "Noticia bibliográfica de primeras ediciones de Juan Ramón Jiménez y de antologías y libros póstumos," pp. 284–85. Contents: I. Ediciones del autor (By year, 1900–1957). II. Antologías y libros póstumos (By year, 1923–1981).

Naharro-Calderón, José María. "Bibliografía de y sobre Juan Ramón Jiménez," *Anthropos* (Barcelona), Suplemento 11 (1989), 146–55.

Palau de Nemes, Graciela. *Vida y obra de Juan Ramón Jiménez: La poesía desnuda*. Segunda edición completamente renovada. Madrid: Editorial Gredos, 1974. 2vs. (Biblioteca Románica Hispánica. II. Estudios y Ensayos, 31). "Indice de obras de Juan Ramón Jiménez que se mencionan o se explican en este trabajo (se da la fecha de composición y entre paréntesis la de publicación cuando no coinciden)," pp. 655–674. Contents: I. Poemas sueltos. A. Miscelánea, 1898–1907. B. Colaboración en *Vida nueva*, 1899–1900. C. Colaboración en *Helio*, 1903–04. D. Libros. E. Colecciones póstumas de la obra suelta y la obra inédita. II. Prosa. A. Prosa suelta. 1. Miscelánea, 1898–1953. 2. Colaboración en *Helios*, 1903–04. 3. Colaboración en *Renacimiento*, 1907. B. Libros. C. Otra publicadas por el autor. D. Colecciones póstumas de la obra suelta y la obra inédita.

Peña, María Teresa de la, and Natividad Moreno. *Catálogo de los fondos manuscritos de Juan Ramón Jiménez*. Madrid: Imprenta del Ministerio de Cultura, 1980. 143p. Manuscripts located in the Archivo Histórico Nacional. Holdings mainly to 1936. Contents: I. Obra poética. II. Epistolario. III. Crítica literaria. IV. Documentos particulares de Juan Ramón Jiménez. V. Documentos de Zenobia. VI. Poesía y prosa de diferentes autores. VII. Dibujos originales. VIII. Indice topográfico.

Sobejano, Gonzalo. "Juan Ramón Jiménez a través de la crítica, II," *Romanistisches Jahrbuch* 9 (1958), 299–330. "Bibliografía sobre J. R. Jiménez," pp. 317–30. Includes 317 items, 1907–58.

Strasburger, Janusz. "La obra de Juan Ramón Jiménez en Polonia: Traducciones, opiniones, afinidades," *Cuadernos Hispanoamericanos*, No. 376/78 (octubre/diciembre de 1981), 946–52. Critical and bibliographical survey.

JIMENEZ MARTOS, LUIS (1926-)
CILH, pp. 69–70. Contents: I. Poesía. II. Crítica y antología. III. Prosa.

JULIA MARTINEZ, EDUARDO (1887–1967)
Esquer Torres, Ramón. "Nuestros filólogos: Eduardo Juliá Martínez," *Boletín de Filología Española*, Nos. 18/19 (enero/junio de 1966), 3–9. "Publicaciones," pp. 5–9. A selected bibliography of 81 items. Incomplete bibliographic information for the journal titles. Contents: I. Ediciones de textos. II. Textos hispanoamericanos. III. Traducciones. IV. Estudios lingüísticos. V. Estudios literarios. VI. Prosa y verso. Obras de creación.

KARR I ALFONSETTI, CARME (1865–1943)
Galerstein, pp. 155–56.

KRUCKENBERG, MARIA DEL CARMEN (1926-
Galerstein, p. 157.

LABORDA MEDIR, CLEMENCIA (1908–1980)
Galerstein, pp. 159–160.

LABORDETA, MIGUEL (1921–1969)
Díaz de Castro, F. J. "La poesía de Miguel Labordeta," *Caligrama* (Palma de Mallorca), No. 1 (1986), 65–90. Includes a bibliography of Miguel Labordeta's unpublished work.
Ferrer Solá, Jesús. *La poesía metafísica de Miguel Labordeta.* Barcelona: Publicacions i Edicions de la Universidad de Barcelona, 1983. 139p. "Bibliografía selecta," pp. 135–39. Contents: I. Ediciones más asequibles (Labordeta's works). II. Estudios críticos.
Pariente, p. 93. Contents: I. Libros de poesía. II. Procedencia de los textos.

LACACI, MARIA ELVIRA (n.d.)
Galerstein, pp. 160–61.

LACARTA, MANUEL (n.d.)
Lacarta, Manuel. *34 posiciones para amar a Bambi*. Prólogo de José Hierro. Barcelona: Anthropos, 1988. 175p. (Ambitos literarios/Poesía, 91). "Bibliografía de Manuel Lacarta," p. 11.

LACASA, CRISTINA (1929-)
Galerstein, pp. 161–64.

LAFFON, RAFAEL (1895–1978)
Cruz Giráldez, Miguel. *Vida y poesía de Rafael Laffón*. Sevilla: Diputación Provincial de Sevilla, 1984. 407p. "Bibliografía," pp. 393–403. Contents: I. Obra poética (By year, 1921–1970). II. Obra en prosa (By year, 1920–1973). III. Sobre Rafael Laffón.

LAFITTE Y PEREZ DEL PUGAR, MARIA DE LOS REYES, CONDESA DE CAMPO ALANGE (1902-)
Galerstein, pp. 164–66.

LAFORET, CARMEN (1921-)
Alarcón, pp. 33–35.
Galerstein, pp. 166–69.
Johnson, Roberta. *Carmen Laforet*. Boston: Twayne Publishers, 1981. 153p. "Selected Bibliography," pp. 147–50. Contents: I. Primary Sources. II. Secondary Sources (criticism; annotated entries). A. Books. B. Articles.
Resnick, p. 219.

LAGOS, CONCHA (1923-)
Agulló Cobo, Mercedes. "Escritores contemporáneos: Concha Lagos," *El Libro Español*, 1 (1958), 303–05. "Bibliografía," p. 305.
Alarcón, p. 35.

LAPESA, RAFAEL (1908-)
"Bibliografía de Rafael Lapesa," III, pp. 13–28 in *Studia hispanica en honorem R. Lapesa* (Madrid: Editorial Gredos, 1975). Includes 180 entries (By year, 1929–75).

LARREA, JUAN (1895–1980)
Bary, David. *Larrea: Poesía y transfiguración*. Barcelona: Editorial Planeta, 1976. 192p. "Bibliografía," pp. 171–89. Contents: I. Textos de Larrea. A. Libros publicados (by year, 1934–1973). B. Poemas sueltos publicados en revistas y antologías (1919–1970). C. Artículos, notas y reseñas (1926–1974). D. Cartas publicadas

(1959–1968). E. Ponencias, conferencias y cursos (1947–1973). F. Traducciones publicadas. G. Textos inéditos. II. Textos publicados sobre Larrea. A. Textos de alcance general (1923–1970). B. Sobre "Rendición de espíritu." C. Sobre "El surrealismo." D. Sobre "The Vision of Guernica." E. Sobre "La espada de la paloma" y "Razón de ser." F. Sobre "César Vallejo, o Hispanoamérica en la cruz de su razón." G. Sobre "Corona incaica." H. Sobre "Del surrealismo o Machupichu." I. Sobre "Versione Celeste." J. Sobre "Versión celeste." K. Sobre la exposición de París. L. Sobre la exposición de Madrid. M. Sobre la Asociación de Amigos de la Arqueología Americana.

Díaz de Guereñu, Juan Manuel. *La poesía de Juan Larrea: Creación y sentido.*, San Sebastián: Universidad de Deusto, Facultad de Filosofía y Letras, 1988. 404p. (Cuadernos Universitarios, Departamento de Literatura, 6). "Bibliografía," pp. 375–401. Contents: I. Bibliografía de Juan Larrea. A. Poesía (1919–1987). B. Prosa. 1. Libros y recopilaciones (1943–1987). 2. Artículos. 3. Cartas. II. Bibliografía sobre Juan Larrea. A. Libros y tesis. B. Artículos y estudios. C. Reseñas, notas y referencias. III. Bibliografía general.

Gurney, Robert. *La poesía de Juan Larrea.* Traducción de Juan Manuel Díaz de Guereñu. Bilbao: Universidad del País Vasco, 1986. 331p. "Bibliografía selecta," pp. 321–31. Includes works by and about Larrea.

Larrea, Juan. *Versión Celeste.* Edición de Miguel Nieto. Madrid: Ediciones Cátedra, 1989. 355p. "Bibliografía," pp. 55–57. Contents: I. Libros de Juan Larrea (By year, 1926–1984). II. Revistas publicadas por iniciativa de Juan Larrea. III. Sobre Juan Larrea (selección).

Pariente, pp. 93–94. Contents: I. Libros de poesía (By year, 1934–1970). II. Estudios sobre su poesía (By year, 1950–76). III. Procedencia de los textos.

LAZARO, MARIBEL (1948–)

"Maribel Lázaro," *O'Connor*, p. 157–58.

LAZARO CARRETER, FERNANDO (1923–)

Abad Nesbot, Francisco. "Nuestros filólogos: el profesor Fernando Lazáro Carreter," *Boletín de Filología Española*, Nos. 50/58 (enero/diciembre de 1974/75), 3–13. "Bibliografía," pp. 10–13. The list does not include newspaper articles or articles within books. Contents: I. Libros. II. Ediciones. III. Folletos. IV. Artículos. V. En prensa.

LEDESMA CRIADO, JOSE (n.d.)
CILH, p. 93.

LEDO ANDION, MARGARITA (1951–)
Galerstein, p. 169.

LEJARRAGA, MARIA DE LA O (1874–1974)
Galerstein, pp. 169–74.
"María de la O Lejarraga," *O'Connor*, pp. 158–59.

LEON, MARIA TERESA (1904–)
Galerstein, pp. 174–77.

LEON, RICARDO (1877–1943)
Romo Arregui, Josefina. "Ricardo León: Bibliografía," *Cuadernos de Literatura Contemporánea*, No. 11/12 (1943), 397–99. Contents: I. Ediciones. A. Obras completas. B. Poesía. C. Obras diversas. D. Prólogos. E. Revistas. II. Estudios. III. Traducciones.

LERA, ANGEL MARIA DE (1912–1984)
Lera, Angel María de. *Novelas*. Prólogo por Luis Escolar Bareño. Madrid: Aguilar, 1966. 1207p. "Bibliografía," pp. xxi-xxiv. Contents: I. Obras de Angel María de Lera. II. Traducciones (by language). III. Sobre Angel María de Lera.
Listerman, Mary Sue. *Angel María de Lera*. Boston: Twayne Publishers, Inc., 1982. 152p. "Selected Bibliography," pp. 146–49. Contents: I. Primary Sources. A. Fiction. B. Non Fiction. C. Articles in *ABC* (Madrid). II. Secondary Sources. A. Books. B. Articles.

LEVERONI, ROSA (1910–1985)
Galerstein, pp. 177–78.

LINARES, LUISA MARIA (1915–)
Galerstein, pp. 178–81.

LOPEZ ALVAREZ, LUIS (1930–)
"Luis López Alvarez: Bibliografía," *Alonso*, p. 181. Poetry books only, by year, 1969–1979.

LOPEZ MORILLAS, JUAN (1913–)
Ilie, Paul. "Bibliografía de Juan López Morillas," pp. 17–20 in *Homenaje a Juan López Morillas: De Cadalso a Aleixandre; Estudios sobre literatura e historia intelectual españolas* (Ma-

drid: Castalia, 1982). Contents: I. Libros. II. Ediciones críticas. III. Traducciones. IV. Colaboraciones en libros. V. Prefacios. VI. Monografías y artículos. VII. Reseñas.

LOPEZ MOZO, JERONIMO (n.d.)

"Jerónimo López Mozo," pp. 27–33 in L. Teresa Valdivieso's *España: Bibliografía de un teatro "silenciado"* (Lincoln, Neb.: Society of Spanish and Spanish-American Studies, 1979). Contents: I. Notas biográficas. II. Obras inéditas. III. Obras publicadas. IV. Traducciones. V. Escritos y declaraciones. VI. Estudios críticos.

Pérez-Stansfield, pp. 342–43.

LOPEZ PACHECO, JESUS (1930–)

Kirschner, Teresa J. "Aproximación a una bibliografía de Jesús López Pacheco," *Revista Canadiense de Estudios Hispánicos*, 10 (1985), 141–49. Contents: I. Poesía (By year, 1953–1982). II. Teatro. III. Narrativa (By year, 1958–81). IV. Artículos (lista parcial, 1958–1985). V. Grabaciones. VI. Traducciones de Jesús López Pacheco. VII. Crítica sobre la poesía de López Pacheco. VIII. Crítica sobre la narrativa de López Pacheco. A. *Central eléctrica*. B. *La hoja de parra*. C. *Lucha por la respiración*. D. Varios.

LOPEZ-PICO, JOSE MARIA (1886–1959)

López-Picó, José María. *Antología de la obra poética de José María López-Picó*. Prólogo y selección: Felip Cid; Versión española: J. Pomar. Barcelona: Ediciones Poligrafa, S.A., 1969. 164p. A bibliography of his published works appears on pp. 159–60.

LOPEZ RUBIO, JOSE (1903–)

Holt, Marion Peter. *José López Rubio*. Boston: Twayne, 1980. 155p. "Selected Bibliography," 145–49. Annotated entries. Contents: I. Primary Sources. A. In English. B. In Spanish. C. Non Dramatic Works by López Rubio. II. Secondary Sources (criticism). A. In English. B. In Spanish. C. In French.

López Rubio, José. *Celos del aire*. Edición, introducción y notas de Marion P. Holt. Salamanca: Ediciones Almar, 1982. 125p. "Bibliografía," pp. 25–26. Contents: I. Las siguientes obras teatrales han sido publicadas en la *Colección Teatro* de Escelicer en Madrid. II. Las siguientes obras han sido publicadas en la antología anual editada por Federico Carlos Sáinz de Robles y publicada por Aguilar en Madrid. III. Las siguientes obras se incluyen en *Teatro selecto* de José López Rubio (Madrid: Escelicer, 1969). IV.

Obra teatral publicada en inglés. V. Otros libros. VI. Estudios (criticism).

LOPEZ SAINZ, CELIA (1927-)
Galerstein, pp. 182–83.

LUCAS, JOAQUIN BENITO DE (1934-)
CILH, pp. 247–48. Contents: I. Poesía. II. Ediciones.

LUIS, LEOPOLDO DE (1918-)
CILH, pp. 107–08. Contents: I. Poesía. II. Antologías. III. Libros de crítica. IV. Libros de su obra.
"Leopoldo de Luis," in Julia Elizabeth Cabey Riley's *Bibliografía de algunos poetas andaluces de posguerra* (Madrid: Universidad Complutense, Departamento de Bibliografía, 1984).

LLAMAZARES, JULIO (1955-)
CILH, p. 209.

MACHADO, ANTONIO (1875–1939). *See also* MACHADO, ANTONIO and MANUEL *below*.
Albornoz, Aurora. "Bibliografía de Antonio Machado," *La Torre*, Nos. 45/46 (enero/junio de 1965), 505–53. Contents: I. Ediciones. A. Obras en verso y prosa. B. Antologías. II. Obras sueltas. A. Poesía. B. Prosa. C. Teatro (con Manuel). D. Arreglos. III. Traducciones (by language). IV. Estudios (Biography and Criticism). V. Homenajes. VI. Poesías dedicadas.
Antonio Machado: Bibliograficesky ukazatel. Moskva: Kniga, 1979. 109p. Mainly titles published in the Soviet Union dealing with Machado and his works, including Russian translations.
Antonio Machado y Baeza a través de la crítica. Edición, introducción y bibliografía por Antonio Chicharro Chamorro. Baeza: Universidad de Verano de Baeza, 1983. 133p. (Aula Antonio Machado, 1). Pages 121–27 includes a bibliographic survey of titles that deal with Machado in Baeza. "Ediciones de la obra de Antonio Machado," pp. 131–33. Contents: I. Ediciones en vida del autor (By year, 1903–1938). II. Ediciones posteriores a 1939 (Selección; by year, 1940–1981). Books only.
Correa, v. 1, pp. 120–21, 516–23. Works by and about the author.
Guerrero Ruiz, Juan, and Casamayor, Enrique. "Bibliografía de Antonio Machado," *Cuadernos Hispanoamericanos*, Nos. 11/12 (septiembre/octubre de 1949), 703–20. Contents: I. Ediciones de

sus obras. A. Poesía. 1. España. 2. Hispanoamérica. 3. Extranjero. B. Prosa. 1. España. 2. Hispanoamérica. C. Teatro. 1. España. 2. Hispanoamérica. II. Obras de conjunto. A. España. B. Hispanoamérica. C. Extranjero. III. Estudios especiales. A. Biografía. B. Retratos poéticos. C. Poesía. D. Prosa. E. Teatro.

Laitenberger, Hugo. *Antonio Machado: Sein versuch einer selbstinterpretation in seinen apokryphen dichterphilosophen.* Wiesbaden: Franz Steiner Verlag GMBH, 1972. 332p. (Untersuchungen zur Sprach- und Literaturgeschichte der romanischen Völker, Band VI). Contents I. Benützte Ausgaben und Abkürzungen. A. Gedichte. B. Prosaschriften. C. Zeitschriften usw. II. Bibliographie zum Werk Machados. Abgrenzung des apokrypen Werks. III. Verzeichnis der benützten Literatur. A. Monographien (Continues Macrì's work). B. Zeitschriften.

Luis, Leopoldo de. *Antonio Machado: Ejemplo y lección.* Madrid: Fundación Banco Exterior, 1988. 243p. "Bibliografía," pp. 231–38.

Machado, Antonio. *Juan de Mairena.* Edición de Antonio Fernández Ferrer. Madrid: Cátedra, 1986. 2vs. (Letras Hispánicas, 240–41). "Bibliografía," v. 1, pp. 53–67. Contents; I. Ediciones principales de *Juan de Mairena* (1936–1985). II. Traducciones. III. Otras obras y ediciones de Antonio Machado (By year, 1903–1971). IV. Estudios sobre Antonio Machado.

______. *Obras: Poesía y prosa.* Edición reunida por Aurora de Albornoz y Guillermo de Torre. Ensayo preliminar por Guillermo de Torre. Buenos Aires: Editorial Losada, S.A., 1964. 1065p. "Bibliografía," pp. 991–1043. Contents: I. Bibliografía de Antonio Machado. A. Ediciones. 1. Obras en verso y prosa. 2. Antologías. B. Obras sueltas. 1. Poesía. 2. Prosa. C. Teatro. 1. Arreglos. D. Traducciones (by language). II. Estudios. III. Homenajes. IV. Poesías dedicadas.

______. *Poesía y prosa.* Edición crítica de Oreste Macrì con la colaboración de Gaetano Chiappini. Madrid: Espasa-Calpe, Fundación Antonio Machado, 1989. 4 vols. "Bibliografía," v. 1, pp. 247–422. Contents: All entries are chronologically arranged under the following headings (works by Machado): I. Fuentes bibliográficas. II. Obras. A. Poesías y prosas en volumenes. B. Poesías sueltas. C. Prosas sueltas. D. Teatro. E. Textos en antologías. F. Traducciones (By language). III. Biografía y crítica. A. Monografías. B. Escritos en colecciones críticas, historias, panoramas, misceláneas, etc. C. Escritos en periódicos, separatas, hojas volantes, etc. 1. Anónimos, colectivos e iniciales. 2. List a nominal. D. Homenajes y colectivos. E. Poesías dedicadas. F.

Sobre la I edición italiana de *Poesie* (1959); II edición; III edición. IV. Adiciones a la bibliografía.

______. *Poesie di Antonio Machado.* Studi introduttivi, testo criticamente riveduto, traduzione, note al testo, commento, bibliografia per Oreste Macrì. II. edizione completa. Milano: Lerici editori, 1961. 1389p. "Bibliografía," pp. 1241–1322. Over 800 items. Contents: I. Fonti bibliografiche. II. Poesie e prose in volume. III. Poesie sparse. IV. Prose sparse. V. Teatro. VI. Testi in antologie. VII. Traduzioni. 1. In italiano. 2. In francese. 3. In iglese. 4. In tedesco. 5. In russo. 6. In arabo. 7. In oco. 8. In romeno. VIII. Monografie. IX. Studi in raccolte, critiche, storie, panorami, etc. X. Studi in periodici. XI. Omaggi. XII. Poesie dedicate. XIII. Sulla i edizione di questo libro. XIV. Aggiunte.

______. *Poésies.* Traduites de l'espagnol par S. Léger et B. Sesé. Paris: Gallimard, 1973. 506p. "Bibliographie," pp. 493–98. The emphasis of the bibliography is on French critical studies and translated works in French.

______. *Soledades. Galerías. Otros poemas.* Edición de Geoffrey Ribbans. Madrid: Cátedra, 1983. 280p. (Letras Hispánicas, 180). "Bibliografía selecta," pp. 63–77. Contents: I. Ediciones de los poemas comprendidos en *Soledades; Galerías; Otros poemas.* II. Estudios generales sobre Antonio Machado y su ambiente. III. Estudios sobre *Soledades; Galerías; Otros poemas.* IV. Homenajes.

Macrì, Oreste. "Algunas adiciones y correcciones a mi edición de las poesías de Antonio Machado," *La Torre*, Nos. 45/46 (enero/junio de 1964), 409–24.

Sesé, Bernard. *Antonio Machado (1875–1939): El hombre, el poeta, el pensador.* Versión española de Soledad García Mouton. Madrid: Editorial Gredos, 1980. 2vs. (Biblioteca Románica Hispánica. II. Estudios y Ensayos, 299.) "Bibliografía," v. 2, pp. 907–29. Contents: I. Obras de Antonio Machado. A. Libros en verso y en prosa aparecidos en vida del autor (by year, 1903–1939). B. Antologías, ediciones diversas y ediciones críticas (by year, 1940–1975). C. Teatro. D. Traducciones al francés de obras de Antonio Machado (by year, 1924–1973). II. Estudios críticos. A. Biografías, estudios de conjunto, monografías. B. Ensayos y artículos. C. Números especiales de revistas o de periódicos, homenajes.

Sippy, Carol. "A Bibliographical Guide to Critical Works on Antonio Machado y Ruiz." Unpublished Ph.D. dissertation, The University of New Mexico, 1978. 481p. "The dissertation is a guide to Hispanic scholars in their study of the poetry, prose, and theater of Antonio Machado. The results of my research are divided into four parts: a chronological bibliography of all criticism, a prose survey of that bibliography, forty-one topical bibliographies, and a name index."

Valle, Rafael Heliodoro. *Antonio Machado (1875–1939). Vida y obra-bibliografía-antología-obra inédita.* New York: Hispanic Institute in the United States, 1951. 212p. "Bibliografía," pp. 91–109. Contents: I. Ediciones. A. Traducciones. B. Teatro (En colaboración con Manuel). C. Refundiciones y traducciones. II. Estudios. A. Sobre el teatro. III. Homenajes. IV. Poesías dedicadas.

MACHADO, ANTONIO and MANUEL. *See also* separate entries for each.

Carrión Gútiez, Manuel, ed. *Bibliografía machadiana: Bibliografía para un centenario.* Madrid: Biblioteca Nacional, 1976. 295p. (Panoramas bibliográficos de España, 2). Includes 4,649 entries. Contents: I. Manuel y Antonio Machado. A. Obras de Manuel y Antonio Machado. 1. Obras completas. 2. Antologías. 3. Teatro. 4. Artículos. B. Obras sobre Manuel y Antonio Machado. 1. Biografía. 2. Crítica. II. Manuel Machado Ruiz. A. Obras de Manuel Machado. 1. Poesía. 2. Prosa. 3. Teatro. B. Obras sobre Manuel Machado. 1. Bibliografía. 2. Biografía. 3. Crítica. 4. Homenajes. Poemas dedicados. III. Antonio Machado Ruiz. A. Obras de Antonio Machado. 1. Obras completas. 2. Obras selectas. Antologías. 3. Poesía. 4. Prosa. B. Obras sobre Antonio Machado. 1. Bibliografía. 2. Biografía. 2. Biografía y crítica. 3. Biografía general. 4. Biografía (estudios parciales). 5. Crítica. 6. Homenajes, coronas, poéticas, etc. 7. Conmemoraciones. 8. Poemas dedicados a Antonio Machado. 9. Algunas dedicatorias a Antonio Machado. IV. Apéndice. V. Indice alfabético (name index).

Guerra, Manuel H. *El teatro de Manuel y Antonio Machado.* Madrid: Editorial Mediterráneo, 1966. 208p. "Bibliografía," pp. 191–201. Contents: I. Obras dramáticas de Manuel y Antonio Machado. A. Dramas originales. B. Traducciones de Manuel y Antonio Machado y sus colaboraciones. C. Adaptaciones de Manuel y Antonio Machado y colaboradores. D. Crítica teatral y notas por Antonio y Manuel Machado. II. Estudios sobre el teatro de los Machado. III. Hechos concernientes al teatro de los Machado. A. Obras originales de Manuel y Antonio Machado. B. Traducciones y adaptaciones de Manuel y Antonio Machado y colaboradores.

MACHADO, MANUEL (1874–1947). *See also* MACHADO, ANTONIO and MANUEL *above.*

Brotherston, Gordon. *Manuel Machado: A Revaluation.* Cambridge: Cambridge University Press, 1968. 162p. "Bibliography," pp. 139–52. Contents: I. Works by Manuel Machado. A. The Poems. B. Prose Works. C. The Plays. D. Translations and Adaptations. II. Works on Manuel Machado.

Carballo Picazo, Alfredo. "Bibliografía de y sobre Manuel Machado," pp. 125–37, in Manuel Machado's *Alma; Apolo* (Madrid: Alcalá, 1967).

Cimon, Monique Anne-Marie. "La poesía de Manuel Machado." Unpublished Ph.D. dissertation, Florida State University, 1972. 213p. "Bibliografía," pp. 199–212. Contents: I. Textos de Manuel Machado. A. Verso. B. Prosa. C. Traducciones. D. Crítica. 1. Libros. 2. Artículos.

Correa, v. 1, pp. 104, 514–16. Works by and about the author.

Ferguson, Joe Irving. "Manuel Machado as a Critic of the Theater: A Study and Classified Bibliography. Unpublished Ph.D. dissertation, University of Tennessee, 1947. 499p. The study concludes with a bibliography which lists all of Machado's reviews and articles plus a more general bibliography.

Machado, Manuel. *Alma. Ars moriendi.* Edición de Pablo del Barco. Madrid: Ediciones Cátedra, 1988. 168p. "Bibliografía," pp. 73–80. Contents: I. Bibliografía de bibliografías. II. Ediciones de *Alma* y *Ars Moriendi.* A. *Alma.* B. *Ars moriendi.* C. Obras completas. D. Poemas sueltos publicados con anterioridad a la edición de *Alma* y *Ars moriendi.* III. Bibliografía crítica esencial. A. Libros. B. Artículos.

MADARIAGA, SALVADOR DE (1886–1978)

Madariaga, Salvador de. *El corazón de Piedra Verde.* Prologo de Luis Suñén. Madrid: Espasa Calpe, 1988. 2 vs. (Colección Austral, 55–56). "Bibliografía selecta," v. 1, pp. 35–37. Contents: I. Historia (By year, 1931–75). II. Política (By year, 1918–82). III. Ensayos de tema diverso (By year, 1921–79). IV. Novelas (By year, 1925–67). V. Teatro (By year, 1939–66). VI. Poesía (By year, 1922–76).

MAEZTU, RAMIRO DE (1875–1936)

"Artículos de Ramiro de Maeztu publicados en *ABC*," *ABC* (2 noviembre de 1952), 2 unnumbered pages.

Fox, E. Inman. "Una bibliografía anotada del periodismo de Ramiro de Maeztu y Whitney (1897–1904)," *Cuadernos Hispanoameri-*

canos, No. 291 (septiembre de 1974), 528–81. Includes 435 items arranged by year and date.

Gamallo Fierros, Dionisio. "Bibliografía acerca de la vida y de la obra literaria y política de Ramiro de Maeztu," *Cuadernos Hispanoamericanos*, Nos. 33/34 (septiembre/octubre de 1952), 239–75. I. Bibliografía (by year, 1898–1936). II. Bibliografía de la fama póstuma de Ramiro de Maeztu (by year, 1937–52).

Landeira, Ricardo. *Ramiro de Maeztu*. Boston: Twayne, 1978. 155p. "Selected Bibliography," pp. 147–51. Contents: I. Primary Sources (Books only; arranged by year, 1911–1975). II. Secondary Sources (criticism; annotated). III. Special Numbers of Journals Devoted to Ramiro de Maeztu.

MALDONADO DE GUEVARA, FRANCISCO (1891–)

"Estudio bio-bibliográfico y crítico de D. Francisco Maldonado de Guevara." Memoria de Licenciatura, Departamento de Bibliografía, Universidad Complutense de Madrid, 1974.

CILH, pp. 131–33. Contents: I. Poesía. II. Novela. III. Monografías. IV. Biografía. V. Ensayo. VI. Teatro. VII. Antologías. VIII. Estudios y preparación de ediciones.

MANRIQUE DE LARA, JOSE GERARDO (n.d.)

Manrique de Lara, José Gerardo. *El crimen fue en Granada (llanto por Federico García Lorca: Tragedia española en dos actos)*. Madrid: Asociación de Escritores y Artistas Españoles, 1985. 85p. "Bibliografía," unpaged. Contents: I. Poesía. II. Novela. III. Monografías. IV. Biografía. V. Ensayo. VI. Antologías. VII. Estudios y preparación de ediciones.

MANTERO, MANUEL (1930–)

"Manuel Mantero," in Julia Elizabeth Cabey Riley's *Bibliografía de algunos poetas andaluces de posguerra* (Madrid: Universidad Complutense, Departamento de Bibliografía, 1984).

Mantero, Manuel. *New Songs for the Ruins of Spain*. Translated by Betty Jean Craige. Lewisburg: Bucknell University Press, 1986. 113p. "Books by Manuel Mantero," pp. 104–05. Contents: I. Poetry. II. Novel. III. Critical Works. IV. Essays, Anthologies. V. Editions. VI. Miscellaneous.

MARANON, GREGORIO (1887–1960)

Almodóvar, Francisco Javier, and Warleta, Enrique. *Marañón o una vida fecunda*. Madrid: Espasa-Calpe, 1952. 468p. "Bibliografía," pp. 393–463. Includes 1287 titles, but excludes newspaper articles.

Gómez-Santos, Marino. *Vida de Gregorio Marañón*. Madrid: Taurus Ediciones, S.A., 1971. 550p. "Bibliografía de Marañón," pp. 417–96. Arranged by year, 1909–70. "Bibliografía sobre Marañón," pp. 496–525.

Keller, Gary D. *The Significance and Impact of Gregorio Marañón: Literary Criticism, Biographies, and Historiography*. Jamaica, New York: Bilingual Press/Editorial Bilingüe, 1977. 310p. "Bibliography," pp. 277–301. A selected bibliography which only includes titles in the areas of literary criticism, biography, and history. Contents: I. Works by Marañón. II. Translations of Marañón's Works into Other Languages. III. Books, Articles, and Pamphlets about Marañón. IV. Book Reviews (About Marañón's Work or About Him). V. Homenajes and Necrologies. VI. General Bibliography.

MARCAL I SERRA, MARIA MERCE (1952–)

Galerstein, pp. 191–92.

MARCH, SUSANA (1918–)

Alarcón, p. 36.

Galerstein, pp. 193–94.

MARCO, CONCHA DE (1916–)

Galerstein, pp. 192–93.

MARIN GUTIERREZ, JOSE. *See* SIJE, RAMON.

MARQUINA, EDUARDO (1879–1946)

Nuez, Manuel de la. *Eduardo Marquina*. Boston: Twayne Publishers, Inc., 1976. 162p. "Selected Bibliography," pp. 153–57. Contents: I. Plays (by year, 1902–1946). II. Plays Not Performed. III. Unpublished Plays Attributed to Marquina. IV. Complete Works. V. Special Editions of Marquina's Plays. VI. Secondary Sources (criticism).

MARSE, JUAN (1933–)

Amell, Samuel. *La narrativa de Juan Marsé, Contador de Aventis*. Madrid: Editorial Playor, 1984. 171p. "Bibliografía," pp. 167–70. Contents: I. Obras de Juan Marsé (1957–1984). II. Obras sobre Juan Marsé.

Marsé, Juan. *Si te dicen que caí*. Madrid: Cátedra, 1982. 368p. (Letras Hispánicas, 167). "Bibliografía," pp. 47–49. Contents: I. Obras de Juan Marsé. A. Novelas (By year, 1961–1982). B.

Cuentos (By year, 1957–1977). C. Miscelánea (By year, 1975–1977). II. Estudios críticos.

MARTEL, CARMEN (1915–)
Galerstein, pp. 194–95.

MARTIN GAITE, CARMEN (1925–)
Alarcón, pp. 36–37.
Brown, Jan Lipman. *Secrets from the Back Room: The Fiction of Carmen Martín Gaite*. University, Miss.: Romance Monographs, Inc., 1987. 296p. (Romance Monographs, 46). "Bibliography," pp. 181–92. Contents: I. Primary Bibliography (In order of publication). A. Novels. B. Novelas and Short Stories. C. Poetry. D. Children's Literature. E. Nonfiction Books. II. Selected Secondary Bibliography. A. Literary Histories and Other Comprehensive Sources. B. Scholarly Articles and Book Reviews. 1. By Work. 2. Thematic and Comparative Studies of Several Works. C. Interviews (In chronological order).
Galerstein, pp. 196–98.
Roger, Isabel M. "Perspectivas críticas; horizontes infinitos: Carmen Martín Gaite; una trayectoria novelística y su bibliografía," *Anales de la Literatura Española Contempóranea*, 13 (1988), 293–317. The first part of the article is a bibliographic essay of major critical studies on Martín Gaite. Contents: I. Bibliografía de Carmen Martín Gaite. A. Ediciones de su obra (by year, 1954–1987). B. Obras prologadas por Carmen Martín Gaite (by year, 1970–1977). C. Obras traducidas por Carmen Martín Gaite (by year, 1968–1984). II. Bibliografía crítica sobre Carmen Martín Gaite. A. Reseñas de sus obras. B. Entrevistas a Carmen Martín Gaite. C. Trabajos críticos sobre Carmen Martín Gaite.

MARTIN RECUERDA, JOSE (1925–)
Martín Recuerda, José. *El engaño. Caballos desbocados*. Edición de Martha T. Halsey y Angel Cobo. Madrid: Cátedra, 1981. 293p. (Letras Hispánicas, 143). "Bibliografía escogida," pp. 65–73. Contents: I. Estrenos de José Martín Recuerda (juntos con datos bibliográficos, 1954–1981). II. Estudios sobre su obra.
______. *La llanura del Cristo*. Estudios preliminares de Antonio Morales. Granada: Los Libros de Maese Pedro; Editorial Don Quijote, 1982. 210p. "Bibliografía," pp. 39–49. Contents: I. La obra dramática de José Martín Recuerda (includes play openings and published versions). II. Artículos y ensayos sobre la obra de Martín Recuerda.
Pérez-Stansfield, p. 343.

Torres, Sixto E. "Social Protest Elements in the Theater of José Martín Recuerda." Unpublished Ph.D. dissertation, Florida State University, 1980. 167p. The appendix offers a chronological listing of the plays by Martín Recuerda through 1977.

MARTIN-SANTOS, LUIS (1924–1964)

Compitello, Malcolm A. "Luis Martín-Santos: A Bibliography," *Letras Peninsulares*, 2 (Fall 1989), 247–69.

Saludes, Esperanza G. *Narrativa de Luis Martin-Santos a la luz de la psicología.* Miami, FL: Universal, 1981. 197p. "Bibliografía," pp. 181–97. Contents: I. Obras de Luis Martín-Santos. A. Literarias. B. Científicas. II. Bibliografía referente a Martín-Santos.

MARTIN VIVALDE, ELENA (1907–)

Alarcón, p. 37.

Galerstein, pp. 198–99.

MARTINEZ BALLESTEROS, ANTONIO (1929–)

"Antonio Martínez Ballesteros," pp. 34–42 in L. Teresa Valdivieso's *España: Bibliografía de un teatro "silenciado"* (Lincoln, Neb.: Society of Spanish and Spanish-American Studies, 1979). Contents: I. Notas biográficas. II. Obras inéditas. III. Obras publicadas. IV. Traducciones. V. Escritos y declaraciones. VI. Estudios críticos.

Pérez-Stansfield, pp. 343–44.

MARTINEZ CIVERA, BEATRIU (1914–)

Galerstein, p. 199.

MARTINEZ MEDIERO, MANUEL (1939–)

"Manuel Martínez Mediero," pp. 43–48 in L. Teresa Valdivieso's *España: Bibliografía de un teatro "silenciado"* (Lincoln, Neb.: Society of Spanish and Spanish-American Studies, 1979). Contents: I. Notas biográficas. II. Obras inéditas. III. Obras publicadas. IV. Escritos y declaraciones. V. Estudios críticos.

Pérez-Stansfield, p. 344.

MARTINEZ RUIZ, JOSE. *See* AZORIN.

MARTINEZ SIERRA, GREGORIO (1881–1947) and MARIA (1880–1974)

O'Connor, Patricia W. *Gregorio and María.* Boston: Twayne Publishers, Inc., 1977. 155p. "Selected Bibiography," pp. 147–52. Contents: I. Primary Sources (Signed by Gregorio Martínez Sierra; by year 1898–1941; signed by María Martínez Sierra, 1899–1960). II. Secondary Sources (annotated). A. Books. B. Articles.

MARTINEZ VALDERRAMA, MARIA LUZ (1918–)
Galerstein, p. 199.

MARURI, JULIO (1928–)
Fernández, Lidio Jesús. "Poemas inéditos de Julio Maruri: Nota bibliográfica y noticias biográficas," *Iris* (Paris), No. 3 (1982), 3–12.

MASIP, PAULINO (1899–1963)
Caballé, Anna. *Sobre la vida y obra de Paulino Masip*. Barcelona: Edicions del Mall, 1987. (Mall Ensayo, Serie Ibérica, 41). "Las publicaciones de Paulino Masip," pp. 50–54. Contents: I. Poesía. II. Prosa (By year, 1924–1954). III. Teatro (By year, 1932–1955). IV. Periodismo (en el exilio). V. Guiones. "Bibliografía," pp. 92–95. Contents: I. Referencias a la obra de Masip (Indice bibliográfico). II. Obras colectivas.

MASOLIVER, LIBERATA (1911–)
Galerstein, pp. 199–203.

MATILLA, LUIS (1939–)
"Luis Matilla," pp. 49–55 in L. Teresa Valdivieso's *España: Bibliografía de un teatro "silenciado"* (Lincoln, Neb.: Society of Spanish and Spanish-American Studies, 1979).
Pérez-Stansfield, p. 345.

MATUTE, ANA MARIA (1926–)
Alarcón, pp. 37–39.
Diaz, Janet W. *Ana María Matute*. New York: Twayne Publishers, Inc., 1971. 165p. "Selected Bibliography," pp. 157–60. Contents: I. Primary Sources (Matute's writings arranged in chronological order). II. Secondary Sources.
Galerstein, pp. 207–11.
Resnick, pp. 219–20.
Roma, Rosa. *Ana María Matute*. Madrid: EPESA, 1971, 206p. "Obras de Ana María Matute," pp. 183–84. Contents: I. Novelas. II. Narraciones. III. Cuentos infantiles. "Esayos críticos y estudios monográficos," pp. 185–88. "Críticas y comentarios (selección)," pp. 191–202.

MAURA, JULIA (1910–1970)
Galerstein, p. 211.
"Julia Maura," *O'Connor*, pp. 161–62.

MAYORAL DIAZ, MARINA (1942–)
Galerstein, p. 212.

MEDINA, VICENTE (1866–1937)
Díez de Revenga Torres, María Josefa. *La poesía popular murciana en Vicente Medina*. Murcia: Universidad de Murcia, Academia "Alfonso X el Sabio," 1983. 286p. "Bibliografía," pp. 281–85. Contents: I. Obras de Vicente Medina (by year, 1895–1981). II. Obras de otros autores (criticism).
Estudios sobre Vicente Medina. Edición de Francisco J. Diéz de Revenga y de Mariano de Paco. Murcia: Academia Alfonso X el Sabio, 1987. 318p. (Biblioteca Murciana de Bolsilo, 92). "Obras editadas por Vicente Medina," pp. 225–26. Works are listed by year, 1895–1932. "Colección de las obras completas," pp. 227–28. The edition published in Rosario de Santa Fe, Argentina.

MEDIO, DOLORES (1914–)
Alarcón, pp. 39–40.
Galerstein, pp. 213–15.
Jones, Margaret E. W. *Dolores Medio*. New York: Twayne Publishers, Inc., 1974. 166p. "Selected Bibliography," pp. 157–61. Contents: I. Primary Sources. A. The Works of Dolores Medio. B. Novelettes and Short Stories. C. Nonfictional Writings. D. Poetry. II. Secondary Sources.

MENENDEZ PIDAL, RAMON (1869–1968)
Arteta y Errasti, Germán. "Bibliografía de don Ramón Menéndez Pidal," in *Homenaje a Menéndez Pidal* (Madrid: Librería y Casa Editorial Hernando, S.A., 1925), III, pp. 655–74. Entries are arranged by year, 1895–1925.
"Bibliografía de d. Ramón Menéndez Pidal," *Ibérida* (Rio de Janeiro), No. 1 (avril de 1959), 164–212. Partially annotated entries arranged by year, 1895–1958.
Serís, Homero. "Apuntes para la bibliografía de Ramón Menéndez Pidal (1932–1968)," *Hispanic Review*, 38, No. 5 (November 1970), 40–46. Arranged by year, 1932–70. Continues his *Supplemento a la bibliografía de don Ramón Menéndez Pidal*. Madrid: Librería y Casa Editorial Hernando, S.A., 1931, 64p., which supplemented Arteta y Errasti's bibliography.

_____, and Arteta y Errasti, Germán. "Ramón Menéndez Pidal: Bibliografía," *Revista Hispánica Moderna*, 4, No. 4 (julio de 1938), 302–30. Contents: I. Bibliografía (by year, 1895–1937). II. Estudios generales sobre Menéndez Pidal.

Vázquez de Parga, María Luisa. "Bibliografía de don Ramón Menéndez Pidal," *Revista de Filología Española*, 47 (1964), 7–127. Contents: I. Bibliografía de Menéndez Pidal (by year, 1891–1964). II. Aportaciones biográficas. III. Estudios generales sobre Menéndez Pidal. IV. Repertorios bibliográficos.

MERCEDER, TRINA (1919–)

Alarcón, p. 40.

Galerstein, p. 216.

MERINO, JOSE MARIA (1941–)

"José María Merino: Bibliografía," *Alonso*, p. 221. Contents: I. Poesía (By year, 1972–1984). II. Narrativa (By year, 1976–1985). Books only.

MIEZA, CARMEN FARRES DE (1931–1976)

Galerstein, pp. 216–17.

MIHURA, MIGUEL (1905–1977)

McKay, Douglas R. *Miguel Mihura*. Boston: Twayne Publishers, Inc., 1977. 154p. "Selected Bibliography," pp. 145–49. Contents: I. Primary Sources. II. Plays and Dates of Their Premières. III. Other Primary Writings. IV. Secondary Sources (criticism). A. In English. B. In Spanish. C. In Norwegian.

Miguel Martínez, Emilio de. *El teatro de Miguel Mihura*. Salamanca: Ediciones Universidad de Salamanca, 1979. 251p. (Acta Salmanticensia; Filosofía y Letras, 112). Contents: I. "Cronología del teatro de Mihura," pp. 13–17. 1932–1968. II. "Bibliografía," pp. 247–48. A. Libros o artículos dedicados a Miguel Mihura. B. Libros y artículos sobre el teatro español contemporáneo, en la mayoría de los cuales puede encontrarse informacíon interesante sobre la obra dramática de Miguel Mihura.

Mihura, Miguel. *The Independent Art: Two Plays by Miguel Mihura: Sublime Decision! The Enchanting Dorotea*. Translated by John H. Koppenhaver and Susan Nelson. San Antonio, Texas: Trinity University Press, 1987. 118p. "Select Bibliography," pp. xxi-xxii. Contents: I. In English. II. In Spanish. III. Mihura's Published Plays (1932–1968).

_____. *Tres sombreros de copa*. Edición de Jorge Rodríguez Padrón. 7.ed. Madrid: Cátedra, 1983. 152p. (Letras Hispánicas, 97).

"Bibliografía," pp. 69–73. Contents: I. Ediciones anteriores. II. Traducciones. III. En televisión. IV. Sobre Mihura.

Ward, Marilyn Italiano. "Themes of Submission, Dominance, Independence and Romantic Love: The Female Figure in the Post-Avant-Garde Plays of Miguel Mihura." Unpublished Ph.D. dissertation, University of Colorado, 1974. 268p. Contains an excellent and detailed bibliography.

MILLAN ASTRAY, PILAR (1892–1949)

Galerstein, pp. 217–19.

"Pilar Millán Astray," *O'Connor*, pp. 163–64.

MIRALES, ALBERTO (1940–)

"Alberto Mirales," pp. 56–59 in L. Teresa Valdivieso's *España: Bibliografía de un teatro "silenciado"* (Lincoln, Neb.: Society of Spanish and Spanish-American Studies, 1979). Contents: I. Notas biográficas. II. Obras inéditas. III. Obras publicadas. IV. Escritos y declaraciones. V. Estudios críticos.

MIRAS, DOMINGO (1934–)

Pérez-Stansfield, p. 345.

MIRO, GABRIEL (1879–1930)

Altisent, Marta. *La narrativa breve de Gabriel Miró y antología de cuentos*. Barcelona: Anthropos, 1988. 319p. "Bibliografía," pp. 299–308. Contents: I. Estudios sobre Gabriel Miró. II. Estudios generales. Apéndice I: Relación de las primeras narraciones de Gabriel Miró (artículos y cuentos; by year, 1899–1911), pp. 311–13. Apéndice II. Relación de cuentos de Miró por orden de publicación (By year, 1908–1920), pp. 315–16.

Coope, Marian G. R. *Reality and Time in the Oleza Novels of Gabriel Miró*. London: Támesis Books, Ltd., 1984. 235p. (Colección Támesis; Serie A-Monografías, 102). "List of Works Cited," pp. 217–22. Contents: I. Works by Gabriel Miró. A. Books. B. Other Writings. C. Letters. D. Interview. II. Works on Miró.

Landeira, Ricardo. *An Annotated Bibliography of Gabriel Miró (1900–1978)*. Lincoln, Neb.: Society of Spanish and Spanish-American Studies, 1978. 200p. Contents: I. The Works by Gabriel Miró. A. Short Pieces and Fragments in Periodicals. B. Full Length Works (by work). C. Novelettes (by work). D. Short Narratives (by work). E. Anthologized Works (by works). F. Collected Works. G. Complete Works. H. Prologues by Miró. I. Translations by Miró. J. Lectures by Miró. K. Interviews. L. Letters. M. Translations of Miró's Work (by work). II. Studies about Gabriel Miró and His Works. A. Biography. B. Death of Miró. C. Miró and the Real Academia Española. D. Miró, Other Writers and Artists. E. General Literary Topics. F. Full Length Works (by work). G. Novelettes (by work). H. Short Narratives (by work). I. Special Literary Topics. 1. Sigüenza varia. 2. Landscape. 3. Prose and Style. J. Homages and Elegies. K. Dissertations. L. Bibliographies. III. Author Index. 2,373 entries. The bibliography also includes a brief biographical section and a chronology of the life of Miró.

______. "Tres cuartos de siglo de crítica mironiana," pp. 265–81 in *Homenaje a Gabriel Miró: Estudios de crítica literaria en el centenario de su nacimiento, 1879–1979.* (Alicante: Publicaciones de la Caja de Ahorros Provincial, 1979). Bibliographic essay arranged by decade, 1900–1979.

MacDonald, Ian R. *Gabriel Miró: His Private Library and His Literary Background.* London: Támesis Books Limited, 1975. 255p. (Coleccion Támesis. Serie A, Monografías, XLI). "Bibliography," pp. 229–36. Contents: I. Books by Gabriel Miró. II. Articles by Gabriel Miró. III. Books and Articles by Others. (Includes unsigned newspaper articles.)

Miró, Clemencia, and Juan Guerrero Ruiz. "Gabriel Miró: Bibliografía," *Cuadernos de Literatura Contemporánea,* Nos. 5/6 (1942), 245–82. Contents: I. Obras de Gabriel Miró (Includes translations). II. Estudios. III. Antologías, enciclopedias, notas y prensa española y extranjera. IV. Iconografía.

Miró, Gabriel. *Años y leguas.* Ed. facsímil. València: Conselleria de Cultura, Educació i Ciència de la Generalitat Valenciana, Diputacions d' Alacant, Castelló i València, 1987. 341p. (Clàssics Valencians, 6). "Bibliografia," pp. 264–68.

______. *Niño y grande.* Edición de Carlos Ruiz Silva. Madrid: Castalia, 1988. 199p. (Clásicos Castalia, 166). "Noticia bibliográfica," pp. 51–62. Contents: I. Obras de Gabriel Miró recogidas en volumen y por orden cronológico (1901–1983). II. Textos de Miró publicados en diarios y revistas y no recogidos en volumen (1901–1954). III. Estudios sobre Gabriel Miró y su obra en general. IV. Homenajes y estudios colectivos dedicados a Gabriel Miró. V. Sobre *Niño y grande.*

______. *Novelas cortas: Nómada, La Palma rota, El hijo santo, Los pies y los zapatos de Enriqueta.* Edición, introducción y notas de Miguel Angel Lozano Marco. Alicante: Excma. Diputación Provincial de Alicante, Instituto de Estudios Juan Gil-Albert, 1986. 382p. "Bibliografía," pp. 83–89. Contents: I. Ediciones (By year). A *Nómada.* B. *La palma rota.* C. *El hijo santo.* D. *Los pies y los zapatos de Enriqueta.* II. Bibliografía selecta (criticism).

_____. *Nuestro Padre San Daniel.* Edición de Manuel Ruiz-Funes. Madrid: Ediciones Cátedra, 1988. 379p. "Bibliografía," pp. 81–88. Contents: I. Sobre la vida y aspectos biográficos. II. Estudios. III. Ensayos. Artículos (no page nos.). IV. Revistas: Números de homenaje a Gabriel Miró.

Ramos, Vicente. *El mundo de Gabriel Miró.* Segunda edición, corregida y aumentada. Madrid: Editorial Gredos, S.A, 1970. 526p. (Biblioteca Románica Hispánica. II. Estudios y Ensayos). "Bibliografía," pp. 459–509. Up-dates the Clemencia Miró bibliography. Contents: I. Ediciones de las obras de Gabriel Miró. II. Traducciones por Gabriel Miró. III. Textos mironianos en antologías. IV. Traducciones de textos de Gabriel Miró. V. Epistolario. VI. Textos de Gabriel Miró no recogidos en volumen. VII. Libros y folletos sobre Gabriel Miró. VIII. Artículos sobre Gabriel Miró.

Rosenbaum, Sidonia C., and Juan Guerrero Ruiz. "Gabriel Miró: Bibliografía," *Revista Hispánica Moderna*, 2, No. 3 (abril de 1936), 207–15. Contents: I. Ediciones. II. Traducciones (by work). III. Estudios.

MOIX, ANA MARIA (1947–)

Alarcón, p. 49.

Galerstein, pp. 219–20.

MOLINA, RICARDO (1917–1968)

Clementson, Carlos. *Ricardo Molina: Perfil de un poeta.* Córdoba: Publicaciones del Monte de Piedad y Caja de Ahorros de Córdoba, 1986. 181p. "Perfil biobibliográfico y humano de Ricardo Molina," pp. 11–29.

Correa, v. 2, pp. 237, 615. Contents: I. Libros. II. Artículos y estudios (criticism).

Mantero, pp. 555–56. Contents: I. Libros de poesía. II. Otras publicaciones. III. Sobre Ricardo Molina.

"Ricardo Molina," in Julia Elizabeth Cabey Riley's *Bibliografía de algunos poetas andaluces de posguerra* (Madrid: Universidad Complutense, Departamento de Bibliografía, 1984).

MOLINA, RODRIGO A. (n.d.)

"Publicaciones de Rodrigo A. Molina," pp. 9–10 in *Estudios de historia*, literatura y arte hispánicos ofrecidos a Rodrigo A. Molina (Madrid: Insula, 1977). Contents: I. Libros (By year, 1961–1973). II. Artículos y reseñas principales (By year, 1943–1975). III. Artículos periodísticos (By year, 1970–1971).

MONTERO, ROSA (1951–)
Galerstein, pp. 223–24.

MONTESINOS, RAFAEL (1920–)
Agulló y Cobo, Mercedes. "Escritores contemporáneos: Rafael Montesinos," *El Libro Español*, No. 14 (febrero de 1959), 71–73. "Bibliografía," p. 73.
Mantero, pp. 556–57. Contents: I. Libros de poesía. II. Otras publicaciones. III. Sobre Rafael Montesinos.
"Rafael Montesinos," in Julia Elizabeth Cabey Riley's *Bibliografía de algunos poetas andaluces de posguerra* (Madrid: Universidad Complutense, Departamento de Bibliografía, 1984).

MONTORIOL I PUIG, CARME (1893–1966)
Galerstein, pp. 224–25.

MORALES, RAFAEL (1919–)
Correa, v. 2, pp. 185, 613. Contents: I. Libros. II. Artículos y estudios (criticism).
Fernández Valladares, Mercedes. *Bibliografía de Rafael Morales*. Madrid: Editorial de la Universidad Complutense, 1981. 24p. (Trabajos del Departamento de Bibliografía; Serie A: Escritores Contemporáneos, 1). Includes 214 entries. Contents: I. Bibliografías. II. Obra completa. III. Ediciones, poemas sueltos, obra crítica (por orden cronológico, 1936–1980). IV. Traducciones (por orden cronológico, 1952–1980). V. Entrevistas (por orden cronológico, 1967–1977). VI. Estudios sobre la obra de Rafael Morales (por orden cronológico, 1943–1979).
López, Julio. *Poesía y realidad en Rafael Morales*. Barcelona: Víctor Pozanco, 1979. 248p. "Bibliografía," pp. 243–47. Contents: I. Bibliografía de Rafael Morales. A. Poesía (1943–1971). B. Narración. C. Ensayo. D. Opiniones de Rafael Morales sobre su poesía. II. Algunas obras sobre Rafael Morales. III. Algunas antologías útiles.
Mantero, pp. 557–59. Contents: I. Libros de Poesía. II. Otras publicaciones. III. Sobre Rafael Morales.

MORENO VILLA, JOSE (1887–1955)
Correa, v. 1, pp. 169–70, 526–27. Works by and about the author.
Moreno Villa, José. *Antología*. Barcelona: Plaza y Janés Editores, 1982. 310p. "Obras de José Moreno Villa," pp. 65–67. Contents: I. Poesía (By year, 1913–1961). II. Prosa (1921–1977). III. Estudios de historia del arte (1920–1948). IV. Ediciones de clásicos con prólogo (1919–1924). V. Traducciones (1919–1945).

_____. *La ola gratinada*. Introducción de Alfonso Canales. Selección y apéndice bio-bibliográfico de Enrique Baena. Málaga: Centro Cultural de la Generación del 27, 1987. 27p.

Pariente, pp. 100–101. Contents: I. Libros de poesía (By year, 1913–61). II. Estudios sobre su poesía (By year, 1925–63). III. Procedencia de los textos.

MORO, EDUARDA (n.d.)

Galerstein, p. 226.

MUGICA CELAYA, RAFAEL. *See* Celaya, Gabriel.

MULDER DE DAUMER, ELISABETH (1904–)

Galerstein, pp. 226–28.

MUNIZ, CARLOS (1927–)

"Carlos Muñiz," pp. 189–90 in Hilde F. Cramsie's *Teatro y censura en la España franquista: Sastre, Muñiz y Ruibal* (New York: Peter Lang, 1985). Contents: I. Obras dramáticas (By year, 1954–1974). II. Ensayos y declaraciones teóricas (By year, 1960–1965).

Muñiz, Carlos. *El tintero. Miserera para medio fraile*. Edición de Loren L. Zeller. Salamanca: Almar, 1980. 142p. "Bibliografía," pp. 29–31. Contents: I. Obras teatrales. II. Crítica.

Pérez-Stansfield, pp. 345–46.

MUNOZ SECA, PEDRO (1881–1936)

Muñoz Seca, Pedro. *La venganza de Don Mendo*. Edición de Salvador García Castañeda. Madrid: Cátedra, 1984. 233p. (Letras Hispánicas, 210). "Noticia bibliográfica," pp. 49–54. Contents: I. El manuscrito. II. Ediciones (By year, 1919–78).

MURCIANO, ANTONIO (1929–)

García Tejera, María del Carmen. *Poesía flamenca (Análisis de los rasgos populares y flamencos en la obra poética de Antonio Murciano.)* Cádiz: Universidad de Cádiz. Servicio de Publicaciones, 1986. 380p. "Bibliografía de Antonio Murciano," pp. 372–80. Contents: I. Obra poética (By year, 1952–85). II. En coloboración con su hermano Carlos (By year, 1954–84). III. Artículos y conferencias sobre flamenco (By year, 1954–85). IV. Bibliografía sobre Antonio Murciano (By year, 1965–83)

MURCIANO, CARLOS (1931–)

CILH, pp. 120–21. Contents: I. Poesía. II. Ensayo. III. Prosa.

MURIA I ROMANI, ANNA (1904–)
Galerstein, pp. 229–30.

NAVALES, ANA MARIA (1939–)
CILH, p. 218.

NAVARRO TOMAS, TOMAS (1884–1979)
Arrigoitia, Luis de. "Bibliografía de don Tomás Navarro Tomás," *Revista de Estudios Hispánicos* (Río Piedras, P.R.), Año 1, No. 1/2 (enero/junio de 1971), 141–50. Contents: I. Ediciones. II. Traducciones. III. Artículos sueltos. IV. Prólogos y ediciones críticas. V. Reseñas. VI. Estudios críticos sobre Navarro Tomás. VII. Noticias.
Beardsley, Theodore S. *Tomás Navarro Tomás: A Tentative Bibliography, 1908–1970*. Syracuse, N.Y.: Centro de Estudios Hispánicos, 1971. 12p. "The following attempt to record all the publications of Don Tomás is arranged chronologically in three major groups: Books, pamphlets, and recordings; articles and notes; reviews." Bibliography also includes work in press, works in preparation, biographical sketches, press notices, and reviews of his work.

NAVAS, JUAN GUALBERTO LOPEZ-VALDEMORO Y DE QUESADA, CONDE DE (1855–1935)
Demidowicz, John P. *El Conde de las Navas, un polígrafo español*. Madrid: Murillo, 1957. 240p. "Obras del Conde de las Navas," pp. 177–89. Contents: I. Bibliografía (listed by year, 1893–1931). II. Cuentos (listed by year 1886–1928). III. Novelas (listed by year 1887–1904). IV. Teatro (listed by year, 1897–1932). V. Casa Real y nobelza española.

NEIRA VILAS, XOSE (1928–)
Lucas, María. *La visión de Galicia en Xosé Neira Vilas*. La Coruña: Ediciones del Castro, 1977. 128p. "Bibliografía de Neira Vilas," pp. 121–22. Contents: I. Narrativa. II. Narrativa para niños. III. Poesía. IV. Poemas en revistas, antologías, etc. V. Traducciones al gallego. VI. Traducciones del gallego al castellano. "Algunos trabajos sobre Neira Vilas," pp. 123–25.

NELKEN Y MAUSBERGER, MARGARITA (1896–1968)
Galerstein, pp. 233–34.

NIEVA, FRANCISCO (1929–)

"Francisco Nieva," pp. 60–66 in L. Teresa Valdivieso's *España: Bibliografía de un teatro "silenciado"* (Lincoln, Neb.: Society of Spanish and Spanish-American Studies, 1979). Contents: I. Notas biográficas. II. Obras inéditas. III. Obras publicadas. IV. Escritos y declaraciones. V. Escritos críticos.

Nieva, Francisco. *La carroza de plomo candente. Coronada y el toro*. Edición, prólogo y notas de Andrés Amorós. Madrid: Espasa-Calpe, 1986. 167p. (Selecciones Austral, 146). "Bibliografía básica," pp. 46–48. Contents: I. Obras dramáticas de Francisco Nieva (By year, 1971–1983). II. Sobre el teatro de Francisco Nieva.

______. *Malditas sean Coronada y su hija. Delirio del amor hostil.* Edición de Antonio González. Madrid: Cátedra, 1980. 274p. (Letras Hispánicas, 119). "Bibliografía," pp. 83–91. Contents: I. Obra publicada de Francisco Nieva (por orden cronológico). A. Teatro. B. Teatro furioso. C. Narrativa. D. Obra inédita. II. Selección de artículos de Francisco Nieva. A. Escritos en francés para las publicaciones del C.N.R.S., París. B. Otros artículos en francés. C. Selección de artículos y notas publicados en revistas especializadas de teatro. 1. *Yorick* (Barcelona). 2. *Primer Acto* (Madrid). 3. *Pipirijaina*. D. Selección de artículos en *Suplemento de Artes y Letras* del diario *Informaciones de Madrid*. E. Selección de artículos publicados en el diario *El País*, de Madrid. F. Publicaciones en otras revistas. G. En otras publicaciones. III. Bibliografía sobre Francisco Nieva. A. Libros. B. Revistas.

______. *Trilogía italiana: teatro de farsa y calamidad*. Edición de Jesús María Barajón. Madrid: Cátedra, 1988. 321p. (Letras Hispánicas, 286). "Bibliografía," pp. 105–09. Contents: I. Obra dramática original (By year, 1971–1988). II. Adaptaciones. III. Artículos de Francisco Nieva sobre su teatro (By year, 1971–1987). IV. Estudios sobre Francisco Nieva (By year, 1971–1987). 54 entries.

Pérez-Stansfield, p. 346.

Signes, Emil George. "The Theatre of Francisco Nieva: A Summary, Analysis, and Bibliography, Together with an Edition and Translation of *La carroza de plomo candente*." Unpublished Ph.D. dissertation, Rutgers University, 1982. 384p. The bibliography section of the dissertation contains "an extensive bibliography, which includes a complete listing not only of Nieva's theatrical work, but also of his essays and other subjects, as well as critical articles about Nieva's work and review of all his staged plays . . . "

NORA, EUGENIO DE (1923–)

Entre la cruz y la espada: en torno a la España de Posguerra; homenaje a Eugenio G. de Nora. Madrid: Editorial Gredos, 1984. 362p. "Bibliografía de Eugenio G. de Nora," pp. 17–18. Entries are arranged by year, 1943–1978. Selective bibliography.

"Eugenio de Nora: Bibliografía," *Alonso*, p. 131. Contents: I. Poesía (By year, 1945–1975). II. Ensayo.

OJEDA, PINO (1916–)

Galerstein, p. 235.

OLIVER, MARIA-ANTONIA (1946–)

Galerstein, pp. 235–37.

OLIVER BELMAS, ANTONIO (1903–1968)

Oliver Belmás, Antonio. *Obras completas* (1923–1965). Madrid: Biblioteca Nueva. 1971. 916p. "Bibliografía," pp. 907–16. Contents: I. Obras (1925–65). II. Otras obras sin fecha de publicación. III. Obras aparecidas después de su muerte. IV. En la revista del *Seminario Archivo Rubén Darío*. V. Libros hispanoamericanos con prólogo o notas del professor Antonio Oliver Belmás. VI. Libros españoles con prólogo de Antonio Oliver Belmás. VII. Premios y distinciones al doctor Antonio Oliver Belmás.

OLIVER I SALLERES, JOAN. *See* QUART, PERE.

OLMO, LAURO (1922–)

Olmo, Lauro. *La camisa. El cuarto poder*. Edición de Angel Berenguer. Madrid: Cátedra, 1984. 353p. (Letras Hispánicas, 208). "Obras de Lauro Olmo," pp. 117–24. Contents: I. Teatro (By work). II. Teatro infantil (By work). III. Narración (By work). IV. Poesía (By work). V. Textos sobre teatro. VI. Otros trabajos. "Artículos y textos sobre Lauro Olmo," pp. 127–28.

______. *La pechuga de Sardina; Mare Nostrum; La señorita Elvira.* Madrid: Plaza y Janés, 1987. 259p. (Colección Clásicos Plaza y Janés, 59). "Bibliografía," pp. 55–64. Contents: I. Obras. A. Obras de teatro (By year, 1953–86). Includes première and publication information. B. Teatro infantil en colaboración con Pilar Enciso (By year, 1954–81). C. Obras para la televisión. D. Adaptaciones teatrales (By year, 1970–85). E. Poesía (By year, 1954–80). F. Novela. G. Cuentos. H. Textos sobre teatro (By year, 1963–84). I. Varios (By year, 1970–84). II. Estudios (criticism).

III. Bibliografía seleccionada sobre *La pechuga de la Sardina* y *Mare Nostrum*.
Pérez-Stansfield, pp. 346–47.

ONIS, FEDERICO DE (1885–1966)
Arrigoitia, Luis de. "Bibliografía de Federico de Onís," *La Torre*, No. 59 (enero/marzo de 1968), 229–62. Contents: I. Ediciones (1909–1963). II. Editor (1912–60). III. Artículos (1900–67). IV. Prólogos (1923–65). V. Reseñas (1909–65). VI. Estudios y homenajes.

OROZCO DIAZ, EMILIO (1909–)
Montes Montes, María José. "Bibliografía del profesor Emilio Orozco Díaz," v. 3, pp. 583–96 in *Estudios sobre literatura y arte ofrecidos al Profesor Emilio Orozco Díaz* (Granada, 1979). Contents: I. Libros (By year, 1937–1978). II. Colaboraciones en obras de conjunto y homenajes (By year, 1953–1975). III. Discursos, conferencias y comunicaciones en congresos (By year, 1947–1979). IV. Artículos en revistas (By year, 1932–1977). V. Fascículos y folletos (By year, 1958–1977). VI. Prólogos (By year, 1958–1978). VII. Artículos en la *Gran Enciclopedia RIALP* (Madrid, 1971–1976).

ORRIOLS, MARIA DOLORS (1914–)
Galerstein, p. 238.

ORS, EUGENIO D' (1882–1954)
Amorós, Andrés, *Eugenio d'Ors, crítico literario*. Madrid: Editorial Prensa Española, 1971. 260p. (El Soto, 17). "Bibliografía," pp. 239–48. Contents: I. Obras de Eugenio d'Ors. A. Obras de D'Ors en que nos hemos basado para nuestro trabajo (21 items). B. Otras obras de D'Ors (35 items). II. Obras sobre Eugenio D'Ors. A. Libros dedicados enteramente a D'Ors (12 items). B. Libros que contienen algún estudio sobre D'Ors (25 items). C. Artículos sobre D'Ors (20 items).
Flórez, Rafael. *D'Ors*. Madrid: EPESA, 1970. 206p. "Bibliografía," pp. 193–203. Contents: I. Obras de Eugenio D'Ors. II. Obras sobre Eugenio D'Ors.
Ors, Eugenio d'. *Diálogos*. Edición de Carlos d'Ors. Prólogo de Jaime Ferrán. Madrid: Taurus Ediciones, 1981. 213p. "Bibliografía," pp. 205–12. Contents: I. Obras de Eugenio d'Ors. II. Obras sobre Eugenio d'Ors.
______. *Introducción a la vida angélica: Cartas a una soledad*. Presentación, cronología y bibliografía de José Jiménez. Madrid:

Tecnos, 1986. 137p. (Colección Metrópolis, 4). "Publicaciones de Eugenio d'Ors," pp. xxxiii-xxxvi.

Sáenz, Pilar. *The Life and Works of Eugenio d'Ors*. Troy, Mich.: International Book Publishers, 1983. 159p. "Selected Bibliography (partially annotated)," pp. 140–52. Contents: I. Primary Sources (only major works). A. Glossary. 1. Collections. 2. Individual Volumes. B. Narrative Works. C. Dramas. D. Philosophy. E. Art Criticism. II. Secondary Sources. A. Books. B. Commemorative Volumes. C. Chapters and Sections of Books. D. Articles in Periodicals (a selection of representative themes, including special issues in commemoration of d'Ors).

Suárez, Ada. *El género biográfico en la obra de Eugenio d'Ors*. Barcelona: Anthropos, 1988. 270p. "Bibliografía," pp. 263–68. Contents: I. Obras del autor. II. Bibliografía general (criticism of d'Ors included). A. Libros. B. Artículos sobre Eugenio d'Ors y Ortega y Gasset.

ORTEGA Y GASSET, JOSE (1883–1955)

Araya, Guillermo. *Claves filológicas para la comprensión de Ortega*. Madrid: Editorial Gredos, S.A., 1971. 248p. (Biblioteca Románica Hispánica. II. Estudios y Ensayos). Contents: "Cronología de las obras de Ortega," pp. 205–26. Contents: I. Recogidas en *Obras completas*. A. Tabla cronológica (1902–62). B. Nómina de libros ordenados por el año de su publicación (1914–62). II. Excluidas de *Obras completas*. A. Tabla cronológica (1908–55). B. Epistolario. "Bibliografía," pp. 243–48 (Criticism, biographies, etc.).

Borel, Jean Paul. *Raison et vie chez Ortega y Gasset*. Neuchâtel, Switzerland: Editions la Baconnière, 1959. 299p. "Bibliographie," pp. 288–95. Contents: Oeuvres d'Ortega y Gasset. II. Ecrits sur Ortega y Gasset. III. Divers. A. Ecrits d'auteurs se rattachant à la tradition ortéguienne. B. Histoire. C. Ecrits philosophiques contemporains ne se rattachant pas à la tradition ortéguienne (les plus importants).

Cirillo, Teresa. "Bibliografía italiana su José Ortega y Gasset," Istituto Universitario Orientale, Napoli (Sezione Romanza, *Annali*), 11 (1969), 87–92. Contents: I. Opere di José María Ortega y Gasset. II. Saggi su José María Ortega y Gasset. A. Libri. B. Articoli di riviste. C. Articoli publicati su quotidiani. D. Recensioni.

Donoso, Anton and Harold C. Raley. *José Ortega y Gasset: A Bibliography of Secondary Sources*. Bowling Green, Ohio: Philosophy Documentation Center, Bowling Green State University, 1986. 449p. Contents: I. Alphabetical Listing (3,937 entries). II.

Appendix I: Late Confirmations/Discoveries/Publications (3,938–4,090). III. Appendix II: In Press (4,090–4,125). IV. Subject Index.

Ortega, hoy: Estudios, ensayos y bibliografía sobre la vida y la obra de José Ortega y Gasset. Xalapa, México: Universidad Veracruzana, 1985. 254p. "Bibliografía," pp. 249–54. Contents: I. Fuentes primarias. A. Obras completas. B. Correspondencia. II. Fuentes secundarias: crítica.

Ortega y Gasset, José. *Espíritu de la letra.* Edición de Ricardo Senabre. Madrid: Cátedra, 1985. 172p. (Letras Hispánicas, 235). "Bibliografía," pp. 45–47. Contents: I. Bibliografía. II. Biografías y obras generales. III. Aspecto literario.

______. *Meditaciones sobre la literatura y el arte (La manera española del ver las cosas).* Edición, introducción y notas de E. Inman Fox. Madrid: Castalia, 1987. 394p. "Bibliografía selecta sobre Ortega y Gasset," pp. 41–45.

Rukser, Ugo, comp. *Bibliografía de Ortega.* Madrid: Ediciones de la *Revista de Occidente*, 1971. 437p. (Estudios orteguianos. 3). "El material reunido en este tomo se ordena del siguiente modo: una primera división afecta a los países que integran la *Bibliografía*, ordenados alfabéticamente; dentro de cada país se ofrecen dos partes, la primera dedicada a las obras del propio Ortega y una segunda que incluya los trabajos a él dedicados; cada una de esas partes está ordenada cronológicamente en anualidades y se divide, a su vez, en dos grupos el primero contiene los libros (total o parcialmente escritos o dedicados a Ortega) y el segundo los escritos aparecidos en revistas o diarios. En los contados casos en que la fecha de edición no exista, el título va colacado al final de los títutulos correspondientes a cada país."

ORTIZ SANCHEZ, LOURDES (1943–)

Galerstein, pp. 238–40.

ORY, CARLOS EDMUNDO DE (1923–)

Correa, v. 2, pp. 287–88, 617. Contents: I. Libros. II. Artículos y ensayos (criticism).

Ory, Carlos Edmundo de. *Energía: Poesía, 1940–1977.* Barcelona: Plaza y Janés, 1978. 234p. "Notas bibliográficas," pp. 233–34. Contents: I. Ediciones de libros cíclicos. II. Ediciones intemporales. III. Ediciones antológicas. IV. Selección de poemas sin formato de libros. V. Folletos.

______. *Miserable ternura: Cabaña.* Madrid: Ediciones Hiperión, 1981. 154p. (Poesía Hiperión, 39). "Bibliografía de Carlos Edmundo de Ory," pp. 151–54. Contents: I. Ediciones. A. Poesía (By year, 1945–1979). B. Monográficos (revistas). II. Narrativa (By year, 1952–1975). III. Ensayo (By year, 1962–1975).

_____. *Poesía, 1945–1969.* Edición preparada por Félix Grande. Barcelona: EDHASA, 1970. 345p. "Bibliografía de Ory," pp. 327–36. Contents: I. Ediciones (By year, 1945–1970). II. Colaboraciones en revistas. A. Poesía. B. Relatos. C. Ensayo. D. Artículos y crítica (By year, 1943–1968). E. Traducciones. III. Obra de Ory traducida. A. Al francés. B. Al alemán. C. Al italiano. D. Al sueco. E. Al portugués. IV. Textos sobre Ory. V. Bibliografía del *postismo*. VI. Libros inéditos.

Pariente, pp. 105–06. Contents: I. Libros de poesía (By year, 1945–71). II. Estudios sobre su poesía (By year, 1945–80). III. Procedencia de los textos.

ORY, EDUARDO DE (1884–1939)

Ramos Ortega, Manuel. *La obra poética de Eduardo de Ory.* Cádiz: UNIMED, 1983. 138p. "Bibliografía," pp. 133–36. Contents: I. Poesía (By year, 1903–1925). II. Antologías (By year, 1909–1936). III. Prosa (By year, 1909–1937). IV. Bibliografía consultada (Includes criticism).

OTERO, BLAS DE (1916–)

Barrow, Geoffrey R. *The Satiric Vision of Blas de Otero.* Columbia: University of Missouri Press, 1988. 160p. "Selected Bibliography," pp. 149–55. Contents: I. Works by Blas de Otero (By year, 1942–1981). II. Secondary Sources (Includes criticism).

Correa, v. 2, pp. 171, 612–13. Contents: I. Libros. II. Artículos y estudios (criticism).

Mantero, pp. 559–60. Contents: I. Libros de poesía. II. Otras publicaciones. III. Sobre Blas de Otero.

Moral, María Asunción. "Bibliografía sobre Blas de Otero," pp. 413–40 in *Al amor de Blas de Otero: Actas de las II Jornadas Internacionales de Literatura; Blas de Otero* (San Sebastián: Universidad de Deusto, Departamento de Literatura, 1986). Entries are arranged chronologically under the following headings: I. Reseñas, Estudios y artículos sobre el autor aprecidos en libros, periódicos y revistas. II. Libros, tesis doctorales, ediciones-homenaje sobre la obra del poeta. III. Estudios más generales donde se estudia o se alude a alguna cuestión de la poesía oteriana.

Puente, Yolanda. "Blas de Otero en las antologías poéticas," pp. 381–412 in *Al amor de Blas de Otero: Actas de las II Jornadas Internacionales de Literatura; Blas de Otero* (San Sebastián: Universidad de Deusto, Departamento de Literatura, 1986). Contents: I. Antologías realizadas por Blas de Otero. II. Antologías consultadas. III. Grupo de unas sesenta antologías. IV. Poemas musicados.

PACHECO, MANUEL (1920–)

Manzano González, Raquel. *La poesía de Manuel Pacheco*. Badajoz: Excma. Diputación Provincial de Badajoz, 1985. 153p. "Obras consultadas," pp. 147–49. Contents: I. De Manuel Pacheco (By year, 1949–1981). II. Estudios críticos (inéditos). III. Estudios críticos (publicados).

Pacheco, Manuel. *Poesía, 1978–1984*. Badajoz: Departamento de Publicaciones, Excma. Diputación Provincial de Badajoz, 1986. 3vs. "Bibliografía," I, pp. 173–94. Includes works by and about the author.

PADRON, JUSTO JORGE (1943–)

CILH, pp. 44–45. Contents: I. Poesía. II. Ensayo, traducción y antologías

Padrón, Justo Jorge. *La visita del mar (1980–1984). Los dones de la tierra (1982–1983)*. Estudio preliminar de Leopoldo de Luis. Madrid: Espasa-Calpe, 1984. 223p. "Bibliografía," pp. 220–23. Contents: I. Obras de Justo Jorge Padrón. A. Poesía (1970–1980). B. Ensayo, traducción y antologías (By year, 1972–1983). C. Obra traducida de Justo Jorge Padrón. 1. *Los círculos del infierno*. 2. Antologías.

PALACIO VALDES, ARMANDO (1853–1938)

Martínez Cachero, José María. "40 fichas para una bibliografía sobre Armando Palacio Valdés," *Boletín del Instituto de Estudios Asturianos* (Oviedo), 7 (1953). 340–59. Contents: I. Notas bibliográficas sobre la personalidad de Palacio Valdés (1853–1938). II. Orden alfabético de autores reseñados.

PALLARES, PILAR (1957–)

Galerstein, p. 243.

PALOU, INES (1923–1975)

Galerstein, p. 242.

PAMIES I BELTRAN, TERESA (1919–)

Galerstein, pp. 243–48.

PANERO, LEOPOLDO (1909–1962)

Aller, César. *La poesía personal de Leopoldo Panero*. Pamplona: EUNSA, 1976. 294p. "Bibliografía," pp. 289–92. Contents: I. Obras principales de Leopoldo Panero. II. Otras obras del poeta. III. Bibliografía sobre Leopoldo Panero. A. Libros. B. Revistas (listed by journal).

Connolly, Eileen. *Leopoldo Panero: La poesía de la esperanza*. Con un prólogo de José Antonio Maravall. Madrid: Editorial Gredos, S.A., 1969. 236p. (Biblioteca Románica Hispánica. VII. Campo Abierto, 25). "Bibliografía," pp. 215–25. Contents: I. Obras de Leopoldo Panero. A. Obras poéticas (orden cronológico). B. Crítica literaria. II. Estudios sobre Leopoldo Panero. III. Bibliografía general (selección).

Correa, v. 2., pp. 97, 608–10. Contents: I. Libros. II. Artículos y estudios (criticism).

Pariente, p. 109. Contents: I. Libros de poesía (By year, 1944–63). II. Estudios sobre su poesía (By year, 1958–65). III. Procedencia de los textos.

Parra Higuera, Alberto. *Investigaciones sobre la obra poética de Leopoldo Panero*. Bern: Herbert Lang; Frankfurt/M.: Peter Lang, 1971. 183p. (Publicaciones universitarias europeas. Serie XXIV: Lenguas y literaturas iberorrománicas, Reihe 24, Vol. I). "Bibliografía consultada," pp. 129–36. "Apéndice," pp. 137–74. Contents: I. Bibliografía de la obra literaria de Leopoldo Panero. Ordenación cronológica. A. Verso. 1. Colecciones hechas y publicadas por Panero. 2. Colecciones hechas por otros, publicadas en revistas, o periódicos o como libro. 3. Publicaciones en antologías e historias de la literatura española. 4. Poemas sueltos en su primera edición y variantes. 5. Traducciones. B. Prosa. 1. Libros. 2. Artículos. 3. Discursos. 4. Prólogos. 5. Entrevistas. 6. Traducciones. II. Bibliografía de crítica, de poemas dedicados y de homenajes a Panero. A. Crítica. B. Poemas dedicados. C. Homenajes.

PARAISO, ISABEL (1942–)

Alarcón, p. 51.

PARCERISAS, FRANCESC (1944–)

"Francesc Parcerisas: Selected Bibliography," *Catalan Writing*, No. 2 (December, 1988), 82–83. Contents: I. Chronology. II. Selected Bibliography (Includes translations).

PEDRERO, PALOMA (1957–)

"Paloma Pedrero," *O'Connor*, pp. 166–67.

PEDROLO, MANUEL DE (1918–)

Arbonès, Jordi. *Pedrolo contra els límits*. Barcelona: Aymà, 1980. 176p. "Obres de Manuel de Pedrolo," pp. 173–76.

"Manuel de Pedrolo," pp. 67–72 in L. Teresa Valdivieso's *España: Bibliografía de un teatro "silenciado"* (Lincoln, Neb.: Society of Spanish and Spanish-American Studies, 1979). Contents: I. Notas biográficas. II. Obras inéditas. III. Obras publicadas. IV. Traducciones. V. Escritos y declaraciones. VI. Estudios críticos.

PEMAN, JOSE MARIA (1897–1981)

En torno a Pemán. Cádiz: Excma. Diputación Provincial de Cádiz, 1974. 657p. "Apuntes biográficos y obras de José María Pemán," pp. 639–56.

Romo Arregui, Josefina. "José María Pemán: Bibliografía," *Cuadernos de Literatura Contemporánea*, No. 8 (1943), 189–190. Contents: I. Ediciones. A. Teatro. B. Poesía. C. Novelas. D. Otras obras. II. Traducciones.

PEREIRA, ANTONIO (1923–)

"Antonio Pereira: Bibliografía," *Alonso*, p. 103. Contents: I. Poesía (By year, 1964–1972). II. Narrativa (By year, 1967–1985). III. Miscelánea. Books only.

PEREZ CASANOVA, SOFIA (1861/62–1958)

"Sofía Pérez Casanova," pp. 168–80 in María del Carmen Simón Palmer's "Tres escritoras españolas en el extranjero," *Cuadernos Bibliográficos*, 47 (1987). Contents: I. Manuscritos, obras impresas (By year, 1885–1945). II. Traducciones. III. Colaboración en publicaciones periódicas (By journal). IV. Colaboraciones en obras colectivas o de otros autores. V. Estudios (criticism).

PEREZ-CLOTET, PEDRO (1902–)

Hernández Guerrero, José Antonio. *La expresividad poética: Análisis de "Signo del Alba" dePedro Pérez-Clotet*. Cádiz: Universidad de Cádiz, 1987. 372p. Footnote 6 on pp. 13–14 includes a list of poetry and prose works in monograph form. "Bibliografía," pp. 275–85 includes a limited number of works about Pérez-Clotet and his work.

PEREZ DE AYALA, RAMON (1880–1962)

Best, Marigold. *Ramon Pérez de Ayala: An Annotated Bibliography of Criticism*. London: Grant and Cutler, 1980. 81p. (Research Bibliographies and Checklists, 33). Contents: I. Books and Parts of Books. II. Articles in Periodicals. III. Articles from Daily

Newspapers (no page nos. given). IV. Unpublished Dissertations and Theses (English and American only). V. Appendix: Works of Pérez de Ayala Not Included in his *Obras Completas* (1964–1969). VI. General Index of Names. Includes 542 entries, most of which contain brief or descriptive annotations.

Bibliografía de Ramón Pérez de Ayala existente en la Biblioteca Pública de Oviedo. Oviedo, 1980. 24p. Contents: I. Obras de Ramón Pérez de Ayala. A. Obras completas. B. Obras selectas. Antologías. C. Poesía. D. Teatro. E. Novela. F. Ensayo. G. Epistolario. II. Obras sobre Ramón Pérez de Ayala. A. Bibliografía. B. Biografía. C. Crítica. 1. Estudios generales. 2. Pérez de Ayala, poeta. 3. Pérez de Ayala, novelista. (a) Estudios generales. (b) Estudios sobre obras sueltas. (c) Pérez de Ayala en sus cartas. D. Conmemoraciones. III. Historias de la literatura, diccionarios, enciclopedias, etc. con mención especial en sus páginas a Ramón Pérez de Ayala.

Billick, David J. "Addendum to the Bibliography of Ramón Pérez de Ayala: Master's Theses and Doctoral Dissertations," *Hispanófila*, No. 59 (enero de 1977), 89–93. An addendum to Pelayo H. Fernández's bibliography. The bibliography is arranged by year, 1932–75. Only U.S. theses and dissertations are included.

Coletes Blanco, Agustín. "Traducciones y selecciones de la obra de Pérez de Ayala publicadas en Gran Bretaña y los Estados Unidos," *Boletín del Instituto de Estudios Asturianos* (Oviedo), 38 (1984), 41–53. "Tabla cronológica de traducciones al inglés y selecciones de su obra publicadas en Gran Bretaña y Los EE. UU.," pp. 45–53. Covers 1920–1972 and includes reviews. Critical entries.

Derndarsky, Roswitha. *Ramón Pérez de Ayala: Zur Thematik und Kunstgestalt seiner Romane.* Frankfurt am Main: Vittorio Klostermann, 1970. 192p. (Studien zur Philosophie und Literatur des Neunzehnten Jahrhunderts, Band 8). "Literaturverzeichnis," pp. 183–90. I. Werke Ayalas. II. Benützte und zitierte Werke.

Feeny, Thomas. *The Paternal Orientation of Ramón Pérez de Ayala.* Valencia: Ediciones Albatros-Hispanófila, 1985. 120p. "Selected Bibliography," pp. 117–19. Contents: I. Works by Pérez de Ayala. II. Studies on Pérez de Ayala.

Fernández, Pelayo H. "Ramón Pérez de Ayala: Bibliografía crítica," *Hispanófila*, No. 55 (septiembre de 1975), 1–31. 343 items arranged by year, 1904–73. Bibliography also includes an author index. This bibliography is updated through 1977 in the author's *Estudios sobre Ramón Perez de Ayala* (Oviedo: Imprenta "La Cruz," 1978), pp. 153–93.

Friera, Florencio. "Crónica y bibliografía del primer centenario del nacimiento de Ramón Pérez de Ayala," *Nueva Conciencia*, Nos.

120/21 (Octubre de 1980), 115–44. "Tras hacer una completa crónica de los diversos actos celebrados con ocasión del centenario del escritor." Includes a bibliography of and about Pérez de Ayala. The 243 items listed cover 1979–1982.

García Domínguez, Elías. "Epistolario de Ramón Pérez de Ayala," *Boletín del Instituto de Estudios Asturianos*, No. 64/65 (mayo/diciembre de 1968), 439–53. Includes an "Obras de Ramón Pérez de Ayala, ediciones en volumen" section.

Lozano Marco, Miguel Angel. *Del relato modernista a la novela poemática: La narrativa breve de Ramón Pérez de Ayala.* Alicante: Caja de Ahorros Provincial; Universidad de Alicante, 1983. 329p. "Bibliografía crítica," pp. 305–24.

Macklin, John. *The Window and the Garden: The Modernist Fictions of Ramón Pérez de Ayala.* Lincoln, Neb.: Society of Spanish and Spanish-American Studies, 1988. 206p. "Select Bibliography," pp. 197–204. Contents: I. Works by Ramón Pérez de Ayala. A. Fiction. B. Essays. II. Critical Studies on Ramón Pérez de Ayala. A. Books. B. Articles. C. Centennial Essays.

Matas, Julio. *Contra el honor: Las novelas normativas de Ramón Pérez de Ayala.* Madrid: Seminarios y Ediciones, S.A., 1974. 240p. "Bibliografía," pp. 229–40. Criticism only.

O'Brien, Mac Gregor. *El ideal clásico de Ramón Pérez de Ayala en sus ensayos en "La Prensa" de Buenos Aires.* Oviedo: Instituto de Estudios Asturianos, 1981. 209p. Includes an apéndice: Los artículos de Ramón Pérez de Ayala en *La Prensa* (pp. 75–206). The 625 articles that appear from 1916–1951 contain brief summaries of their contents.

Pérez de Ayala, Ramón. *A.M.D.G.* Edición de Andrés Amorós. Madrid: Ediciones Cátedra, 1983. 345p. Contents: I. Ediciones de la novela (p. 100). II. Traducciones (p. 100). III. Bibliografía de Pérez de Ayala (p. 101). IV. Sobre *A.M.D.G.* (p. 102). V. Libros dedicados a Pérez de Ayala (pp. 102–103). VI. Publicaciones con motivo del centenario (p. 104). VII. Estudios sobre Pérez de Ayala en libros de conjunto (pp. 104–07). VIII. Algunos artículos (pp. 107–10).

______. *Artículos y ensayos en los semanarios "España", "Nuevo Mundo" y "La Esfera".* Prólogo y recopilación por Florencio Friera Suárez. Oviedo: Universidad, 1986. 230p.

______. *Crónicas londineses.* Edición, introducción, bibliografía y notas de Agustín Coletes Blanco. Murcia: Universidad de Murcia, 1985. 180p. "Noticia bibliográfica," pp. 37–43. Content: I. Repertorios bibliográficos. II. Bibliografía ayalina (1982–1984; arranged by year).

______. *El ombligo del mundo*. Estudio preliminar y edición crítica por Angeles Prado. 5. ed. Madrid: Orígenes, 1982. 281p. "Noticia bibliográfica (varias ediciones de *El ombligo del mundo* y de los cuentos que integran la colección)," p. 69. "Bibliografía sobre el autor," pp. 71–76. Contents: I. Libros. II. Estudios y artículos.

______. *Tigre Juan. El curandero de su honra*. Edición, introducción y notas de Andrés Amorós. Madrid: Castalia, 1980. (Clásicos Castalia, 103). "Noticia bibliográfica (Las principales ediciones y traducciones de *Tigre Juan* y *El curandero de su honra*)," pp. 73–74. "Bibliografía," pp. 75–82. Contents: I. Sobre *Tigre Juan* y *El curandero de su honra*. II. Sobre Pérez de Ayala en general, incluyendo algún estudio sobre este novela. A. Libros dedicados a Pérez de Ayala. B. Estudios sobre Pérez de Ayala en libros de conjunto. C. Artículos. D. Algunas obras de referencia. E. Ediciones de obras de Pérez de Ayala que se han utilizado.

Pol Stock, Margaret. *Dualism and Polarity in the Novels of Ramón Pérez de Ayala*. London: Támesis, 1988. 153p. (Coleccion Támesis, Serie A, Monografías, 127). "Selected List of Works Consulted," pp. 151–53. Contents: I. Primary Sources. II. Secondary Sources.

Rand, Marguerite C. *Ramón Pérez de Ayala*. New York: Twayne Publishers, Inc., 1971. 175p. "Selected Bibliography," pp. 163–69. Contents: I. Primary Sources. A. Books by Pérez de Ayala (A few minor works omitted). B. English Translations. II. Secondary Sources.

Urrutia, Norma. *De "Troteras" a "Tigre Juan": dos grandes temas de Pérez de Ayala*. Madrid: Insula, 1960. 126p. "Apéndice bibliográfico," pp. 117–24. Contents: I. Obras. II. Traducciones. III. Estudios.

PEREZ DE LA DEHESA, RAFAEL (1913–1974)

"Bibliografía de Rafael Pérez de la Dehesa," pp. 304–05, in *La crisis de fin de siglo: Ideología y literatura: Estudios en memoria de R. Pérez de la Dehesa* (Esplugues de Llobregat-Barcelona: Editorial Ariel, 1975). Contents: I. Libros. II. Ediciones. III. Artículos.

PEREZ-GOMEZ, ANTONIO (1902–1976)

Díez de Revenga, Francisco Javier. "Bibiófila y bibliografía de Antonio Pérez-Gómez," v. 1, pp. 211–38 in *Libro-Homenaje a Antonio Pérez-Gómez* (Cienza, 1978). Contents: I. Publicaciones de Antonio Pérez-Gómez. A. " . . . La Fonte que mana y corre . . . " B. Libros raros de poesía de los siglos XVI y XVII. C. Reproducciones facsimilares de ejemplares únicos. D. Obras fuera de serie. E. Incunables poéticos castellanos. F. Duque y

Marqués. G. Colecciones de romances. H. El ayre de la almena. I. Ediciones conmemorativas. J. Libros sobre libros. K. Pliegos conmemorativos de la Navidad. II. Literatura murciana de Cordel: revista *Monteagudo* de la Cátedra Saavedra Fajardo de la Universidad de Murcia (Tomos I, 1953–Tomo III, 1970). III. Otras publicaciones (1948–1976).

PEREZ VALIENTE, SALVADOR (1919–)
CILH, p. 260. Contents: I. Poesía. II. Prosa. III. Erudición.

PEREZ Y PEREZ, RAFAEL (1891–)
Azorín Fernández, María Dolores. *La obra novelística de Rafael Pérez y Pérez*. Alicante: Instituto de Estudios Alicantinos, 1983. 171p. (*Its* Publicaciones, Serie I, No. 77). "Novelas de Rafael Pérez y Pérez," pp. 149–50.

PERUCHO, JUAN (1920–)
Pujol, Carlos. *Juan Perucho: El mágico prodigioso*. Bellaterra: Universidad Autónoma de Barcelona, Escuela Universitaria de Traductores e Intérpretes, 1986. 97p. (Monografies de Quaderns de Traducció i Interpretació, 3). "Bibliografía de Juan Perucho por Lourdes Güell," pp. 83–97. Contents: I. Obras de Juan Perucho (By year, 1947–1986). Includes reviews. II. Incluidas en antologías. III. Sobre Juan Perucho. A. Artículos. B. Entrevistas. IV. Obras generales. V. Bibliografía particular.

PESSARRODONA I ARTIGUES, MARTA (1941–)
Galerstein, pp. 255–56.

PINILLOS, MANUEL (n.d.)
Calvo Carilla, José Luis. *Introducción a la poesía de Manuel Pinillos: Estudio y antología*. Zaragoza: Prensas Universitarias de Zaragoza, Universidad de Zaragoza, 1989. 191p. (Humanidades, 10). "Breve (y provisional) noticia bibliográfica," pp. 105–12.

PLA, JOSEP (1897–1981)
Casasús, Josep Maria. *Lliçons de periodisme en Josep Pla: La modernització dels gèneres periodístics a Catalunya*. Barcelona: Destino, 1986. 312p. (Collecció El Dofí, 1). "Bibliografia," pp. 299–312. Contents: I. Edicions consultades de l'obra completa de Josep Pla (By year, 1969–1984). II. Obres sobre Josep Pla. III. Articles sobre Josep Pla. IV. Obres sobre gèneres periodisme i pensament català. A. Llibres. B. Articles.

Manent, Albert. *Tres escritores catalanes: Carner, Riba, Plá*. Madrid: Editorial Gredos, S.A., 1973. 338p. (Biblioteca Románica Hispánica. II. Estudios y ensayos, 187). "Bibliografía de Josep Plá," pp. 325–30. Contents: I. En catalán. II. En castellano. III. Traducciones.

PLA Y BELTRAN, PASCUAL (1908–1961)
Gracia, Antonio. *Pascual Pla y Beltrán*. Alicante: Instituto de Estudios Alicantinos, Excma. Diputación Provincial de Alicante, 1984. 185p. (Publicaciones del Instituto de Estudios Alicantinos, Serie I, Número 92). "Bibliografía," pp. 177–85. Contents: I. Obras de Pla y Beltrán. A. Libros y folletos (By year, 1929–60). B. En periódicos y revistas. 1. Poemas (selected; by year, 1929–60). 2. Cuentos (By year, 1956–60s). 3. Artículos (Selected, by year, 1936–62). II. Sobre Pla y Beltrán.

POMBO, PILAR (1953–)
"Pilar Pombo," *O'Connor*, pp. 167–68.

POMPEIA, NURIA (1938–)
Galerstein, pp. 256–58.

PORCEL, BALTASAR (1937–)
"Baltasar Porcel: Selected Bibliography," *Catalan Writing*, No. 2 (December, 1988), 60–61. Contents: I. Chronology. II. Fiction. II. Theatre, Prose, and Travel. III. Translations (By language).

PORPETTA, ANTONIO (1936–)
CILH, pp. 191–92. Contents: I. Poesía. II. Ensayo.

PORQUERAS MAYO, ALBERTO (1930–)
Laurenti, Joseph L. "Bibliografía de Alberto Porqueras Mayo," pp. 489–505 in *Varia Hispánica: Homenaje a Alberto Porqueras Mayo* (Kassel: Edition Reichenberger, 1989). Contents: I. Libros (By year, 1957–1989). II. Ediciones (By year, 1958–1989). III. Artículos (By year, 1954–1989). IV. Reseñas (By year, 1953–1989). V. En prensa. 181 entries.

PORTAL, MARTA (1930–)
Alarcón, p. 60.
Galerstein, pp. 258–59.

POZO GARZA, LUZ (1922–)
Galerstein, p. 259.

PRADOS, EMILIO (1899–1962)

"Bibliografía de Emilio Prados," *Litoral* (Málaga), No. 100 (1981), 97–98.

Blanco Aguinaga, Carlos. "Emilio Prados: Bibliografía," *Revista Hispánica Moderna*, 25, No. 3/4 (julio/octubre de 1960), 105–07. Contents: I. Libros. II. Otras publicaciones. III. Poesías sueltas. IV. Estudios.

______. *Lista de los papeles de Emilio Prados en La Biblioteca del Congreso de los Estados Unidos de América.* Baltimore: The Johns Hopkins Press, 1967. 47p. Contents: I. Los papeles. A. España (1925–1939). 1. Obras escritas en España casi todas sin revisión posterior. 2. Obras escritas en España en versiones revisadas en México. B. México. 1. Poesía de 1939–47. 2. Poesía de 1947–62. 3. Poesía de fecha incierta. C. Notas autobiográficas y papeles de menor importancia. II. Apéndices. A. Indice de libros publicados de Emilio Prados. B. Indice de títulos de libros, publicados o no, que aparecen en este catálogo. C. Títulos de libros que Prados dijo alguna vez haber escrito y que no aparecen ni en este catálogo ni entre las obras publicadas del poeta.

Correa, v. 1, pp. 429–30, 550. Works by and about the author.

Ellis, P. J. *The Poetry of Emilio Prados.* Cardiff: University of Wales Press, 1981. 332p. "Published Works of Emilio Prados," p. 294 (By year, 1925–1976, books only). "Bibliography of Articles and Books on the Work and Life of Emilio Prados Referred to in the Text," pp. 297–99.

González Muela, pp. 73–75. Works by and about Prados are arranged chronologically.

Hernández, Patricio. *Emilio Prados: La memoria del ovido.* Zaragoza: Secretariado de Prensas Universitarias, Universidad de Zaragoza, 1988. 2 vs. "Bibliografía," v. 2, pp. 299–517. Contents: I. Obras de Emilio Prados. (By year, 1925–1978). II. Otras publicaciones (By year, 1937–1941). III. Papeles y epistolario. IV. Estudios (criticism). V. Páginas dedicadas.

Pariente, pp. 113–14. Contents: I. Libros de poesía (By year, 1927–65). II. Estudios sobre su poesía (By year, 1940–68). III. Procedencia de los textos.

Prados, Emilio. *Poesías completas.* Edición y prólogo de Carlos Blanco Aguinaga y Antonio Carreira. México, D. F.: Aguilar, 1975. 2 vs. "Bibliografía," v. 1, pp. lxix–xcv. Contents: I. Obras (By year, 1925–1971). II. Otras publicaciones (1937–1941). III. Poemas sueltos (1923–1969). IV. Antologías. V. Estudios (criticism). VI. Páginas dedicadas.

Reina, Elena. *Hacia la luz: Simbolización en la poesía de Emilio Prados.* Amsterdam: Rodopi, 1988. 283p. (Biblioteca Hispanoamericana y Española de Amsterdam, 6). "Bibliografía," pp. 259–70. Contents: I. Obras de Emilio Prados (By year, 1925–1987). II. Otras publicaciones (By year, 1937–1940). III. Papeles (By year, 1967–1985). IV. Estudios (criticism).

PRAT, IGNACIO (1945–)
Navarro, Rosa. "Bibliogafía de Ignacio Prat," *El Ciervo* (Barcelona), No. 375 (1982), 33.

PUCHE, ELIODORO (1885–1964)
Díez de Revenga, Francisco Javier. *Eliodoro Puche: Historia y crítica de un poeta.* Murcia: Academia "Alfonso X El Sabio," 1980. 293p. "Bibliografía sobre Eliodoro Puche," pp. 291–93.

PUERTOLAS VILLANUEVA, SOLEDAD (1947–)
Galerstein, p. 260.

QUART, PERE (pseud. of Joan Oliver i Salleres, 1899–1986)
A biobibliography of the author, including translations, appears in David Herschel Rosenthal's "Modern Catalan Poetry: A Critical Introduction with Translations" (Unpublished doctoral dissertation, City University of New York, 1977).
Turull, Antoni. *Pere Quart, poeta del nostre temps.* Barcelona: Edicions 62, 1984. 231p. "Cronologia i bibliografia (1899–1983)," pp. 227–31.

QUINONES, FERNANDO (1930–)
"Fernando Quiñones," in Julia Elizabeth Cabey Riley's *Bibliografía de algunos poetas andaluces de posguerra* (Madrid: Universidad Complutense, Departamento de Bibliografía, 1984).

QUIROGA, ELENA (1921–)
Alarcón, pp. 60–61.
Boring, Phyllis Zatlin. *Elena Quiroga.* Boston: Twayne Publishers, 1977. 151p. "Selected Bibliography," pp. 143–47. Contents: I. Primary Sources. A. Novels and Novelettes (By year, 1949–1977). B. Miscellaneous and Privately Printed Works (By year, 1952–1963). II. Secondary Sources (criticism; annotated entries).
Galerstein, pp. 261–64.

RAFAEL MARES KURZ, CARMEN (1911–)
Galerstein, pp. 265–69.

RAGUE-ARIAS, MARIA JOSE (1941–)
"María José Rague-Arias," *O'Connor*, p. 168.

RAMON Y CAJAL, SANTIAGO (1852–1934)
Ramón y Cajal, Santiago. *Obra literaria*. México: Ediciones De Andrea, 1965. 144p. (Colección Studium, 53). "Bibliografía," pp. 141–44. Contents: I. Obras de Santiago Ramón y Cajal. II. Obras sobre Ramón y Cajal.

REINA, MARIA MANUELA (1958–)
"María Manuela Reina," *O'Connor*, p. 169.

REJANO, JUAN (1903–1976)
Rejano, Juan. *La mirada del hombre: Nueva suma poética (1943–1976)*. Madrid: Anthropos, 1988. 493p. (Memoria rota; Exilios y heterdoxias, 12). "Juan Rejano, nota biográfica y bibliográfica," pp. 481–84.

RESINO, CARMEN (1941–)
"Carmen Resino," *O'Connor*, pp. 169–71.

REY, AGAPITO (1892–)
"Bibliografía," pp. 21–24 in *Homenaje a Don Agapito Rey: Trabajos publicados en su honor a cargo de Josep Roca-Pons* (Bloomington: Department of Spanish and Portuguese, Indiana University, 1980). Contents: I. Libros (By year, 1927–1966). II. Artículos (By year, 1927–1976). III. Reseñas (lista parcial).

REY SOTO, ANTONIO (1879–)
"Bibliografía de Antonio Rey Soto (Obras anunciadas e incompletas)," *Filología Moderna* (Barcelona), No. 69 (1965), 273–89.

RIAZA, LUIS (1925–)
"Luis Riaza," pp. 73–76 in L. Teresa Valdivieso's *España: Bibliografía de un teatro "silenciado"* (Lincoln, Neb.: Society of Spanish and Spanish-American Studies, 1979). Contents: I. Notas biográficas. II. Obras inéditas. III. Obras publicadas. IV. Escritos y declaraciones. V. Estudios críticas.
Pérez-Stansfield, p. 347.

RIBA, CARLES (1893–1959)

"Carles Riba: Selected Bibliography," *Catalan Writing*, No. 3 (October 1989), 60–63. Contents: I. Chronology. II. Poetry. III. Criticism. IV. Translations (By language).

Friese, Birgit. *Carles Riba als übersetzer aus dem deutschen*. Frankfurt am Main: Verlag Peter Lang, 1985. 265p. (Hispanistische Studien, 16). Contents: "Literaturverzeichnis," pp. 257–65. Contents: I. Carles Riba. A. Primärwerke. B. Ubersetzungen. II. Sekundärliteratur.

Marti i Bas, M. Montserrat. "Bibliografía de Carles Riba," pp. 569–83 in *In Memoriam Carles Riba, 1959–1969* (Barcelona: Editorial Ariel, S.A., 1973). Contents: I. Obres originas. A. Obres completes. B. Poesía. C. Prosa narrativa. D. Crítica i assaig. E. Antologies i pròlegs. F. Manuals. G. Traducciones. 1. Biblia. 2. Llengües clàssiques. 3. Llengües modernes. H. Obres per a infants i adolescents. II. Obres de Carles Riba tradüides a diverses llengües.

RIDRUEJO, DIONISIO (1912–1975)

Correa, v. 2, pp. 113–14, 610. Contents: I. Libros. II. Artículos y estudios (criticism).

Doménech, Francisco. *Bibliografía de Dionisio Ridruejo*. Madrid: Universidad Complutense, 1982. 36p. (Trabajos del Departamento de Bibliografía; Serie A, Escritores Contemporáneos, 7). 705 entries. Contents: I. Bibliografías. II. Obras completas. III. Ediciones, poemas sueltos, obra crítica, prólogos (By year, 1933–1979). IV. Colaboraciones sistemáticas en publicaciones periódicas: A. *Arriba* (1939–1953). B. *Solidaridad Nacional* (1945–1951). C. *Destino* (1971–1975). V. Crítica e interpretación literaria de la obra de Dionisio Ridruejo. VI. Apéndice: Colaboraciones sistemáticas en publicaciones periódicas (By year, 1952–1975). Homenajes (By year, 1974–1977).

Ridruejo, Dionisio. *Cuadernos de Rusia. En la soledad del tiempo. Cancionero de Ronda. Elegías*. Edición, introducción y notas de Manuel A. Pinilla. Madrid: Castalia, 1981. 324p. (Clásicos Castalia, 106). "Noticia bibliográfica," pp. 57–64. Contents: I. Ediciones de poesía (By year, 1935–1976). II. Poemas dispersos en libros, periódicos, revistas y folletos (selected, by year, 1933–1975). III. Otras obras (By year, 1944–1978). "Bibliografía selecta (criticism)," pp. 65–66.

Rubio, María, and Solana, Fermín. "Aproximación a una bibliografía de Dionisio Ridruejo," pp. 431–98 in *Dionisio Ridruejo, de la Falange a la opisición* (Madrid: Taurus Ediciones, 1976). Annotated contents, notes, etc. Contents: I. Obras y folletos,

1935–75. II. Colaboraciones en escritos colectivos. Prólogos. III. Corresponsal en Roma, 1949–51. IV. Algunas colaboraciones sistemáticas. A. *Escorial.* Revista de cultura y letras. B. *Solidaridad Nacional.* C. *Revista:* Seminario de información, artes y letras. D. *Destino.* V. Anotaciones de literatura comprometida: A. *Bohemia.* B. *Boletín informativo.* C. *Mañana,* tribuna democrática española. D. *Ibérica.* E. *Opiniones y noticias;* hojas informativas de política y democracia. VI. Colaboraciones y artículos diversos (1933–1975). A. Etapa de 1933–1942. B. Etapa de 1942–1955. C. Etapa de 1955–1975.

Schmidt, Hans-Peter. *Dionisio Ridruejo: Ein Mitglied der spanischen "Generation von 36."* Bonn: Romanisches Seminar der Universität Bonn, 1972. 334p. (Romanistische Versuche und Vorarbeiten, 41). "Literaturverzeichnis," pp. 325–34. Contents: I. Ridruejos Werke (Chronologisch Geordnet). A. Einzelveröffentlichungen. B. Nichtselbaständige Veröffentlichungen. II. Sekundärliteratur. A. Alphabetisches Namensverzeichnis. B. Zeitungs- und zeitschriftenmaterial ohne Autorenangabe.

RIERA, MIQUEL-ANGEL (1930–)

"Miquel-Angel Riera," *Catalan Writing,* No. 2 (December 1988), 43–45. Contents: I. Chronology. II. Poetry. III. Fiction. IV. Translations (By language).

RIERA GUILERA, CARME (1948–)

Galerstein, pp. 270–71.

RINCON, MARIA EUGENIA (1926–)

Galerstein, p. 272.

RIO, ANGEL DEL (1900–1962)

Florit, Ricardo. "Angel del Río: Bibliografía," *Revista Hispánica Moderna,* 31, No. 1/4 (enero/octubre de 1965), 455–59. Contents: I. Libros (Includes reviews). II. Ediciones y prólogos. III. Artículos y monografías. IV. Reseñas.

_____. *Bibliografía de Angel del Río.* New York: Hispanic Society of America, Department of Spanish and Portuguese, Columbia University, 1979. (Bibliotheca Hispana Novissima, 3). Contents: I. Libros (By year, 1935–1972). Includes reviews. II. Ediciones y prólogos (By year 1930–1957). Includes reviews. III. Artículos y monografías. IV. Reseñas. V. Artículos dedicados y notas necrológicas.

RIOS, JULIAN (n.d.)

Palabras para "Larva." Edición al cuidado de Andrés Sánchez Robayna y Gonzalo Díaz-Migoyo. Barcelona: Edicions del Mall, 1985. 257p. "Bibliografía," pp. 253–57. Contents: I. Modalidades de la primera edicion de *Larva*. (Edicions del Mall, 1983). II. Fragmentos de *Larva* en revistas. III. Traducciones de *Larva*. A. Inglés. B. Francés. C. Alemán. IV. Textos críticos sobre *Larva*. V. Entrevistas con Julián Ríos.

RIOS RUIZ, MANUEL (1934–)

CILH, pp. 51–52.

RISCO, VICENTE (1884–1963)

Risco, Vicente. *Obra completa*. Acercamento biográfico e bibliografía por Fernando Salgado. Edición e limiar de "Teoría Nacionalista" de Francisco J. Bobillo. Madrid: Akal Editor, 1981. 2vs. "Bibliografía de Risco," v. 1, pp. xv–xxii. Contents: I. Teoría nacionalista. II. Narrativa galega. III. Narrativa castelán. IV. Teatro. V. Viaxes. VI. Outras prosas galegas. VII. Folklore, etnografía, mitoloxía. . . . VIII. Historiografía e teoría de historia. IX. Lingua, literatura e pedagoxía. X. Outras prosas en castelán. "Algúns traballos sobre Risco," v. 1, pp. xxiii–xxiv.

RIVERA TOVAR, ASUNCION (1919–)

Galerstein, pp. 272–73.

ROCA FRANQUESA, JOSE MARIA (1915–1983)

Ruiz de la Peña Solar, Alvario. "Bio-bibliografía del profesor D. José María Roca Franquesa," *Archivium* (Oviedo), 33 (1983), 7–12. Contents: I. Datos biográficos. II. Estudios de literatura española (By year, 1944–1980). III. Estudios de literatura asturiana (By year, 1949–1980). IV. Escritos sobre la vida y la obra del Profesor Roca Franquesa.

RODOREDA, MERCE (1909–1983)

Galerstein, pp. 273–75.
Resnick, pp. 221–22.

RODRIGUEZ, CLAUDIO (1934–)

Correa, v. 2, pp. 425, 620–21. Works by and about the author.
Mayhew, Jonathan. *Claudio Rodríguez and the Language of Poetic Vision*. Cranbury, N.J.: Bucknell University Press, 1990. 158p. "Bibliography," pp. 153–56. Contents: I. Works by Claudio

Rodríguez. II. Works about Claudio Rodríguez and Other Works Cited in the Text.

Rodríguez, Claudio. *Antología poética*. Introducción y selección de Philip W. Silver. Madrid: Alianza Editorial, 1981. 141p. "Bibliografía asequible," pp. 21–22. Contents: I. Primeras ediciones (By year, 1953–1976). II. Estudios (criticism).

RODRIGUEZ ALVAREZ, ALEJANDRO. *See* CASONA, ALEJANDRO.

RODRIGUEZ BUDED, RICARDO (1926–)

Pérez-Stansfield, p. 347.

RODRIGUEZ CASTELAO, ALFONSO (1886–1950)

Rodríguez Castelao, Alfonso. Cuatro obras (teatro, relatos, fantasia, macabra, ensayos). Edición de Jesús Alonso Montero. Tercera edición. Madrid: Cátedra, 1982. 181p. (Letras Hispánicas, 1). "Bibliografía de Rodríguez Castelao," pp. 33–36. Contents: I. Estudios (By year, 1915–50). II. Narrativa (By year, 1920–67). III. Teatro. IV. Volumenes de dibujos con textos al pie (By year, 1930–62). V. Antologías. VI. Traducciones. "Bibliografía sobre su obra," pp. 36–39. Contents: I. Trabajos generales (By year, 1932–71). II. El escritor (By year, 1956–70). III. Teatro (By year, 1959–70). IV. Arte. V. Otros aspectos (By year, 1952–70).

Schreiner, Kay-Michael. *Alfonso Rodríguez Castelao: Eine Untersuchung der erzählerischen Werkes unter dem Aspekt von Literatur und Politik*. Frankfurt am Main: Peter Lang, 1980. 192p. "Literaturverzeichnis," pp. 184–92. Contents: I. Werke Alfonso Rodríguez Castelao's. A. Die Erzählungen. B. Die Schriften zur Politik und Kunst. II. Sekundärliteratur. III. Sammelbände (Homenajes).

RODRIGUEZ MENDEZ, JOSE MARIA (n.d.)

Martín Recuerda, José. *La tragedia de España en la obra dramática de José María Rodríguez Méndez (desde la restauración hasta la dictadura de Franco*. Salamanca: Ediciones Universidad de Salamanca, 1979. 227p. "Bibliografía," pp. 225–27. Contents: I. Bibliografía del autor (1953–1978). II. Bibliografía sobre el autor.

Pérez-Stansfield, pp. 347–48.

Rodríguez Méndez, José María. *Los inocentes de la Moncloa*. Introducción, edición y notas de Martha Halsey. Salamanca: Almar, 1980. 107p. (Colección Almar Teatro, 6). "Bibliografía selecta," pp. 45–50. Contents: I. Obras de José María Rodríguez Méndez. A. Drama (By year, 1961–1979). B. Libros sobre teatro

(By year, 1972–1974). C. Artículos sobre teatro. D. Entrevistas y coloquios en que interviene Rodríguez Méndez. II. Estudios críticos sobre Rodríguez Méndez. III. Sobre *Los inocentes de la Moncloa*. IV. Estudios de José María Rodríguez Méndez.

RODRIGUEZ-MONINO, ANTONIO (1910–1970)
"Actualización de la bibliografía de don Antonio Rodríguez-Moñino (1955–1978)," *Cuadernos de Bibliófilia* (Valencia), No. 3 (1980), 49–56.

ROIG, MONTSERRAT (1946–)
Galerstein, pp. 275–77.
"Montserrat Roig: Selected Bibliography," *Catalan Writing*, No. 3 (October 1989), 41–43. Contents: I. Chronology. II. Fiction. III. Non Fiction. IV. Translations.

ROJAS, CARLOS (1928–)
En torno al hombre y a los monstruos: Ensayos críticos sobre la novelística de Carlos Rojas editados por Cecilia Castro Lee y C. Christopher Soufas, Jr. Potomac, Md: Scripta Humanistica, 1987. 183p. "Carlos Rojas: Bibliografía selecta," pp. 176–80. Contents: I. Novelas (primeras ediciones). II. Obras selectas. III. Obras críticas. IV. Novelas cortas. V. Ediciones críticas. VI. Prólogos. VII. Traducciones. VIII. Libros de textos. IX. Traducciones de las novelas de Carlos Rojas. X. Cuentos misceláneos. XI. Artículos sobre la literatura (Very selective listing). XII. Contribuciones a la prensa. "Bibliografía muy selecta de ensayos y estudios sobre Carlos Rojas," pp. 180–82.

ROLAN, FELICIANO (1907–1935).
Caimotto, Oreste. *Feliciano Rolán: Su obra poética*. Madrid: Editorial Mezquita, 1984. 358p. (Serie Ensayo Literario, 33). "Obras de Feliciano Rolán," pp. ix–xxiii. Contents: I. Obras publicadas. A. *Huellas*. B. *De Mar a Mar*. C. *Tierra*. D. *Apios*. II. Obras inéditos. III. Ensayos y homenajes a Feliciano Rolán. Includes manuscript citations. "Bibliografía sobre Feliciano Rolán," pp. 355–58. Contents: I. Ediciones de obras de Feliciano Rolán. II. Estudios, homenajes, conferencias, artículos. "De los escritos de Feliciano Rolán (en orden alfabético)," (unpaged).

ROLDAN, MARIANO (1932–)
"Mariano Roldán," in Julia Elizabeth Cabey Riley's *Bibliografía de algunos poetas andaluces de posguerra* (Madrid: Universidad Complutense, Departamento de Bibliografía, 1984).

ROMERO, CONCHA (1945-)
"Concha Romero," *O'Connor*, pp. 171–72.

ROMERO, LUIS (1916–)
González-del-Valle, Luis, and Bradley A. Shaw. *Luis Romero*. Boston: Twayne Publishers, Inc., 1979. 151p. "Selected Bibliography," pp. 131–35. Contents: I. Primary Sources (in chronological order and by genres). A. Novels. B. Short Stories. C. Historical Works. D. Other Creative Works. E. Travel Books. F. Essays and Lectures. II. Secondary Sources (criticism).

ROMERO ESTEO, MIGUEL (1930–)
"Miguel Romero Esteo," pp. 77–82 in L. Teresa Valdivieso's *España: Bibliografía de un teatro "silenciado"* (Lincoln, Neb.: Society of Spanish and Spanish-American Studies, 1979). Contents: I. Notas biográficas. II. Obras inéditas. III. Obras publicadas. IV. Traducciones. V. Escritos y declaraciones. VI. Estudios críticos.
Pérez-Stansfield, p. 348.

ROMERO SERRANO, MARINA (1908–)
Galerstein, pp. 277–79.

ROMO ARREGUI, JOSEFINA (1913–)
Galerstein, pp. 279–80.

ROS, SAMUEL (1904–1945)
Fraile, Medardo. *Samuel Ros (1904–1945): Hacia una generacion sin crítica*. Madrid: Editorial Prensa Española, 1972. 230p. "Obra consultada de Samuel Ros," pp. 177–88. Ros' works are listed by year, 1923–1962, but there are many incomplete bibliographical entries. "Sin firma," pp. 189–92. "Obra consultada sobre Samuel Ros," pp. 192–97.

ROSALES, LUIS (1910–)
"Bibliografía de y sobre Luis Rosales," *Anthropos (Barcelona), No. 25 (1983), 26–32.*
Correa, v. 2, pp. 81, 608. Contents I. Libros. II. Artículos y estudios (criticism).
Porlán, Alberto. "Bibliografía de Luis Rosales," *Cuadernos Hispanoamericanos*, Nos. 257/258 (mayo/junio de 1972), 694–702. Contents: I. Obra de Luis Rosales (por orden cronológico). A. Libros: poesía, ensayos, teatro, traduccionies. B. Textos de

creación aparecidos en publicaciones diversas. II. Textos sobre Luis Rosales (por orden alfabético de autores).

Rosales, Luis. *Antología poética*. Preámbulo y selección de Alberto Porlán. Madrid: Alianza Editorial, 1984. 212p. (el Libro de Bolsillo, 1032). "Bibliografía básica de Luis Rosales," pp. 18–19. Contents: I. Poesía (By year, 1935–83). II. Ensayos (By year, 1947–78). Books only.

Sánchez Zamarreño, Antonio. *La poesía de Luis Rosales (1935–1980)*. Salamanca: Ediciones Universidad de Salamanca, 1985. 399p. (Acta Salmanticensia, Filosofía y Letras, 187). "Bibliografía," pp. 375–83. Contents: I. Corpus poético fundamental (By year, 1935–1984). II. Varia (By year, 1934–1985). III. Bibliografía sobre Luis Rosales.

RUBIA BARCIA, JOSE (1914–)

"Selected Bibliography of Works by José Rubia Barcia," pp. 11–12 in *Studies in Honor of José Rubia Barcia* (Lincoln, Neb.: Society of Spanish and Spanish-American Studies, 1982). Contents: I. Books (By year, 1940–1978). II. Essays (By year, 1940–1980).

RUBIO Y LOPEZ GUIJARRO, MARIA DEL CARMEN (1915–)

Galerstein, pp. 281–82.

RUEDA, SALVADOR (1887–1933)

Espejo-Saavedra, Rafael. *Nuevo acercamiento a la poesía de Salvador Rueda*. Sevilla: Servicio de Publicaciones de la Universidad de Sevilla, 1986. 171p. (Serie: Filosofía y Letras, 91). "Bibliografía," pp. 163–67. Contents: I. Obras de Salvador Rueda. II. Estudios sobre Salvador Rueda. The bibliography includes very few entries published after 1976, the year the author completed his dissertation.

Romo Arregui, Josefina. "Salvador Rueda: Bibliografía," *Cuadernos de Literatura Contemporánea*, No. 7 (1943), 84–88. Contents: I. Ediciones. A. Poesías. B. Novelas. C. Otras obras. D. Prólogos. II. Estudios.

RUIBAL, JOSE (1925–)

"José Ruibal," pp. 190–91 in Hilde F. Cramsie's *Teatro y censura en la España franquista: Sastre, Muñiz y Ruibal*. New York: Peter Lang, 1985. 205p. "Bibliografía," pp. 189–205. Contents: I. Obras dramáticas (By year, 1969–1975). II. Ensayos y declaraciones teóricas (By year, 1968–1977).

"José Ruibal," pp. 83–91 in L. Teresa Valdivieso's *España: Bibliografía de un teatro "silenciado"* (Lincoln, Neb.: Society of Spanish and Spanish-Amrican Studies, 1979). Contents: I. Notas biográficas. II. Obras inéditas. III. Obras publicadas. IV. Traducciones. V. Escritos y declaraciones. VI. Estudios críticos.

Pérez-Stansfield, p. 348.

Phillips, Elda María. *Idea, signo y mito: El teatro de José Ruibal.* Madrid: Ediciones Orígenes, 1984. 139p. "Bibliografía," pp. 135–36. Contents: Fuentes primarias. A. Obras publicadas de José Ruibal. B. Obras inéditas de José Ruibal. C. Artículos publicados de José Ruibal. II. Fuentes secundarias: Artículos sobre el teatro de José Ruibal.

RUIZ IRIARTE, VICTOR (1912–1982)

Boring, Phyllis Zatlin. *Víctor Ruiz Iriarte.* Boston: Twayne Publishers, Inc., 1980. 151p. "Selected Bibliography," pp. 140–45. Contents: I. Primary Sources (Plays are listed chronologically, 1943–1975). II. Other Published Dramatic Works. III. Selected Essays. IV. Secondary Sources (criticism; annotated entries).

García Ruiz, Víctor. *Víctor Ruiz Iriarte: Autor dramático.* Madrid: Editorial Fundamentos, 1987. 300p. "Bibliografía de Víctor Ruiz Iriarte," pp. 49–119. Contents: I. Bibliografía primaria. A. Obras dramáticas. 1. Estrenadas (By work in chronological order, 1943–75). 2. No estrenadas. 3. Adaptaciones y versiones. a. Estrenadas (By year, 1955–73). b. No estrenadas. 4. Colaboraciones. a. Estrenadas (By year, 1959–63). b. No estrenadas. 5. Proyectos de obras sin terminar. 6. Colectaneas. B. Obras para televisión. 1. Series originales. 2. Adaptaciones para TV de obras dramáticas de otros autores. 3. Adaptaciones a TV de obras dramáticas de Ruiz Iriarte. 4. Ediciones de obras para televisión. C. Guiones de cine. D. Artículos en publicaciones periódicas. 1. Artículos literarias. a. Autobiográfico. b. Sobre temas teatrales. c. Géneros dramáticos. d. Crítica teatral. e. De circunstancias. f. Sobre figuras del teatro y literarias. g. Temas artísticos diversos. 2. Artículos costumbristas y de circunstancias. 3. Curso delineante. 4. Comentarista de los cambios sociales. 5. Sobre el progreso técnico. 6. Comentarios de actualidad. E. Prólogos. F. Conferencias y charlas. G. Entrevistas (selección). II. Bibliografía secundaria. A. Libros de conjunto sobre Ruiz Iriarte. B. Artículos sobre Ruiz Iriarte. C. Referencias dentro de obras no dedicadas exclusivamente a Ruiz Iriarte. D. Críticas a estrenos.

RUIZ PENA, JUAN (1915-)

"Juan Ruiz Peña," in Julia Elizabeth Cabey Riley's *Bibliografía de algunos poetas andaluces de posguerra* (Madrid: Universidad Complutense, Departamento de Bibliografía, 1984).

SAENZ-ALONSO, MERCEDES (1917-)

Galerstein, pp. 284–85.

SAGARRA, JOSEP MARIA DE (1894–1961)

Permanyer, Lluís. *Sagarra*. Barcelona: Edicions de Nou Art Thor, 1982? 32p. (*Gent Nostra*, v. 15, no. 4). "Bibliografía y cronología" pp. 26–29.

______. *Sagarra vist pels seus íntims*. Barcelona: Edhasa, 1982. 386p. "Bibliografia de Josep Maria de Sagarra," pp. 359–70. Includes works by title and by translation. "Bibliografia essencial," pp. 355–58. Includes works about Sagarra.

SAHAGUN, CARLOS (1938-)

Correa, v. 2, pp. 481, 622–23. Works by and about the author.

SALABERT, MIGUEL (1931-)

Salabert, Miguel. *El exilio interior*. Barcelona: Anthropos, 1988. 260p. (Memoria rota; Exilios y heterodoxias, 13). "Miguel Salabert: bio-bibliografía," pp. 259–60.

SALAVERRIA, JOSE MARIA (1873–1940)

Caudet Roca, Francisco. *Vida y obra de José Marí Salaverría*. Madrid: C.S.I.C., Instituto "Miguel de Cervantes" de Filología Hispánica, 1972. 229p. (*Anejos de Revista de Literatura*, 33). "Apéndice bibliográfico," pp. 185–224. Contents: I. Contribución a la bibliografía de artículos de José María Salaverría. A. *El Gráfico*, Madrid (1904). B. *España Nueva* (Madrid 1906). C. *El Imparcial*, Madrid (1906). D. *ABC*, Madrid (by year, 1907–40). E. *La Vanguardia*, Barcelona (1914–36). F. *El Público vasco*, Bilbao (1926–36). G. *España* (1939). *El Heraldo de Aragón* (1938). H. *ABC* (Sevilla, 1937–39). I. *La Nación* (Buenos Aires, 1939–40). J. *El Diario de la Marina*, Habana (1921–23). II. Indice de obras. III. Bibliografía (Includes criticism, biographies, and general literary studies).

Petriz Ramos, Beatrice. *Introducción crítico-biografíca a José María Salaverría* (1873–1940). Madrid: Editorial Gredos, 1960. 353p. "Bibliografías," pp. 311–53. Contents: I. Bibliografía de las obras publicadas de José Salaverría de las obras publicadas de José Salaverría. II. Bibliografía de los artículos periodísticos de Salaverría en *ABC* de Madrid (by year, 1906–40). III. Fuentes inéditas. IV. Bibliografía general.

SALINAS, PEDRO (1891–1951)

Arce, M., and Sidonia C. Rosenbaum. "Pedro Salinas: Bibliografía," *Revista Hispánica Moderna*, 7, No. 1/2 (enero/abril de 1941), 69–73. Contents: I. Ediciones. A. Poesía. B. Novela. C. Crítica. D. Ediciones. E. Traducciones. II. Estudios (General and by work).

Becco, Horacio Jorge. "Acercamiento bio-bibliográfico a la obra de Pedro Salinas," *Buenos Aires Literaria*, 2 (1953), 115–142. Contents: I. Ediciones. A. Poesía. B. Prosa. 1. Ensayos y estudios literarios. 2. Teatro. 3. Ediciones. 4. Traducciones. 5. Prólogos. II. Traducciones. III. Discografía. IV. Estudios sobre Salinas. V. Estudios sobre cada obra. VI. Antologías. VII. Poemas dedicados.

Brehm Carstensen, Luis Fernando Carlos. "Pedro Salinas: La búsqueda del lenguaje." Unpublished Ph.D. dissertation, Cornell University, 1975. 259p. "Bibliografía," pp. 243–52. Contents: I. Primeras ediciones de las poesías de Pedro Salinas. II. Crítica sobre la obra poética de Pedro Salinas. III. Números de homenaje.

Correa, v. 1, pp. 278, 538–41. Works by and about the author.

Debicki, Andrew P., comp. *Pedro Salinas*. Madrid: Taurus Ediciones, 1976. 275p. "Bibliografía selecta," pp. 269–75. Contents: I. Obras de Pedro Salinas. A. Libros de poesía. B. Prosa narrativa y teatro. C. Crítica y ensayo. II. Obras acerca de Salinas. A. Artículos y capítulos de libros. B. Estudios de la época. C. Biografía y bibliografía. D. Libros de crítica dedicados a Salinas.

González Muela, pp. 75–78. Works by and about Salinas are arranged chronologically.

Helman, Edith F. "Pedro Salinas: A Tentative Bibliography," *Hispania*, 35 (May 1952), 156–58. Updates the Arce and Rosenbaum bibliography. Contents: I. Books. A. Poetry. B. Fiction. C. Essays and Literary Studies. II. Uncollected Essays and Articles. III. Criticism and Reviews of His Works. A. Poetry and Prose in General. B. Individual Works.

Newman, Jean Cross. *Pedro Salinas and His Circumstance*. San Juan, P.R.: Interamerican University Press, 1983. 274p. "Bibliography," pp. 243–51. Contents: I. Works by Salinas. A. Poetry (1923–1975). B. Prose Narrative, Drama (1926–1957). C. Critical Works, Essays (1940–1961). II. Bibliography on Salinas. III. Critical Studies on Salinas. IV. Collected Articles on Salinas. V. Homage Issues of Journals. VI. Critical Editions by Salinas. VII.

Translations by Salinas. VIII. Translations into English of Salinas (Complete Volumes Only). IX. Salinas Translated in Anthologies of Poetry, Including Other Poets. X. Articles on Salinas.

Palley, Julián. *La luz no usada: La poesía de Pedro Salinas*. México: Ediciones De Andrea, 1966. 115p. "Bibliografía" pp. 105–13. Contents: I. Obras de Pedro Salinas. A. Poesía. B. Ensayo y crítica (No están incluidas los artículos aparecidos en revistas). C. Teatro. D. Ficción. E. Ediciones. F. Traducciones hechas por Salinas. II. Traducciones de obras de Salinas. III. Estudios sobre Pedro Salinas. IV. Biografía y bibliografía.

Pane, Remigio U. "A Bibliography of Salinas' Works in English Translation," *Hispania*, 35 (May 1952), 159–60. Contents: I. Anthologies. II. Individual Poems. III. Miscellaneous.

Salinas, Pedro. *Aventura poética (Antología)*. Edición de David L. Stixrude. Madrid: Ediciones Cátedra, 1980. 277p. "Bibliografía selecta," pp. 54–58. Contents: I. Libros de poesía de Pedro Salinas. II. Libros narrativos y dramáticos de Pedro Salinas. III. Obras críticas de Pedro Salinas. IV. Ediciones hechas por Pedro Salinas. V. Libros sobre el poesía de Pedro Salinas. VI. Artículos sobre la poesía de Pedro Salinas. VII. Estudios sobre la generación de 1927.

______. *Ensayos completos*. Edición preparada por Solita Salinas de Marichal. Madrid: Ediciones Taurus, 1983. 3 vs. "Cronología bibliográfica," v. 1, pp. 37–44. Eighty-two entries are arranged by year, 1924–1983.

Stixrude, David L. *The Early Poetry of Pedro Salinas*. Madrid: Editorial Castalia, 1975. 166p. "List of Works Cited," pp. 165–66. Contents: I. Works by Pedro Salinas. II. Studies Pertaining to Salinas.

Zubizarreta, Alma de. *Pedro Salinas: El diálogo creador*. Prólogo de Jorge Guillén. Madrid: Editorial Gredos, 1969. 423p. (Biblioteca Románica Hispánica, 2. Estudios y ensayos, 128). "Bibliografía," pp. 369–404. Contents: I. Obras de Pedro Salinas. A. Obras poéticas. B. Obras poéticas traducidas. C. Obras narrativas. D. Traducciones de obras narrativas. E. Obras dramáticas. F. Obras dramáticas traducidas. G. Sátiras (inéditas). H. Ensayo y crítica literaria. I. Prólogos. J. Traducciones. K. Epistolario. L. Discografía. M. Obras poéticas recogidas en antologías. II. Bibliografía sobre la obra poética. A. Crítica sobre la obra poética y crítica general. B. Crítica sobre la obra narrativa. C. Crítica sobre la obra dramática. D. Crítica sobre la obra de ensayo y crítica literaria. E. Sobre ediciones críticas. F. Sobre obras traducidas. G. Números de homenaje. H. Bibliografías. I. Biografías. J. Poemas dedicados a Salinas.

SALISACHS, MERCEDES (1916–)
Galerstein, pp. 286–88.
Resnick, p. 222.

SALOM, JAIME (1925–)
Marquerie, Alfredo. *Ensayo crítico del teatro de Jaime Salom*. Madrid: Editorial Escelicer, S.A., 1973. 320p. "Obras editas," pp. 315–16. "Fichas de estreno y repartos," pp. 316–20.
Salom, Jaime. *La piel del limón*. Introducción y notas de Phyllis Zatlin Boring. Salamanca: Almar, 1980. 99p. (Colección Almar-Teatro, v. 3). "Bibliografía," pp. 25–27. Contents: I. Ediciones. II. Obra en catalán. III. Estudios (criticism). "Tabla cronológica (unpaged)." Contents: I. Año. II. Vida y obra de Salom. III. Acontecimientos culturales. IV. Acontecimientos históricos.
Zatlin-Boring, Phyllis. *Jaime Salom*. Boston: Twayne, 1982. 163p. "Selected Bibliography," pp. 155–58. Contents: I. Primary Sources. A. Original Plays (In order of performance). B. Adaptations. C. Collections of Plays by Salom. D. Other Editions. II. Secondary Sources (Annotated criticism entries).

SALVA, MARIA ANTONIO (1869–1957)
Galerstein, pp. 288–90.

SALVAT-PAPASSEIT, JOAN (1894–1924)
A biobibliography of the author, including translations, appears in David Herschel Rosenthal's "Modern Catalan Poetry: A Critical Introduction with Translations" (Unpublished doctoral dissertation, City University of New York, 1977).
Salvat-Papasseit, Joan. *El poema de la rosa als llavis*. A cura de Joaquim Molas. 2. ed. Barcelona: Ariel, 1982. 96p. "Cronología (1894–1925)," pp. lv–lxxvii. Bio-bibliographical information included.
______. *Poesies completes*. Edició a cura de Joaquim Molas. Barcelona: Editorial Ariel, 1983. 270p. (Clàssics Catalans Ariel, 2). "Bibliografia," pp. lxxix–xcii. Contents: I. Bibliografies. II. Obres de Joan Salvat-Papasseit. A. Poesies completes. B. Obres soltes de poesia. C. Antologies i traduccions. D. Obras en prosa. E. Revistes. F. Montatges teatrals. G. Discografia. II. Assaigs i notes sobre Joan Salvat-Papasseit.

SANCHEZ, ALBERTO (1915–)
García Lorenzo, Luciano. "Biobibliografía de Alberto Sánchez," *Anales Cervantinos*, 25/26 (1987/88), 9–18. Contents: I. Biografía. II. Bibliografía. A. Trabajos de crítica literaria. 1. Sobre

Cervantes. 2. Sobre Lope de Vega. 3. Sobre Quevedo. 4. Sobre Góngora. 5. Sobre M. Menéndez Pelayo. 6. Sobre Blasco Ibáñez. 7. Sobre Antonio Machado. 8. Sobre Ramón Gómez de la Serna. 9. Sobre Ramón de Garciasol. B. Otros trabajos.

SANCHEZ-CUTILLAS I MARTINEZ, CARMELINA (1927–)
Galerstein, p. 291.

SANCHEZ ESCRIBANO, FEDERICO (1898–1969)
Porqueras-Mayo, Alberto. "Bibliografía de Federico Sánchez Escribano," *Revista de Filología Española*, 53 (1970, i.e., 1972), 310–16. 117 items. Contents: I. Libros. A. Investigación. B. Ediciones. C. Poesías. II. Artículos. III. Poemas sueltas. IV. Reseñas.

SANCHEZ ESPESO, GERMAN (1940–)
"Germán Sánchez Espeso: Bibliografía," pp. 323–25 in José Luis Martín Nogales' *Cincuenta años de novela española (1936–1986): Escritores navarros* (Barcelona: PPU, 1989). Contents: I. Novelas. II. Cuentos. III. Artículos, entrevistas y reseñas.

SANCHEZ FERLOSIO, RAFAEL (1927–)
Hernando Cuadrado, Luis Alberto. *El español coloquial en "El Jarama."* Madrid: Playor, 1988. 154p. "Bibiografía," pp. 135–52. Includes critical studies about Sánchez Ferlosio and *El Jarama*.
Villanueva, Darío. *El "Jarama" de Sánchez Ferlosio*. Santiago de Compostela: Universidad de Santiago de Compostela, 1973. 167p. (Monografías de la Universidad de Santiago de Compostela, 25). "Apéndice bibliográfico," pp. 154–64. Contents: I. La obra de Rafael Sánchez Ferlosio. A. Narrativa. B. Artículos. C. Prólogos y versiones. D. Inéditos. E. Traducciones de sus novelas. II. Artículos sobre la obra de Rafael Sánchez Ferlosio. A. Sobre *Industrias y andanzas de Alfanhuí*. B. Sobre *El jarama*. C. Varios. III. Bibliografía general. A. Ensayos. B. Artículos. C. Varios. IV. Adición.

SANCHEZ MEJIAS, IGNACIO (1891–1934)
Sánchez Mejías, Ignacio. *Teatro. Edición, prólogo y bibliografía de Antonio Gallego Morrell*. Madrid: Ediciones del Centro, 1976. 139p. "Bibliografía," pp. 35–39. Contents: I. El torero y el hombre (Criticism and biographical sketches). II. El autor teatral (Criticism and biographical sketches). III. Poemas en su honor. IV. Iconografía.

SANCHEZ-OSTIZ, MIGUEL (1950-)

"Miguel Sánchez-Ostiz: Bibliografía," pp. 325–27 in José Luis Martín Nogales' *Cincuenta años de novela española (1936–1986): Escritores navarros* (Barcelona: PPU, 1989). Contents: I. Poesía. II. Novelas. III. Artículos y diario. IV. Otros textos. V. Artículos, entrevistas y reseñas.

SANCHIS GUARNER, MANUEL (1911–1981)

Llopis Bauset, Frederic V. "Bibliografia de Manuel Sanchis Guarner," v. 1., pp. xv-xviii in *Estudis en memória del professor Manuel Sanchis Guarner: Estudis de llengua i literatura catalanes* (València: Universitat de València, 1984). Contents: I. Llibres i opuscles. II. Introduccions. Pròlegs i edicions de textos. III. Extrets o capítols de revistes, congressos, miscellànies, etc. All 116 entries are listed chronologically under each section.

SANTIAGO, ELENA (n.d.)

"Elena Santiago: Bibliografía," *Alonso*, p. 287. Contents: I. Narrativa (By year, 1977–1985). II. Biografía. III. Poesía. Books only.

SASTRE, ALFONSO (1926-)

"Alfonso Sastre," pp. 191–93 in Hilde F. Cramsie's *Teatro y censura en la España franquista: Sastre, Muñiz y Ruibal*. New York: Peter Lang, 1985. 205p. Contents: I. Obras dramáticas (By year, 1949–1979). II. Obras teóricas y ensayos (By year, 1951–1978).

Anderson, Farris. *Alfonso Sastre*. New York: Twayne Publishers, Inc., 1971. 164p. "Selected Bibliography," pp. 159–61. Contents: I. Primary Sources: Major Works of Alfonso Sastre. II. Secondary Sources.

_____. "The Dialectics of Alfonso Sastre." Unpublished Ph.D. dissertation, University of Wisconsin, 1968. 337p. Work includes an extensive bibliography: 132 essays and articles by Sastre, 73 studies and articles about Sastre, and 48 reviews of Sastre's plays.

Bryan, T. Avril. *Censorship and Social Conflict in the Spanish Theatre: The Case of Alfonso Sastre*. Washington, D.C.: University Press of America, 1982. 145p. "Bibliography," pp. 133–42. Contents: I. Primary Sources. A. Plays by Alfonso Sastre. B. Books and Articles by Alfonso Sastre (1956–1974). II. Secondary Sources (criticism).

Etudes Ibériques XII: Théatre en Espagne II-Alfonso Sastre. Rennes: Centro d'Etudes Hispaniques, Hispano-Américaines et Luso-Brésiliennes, 1977. 80p. "Bibliografía," pp. 73–80. Contents: I. Obras de Alfonso Sastre. A. Teatro (by year, 1948–1976).

B. Narrativa. C. Ensayo. D. Poesía. II. Obras de referencia (bibliografía escogida).

Forys, Marsha. *Antonio Buero Vallejo and Alfonso Sastre: An Annotated Bibliography*. Metuchen, N.J.: Scarecrow Press, 1988. 209p. The entries for Sastre number 453 and cover pages 151–95 of this bibliography. The bibliography is divided into: Books, theses, and dissertations; Journals, magazines, and newspapers; and Unverified citations (those that the compiler was unable to check personally). Only criticism is included. Coverage is through 1986. Descriptive annotations are included only when the main idea is not readily apparent from the title of the work.

Ruggeri Marchetti, Magda. *Il teatro di Alfonso Sastre*. Roma: Bulzoni Editore, 1975. 330p. "Bibliografia," pp. 273–303. Contents: I. Teatro. A. Raccolte. B. Drammi singoli (By year, 1948–1973). C. Traduzioni. II. Narrativa. III. Poesia (by year, 1965–1973). IV. Prose critiche e polemiche (By year, 1946–1973). V. Opere inedite. VI. Critica.

Sastre, Alfonso. *La taberna fantástica*. Edited by Mariano de Paco. Madrid: Taurus, 1986. 162p. "Bibliografía," pp. 33–44. Contents: I. De Alfonso Sastre. A. Obras dramáticas (By year, 1946–1985). B. Versiones estrenadas (By year, 1958–1972). C. Libros de narrativa. D. Libros de ensayo y opinión. II. Sobre Alfonso Sastre: Libros dedicados a Sastre y al teatro español de posguerra (selected).

Seator, Lynette Hubbard. "A Study of the Plays of Alfonso Sastre: Man's Struggle for Identity in a Hostile World." Unpublished Ph.D. dissertation, University of Illinois, 1972. 283p. "Bibliography," pp. 271–80. Contents: I. Primary Sources. A. Plays by Alfonso Sastre. B. Books and Articles by Alfonso Sastre. II. Secondary Sources. "Appendix," pp. 281–282, contains a list of "The Plays of Alfonso Sastre with the Dates of Their Completion and their Performances in Spain."

SEDANO, DORA (1912–)

Galerstein, pp. 294–95.

"Dora Sedano," *O'Connor*, pp. 172–73.

SEGOVIA, TOMAS (1927–)

Correa, v. 2, p. 401. Works by the author.

SENDER, RAMON (1901–1982)

Alvarez, Elsa Delia. "La obra de Ramón Sender (estudios de los personajes femeninos)." Unpublished Ph.D. dissertation, Michigan State University, 1971. 342p. "Bibliografía," pp. 297–325.

Contents: I. Obras de Sender. A. Novelas. B. Poesía, cuentos, teatro. C. Ensayos. D. Artículos en revistas. II. Bibliografía sobre Sender. III. Otras obras consultadas. "Apéndice: recopilación de artículos de Sender y sobre Sender publicados en revistas y periódicos españoles hasta 1936," pp. 326–42. Contents: I. Artículos o reseñas de Ramón Sender en *el Sol*. II. Artículos de *La Libertad* firmados todos ellos por Ramón J. Sender. III. Artículos de R. J. Sender en *Levitán*. IV. Artículos sobre Sender publicados en *La Libertad*. V. Artículos sobre Sender publicado en *Leviatán*.

Carrasquer, Francisco. *"Inmán" y la novela histórica de Sender*. London: Támesis Books, Ltd., 1970. 304p. (Colección Támesis. Serie A. Monografías, XVII). "Bibliografía," pp. 281–95. Contents: I. Obras de Sender (annotated contents of works). A. Novelas. B. Cuentos y novelas cortas. C. Teatro. II. Obras sobre Sender o en las que se habla de Sender (annotated). III. Otras fuentes de este trabajo.

Collard, Patrick. *Ramón J. Sender en los años 1930–1936: sus ideas sobre la relación entre literatura y sociedad*. Gent: Rijksuniversiteit te Gent, 1980. 236p. "Bibliografía (obras citadas en este trabajo)," pp. 213–23. Contents: I. Narrativia, poesía, teatro (by year, 1919–1976). II. Ensayos, colecciones de artículos, recuerdos autobiográficos (libros, by year, 1928–1975). III. Artículos en periódicos y revistas (1927–1936, by journal and newspaper). IV. Libros artículos dedicados enteramente o en parte a Ramón J. Sender.

Espadas, Elizabeth. "Ensayo de una bibliografía de Ramón J. Sender," *Papeles de Son Armadans*, Año 19, tomo 74, No. 220 (julio de 1974), 90–104; No. 221/222 (agosto/septiembre de 1974), 232–62. Contents: I. Estudios sobre su obra en general (libros, artículos y tesis de orientación biografíca, panorámica, temática y bibliográfica). II. Estudios sobre obras individuales: Novelas, cuentos, teatro, ensayos, poesía, colecciones de artículos.

_____. _____: "Addendum," *Papeles de Son Armadans*, Año 20, tomo 78, Nos. 233/234 (agosto/septiembre de 1975), 247–59. Same format as original article.

_____. "Bibliografía," pp. 121–77 in Francisco Carrasquer's *La verdad de Ramón J. Sender con bibliografía de Elizabeth Espadas* (Leiden: Ediciones CINCA, 1982). Contents: I. Obras de Sender. A. Novelas (By year, 1933–1980). B. Cuentos y novelas cortas (By year, 1940–1972). C. Teatro (By year, 1935, 1968). D. Ensayos (By year, 1925–1978). E. Poesía (By year, 1960–1974). F. Colecciones de artículos. II. Hacia una bibliografía sobre la obra de Ramón J. Sender. A. Estudios sobre su obra en general (libros, artículos y tesis de orientación biográfica, panorámica, temática y bibliográfica). Some critical and content annotations and reviews are included. B. Estudios sobre obras individuales. 1. Novelas (By work, arranged chronologically; includes some reviews). 2. Cuentos (arranged chronologically). 3. Teatro. 4. Ensayos. 5. Poesía. 6. Colecciones de artículos.

_____. "La vision crítica de la obra de Ramón J. Sender: ensayo bibliográfico," pp. 227–87 in *Homenaje a Ramón J. Sender* (Newark, Del.: Juan de la Cuesta, 1987). Contents: I. Estudios sobre su obra en general. A. Estudios bibliográficos. B. Estudios biográfios, entrevistas y personalia. C. Libros, artículos y tesis de orientación temática o panorámica. II. Estudios sobre obras individuales. A. Novelas. B. Cuentos. C. Teatro. D. Ensayos. E. Poesía. F. Colecciones de artículos; miscelánea.

King, Charles L. *Ramón J. Sender: An Annotated Bibliography, 1928–1974*. Metuchen, N.J.: Scarecrow Press, 1976. 287p. Includes 1,357 briefly annotated entries. Only English and Spanish language citings are included. By far, the most important bibliography published to date of works by and about Sender. Contents: I. Works by Sender. A. Books. 1. Novels. 2. Short Stories. 3. Drama. 4. Essays, Journalism and Personal Narrative. 5. Poetry. 6. Anthology. B. Pamphlets and other Short Separate Publications. 1. Drama. 2. Journalistic Essays. C. Contributions in Books. 1. Fiction. 2. Drama. 3. Articles. 4. Prologues. D. Contributions in Periodicals. 1. Fiction. 2. Drama. 3. Poetry. 4. Articles in *La Libertad*. 5. Articles in Periodicals other than *La Libertad* and Not as Syndicated Column, "Los Libros y los días." 6. Syndicated Column, "Los Libros y los días." (Over 667 entries). II. Works about Sender (Including reviews about them). A. Books. B. Special Issue of a Journal. C. Contributions in Books. D. Contributions in Periodicals. 1. Bibliographies. 2. Critical Articles, Essays and Abstracts. 3. News Articles. E. Theses. 1. Licentiate. 2. Master's. 3. Doctor's. This work up-dates the author's "Una bibliografía senderiana española (1928–1967)," *Hispania*, 50 (1967), 629–45 and "A Senderian Bibliography in English, 1950–1968, With an Addendum," *The American Book Collector*, 20, No. 6 (March/April 1970), 23–29.

_____. "A Partial Addendum (1975–82) to *Ramón J. Sender: An Annotated Bibliography (1928–1974)*," *Hispania*, 66 (May 1983), 209–16. The bibliography is limited to listing reprints or *ediciones nuevas* as well as new works of Sender. Contents: I. Reprints or *Ediciones Nuevas*. A. Novels (reviews are included). B. Short Stories (reviews included). C. Drama (reviews included).

D. Essays, Journalism and Personal Narrative (reviews included). E. Poetry. II. New Books, 1975–1982. A. Novels and Short Novels (synopses and reviews included). B. Essays, Journalism, and Personal Narrative (synopses and reviews included). There are 59 total entries.

_____. "Sender's Column: Los libros y los días, 1975–1982: An Annotated Bibliography," pp. 201–25 in *Homenaje a Ramón J. Sender* (Newark, Del.: Juan de la Cuesta, 1987). The annotated 140 enries are arranged by year, 1975–1982. The topic and content of the column are included.

Ruiz Gallego-Largo, Jesús. "Artículos de R. J. Sender en el diario *Solidaridad Obrera*," *Cuadernos de Historia Moderna y Contempóraneo* (Madrid), 6 (1985), 281–312.

Sender, Ramón José. *Mister Witt en el cantón*. Edición, introducción y notas de José María Jover. Madrid: Castalia, 1987. (Clásicos Castalia, 148). "Bibliografía selecta," pp. 141–46. Contents: I. Repertorios bibliográficos. II. Sobre la posición de Sender en la literatura española. III. Obras fundamentales sobre el primer Sender. IV. Sobre el horizonte histórico del primer Sender (By year, 1928–1939). V. Bibliografía relativa a *Mister Witt en el Cantón*. A. Trayectoría literatura del tema cantonal. B. El tema cantonal en la historiografía. C. Referencias críticas a *Mister Witt en el Cantón*.

Trippet, Anthony M. *Adjusting to Reality: Philosophical and Psychological Ideas in the Post Civil War Novels of Ramón J. Sender*. London: Támesis Books, 1986. 185p. (Colección Támesis, Serie A., Monografías, CXXII). "List of Works Cited," pp. 179–83. Contents: I. Works by Sender. A. Novels (By year, 1930–1984). B. Stories in Collections (By year, 1960–1970). C. Theatre. D. Poetry. E. Non Fiction (By year, 1928–1982). II. Works on Sender. A. Bibliographies. B. Completed Books. (By year, 1967–1982). C. Articles, Chapters or References in Books (By year, 1962–1983). D. Articles and Reviews Appearing in Journals (By year, 1963–1984). E. Theses (By year, 1960–1976).

Vieches de Frutos, María. "Bibliografía crítica sobre el primer Sender," pp. 121–42 in *Censo de Escritores al Servicio de los Austrias y otros estudios bibliográficos* (Madrid: C.S.I.C., 1983). The 157 entries cover 1928–1936. Includes annotations and reviews. Contents: I. Narrativa. Novelas (By year, 1930–1936). II. Ensayos (By year, 1928–1936). III. Prólogos y epílogos. IV. Cartas (By year, 1933–1936). V. Estudios sobre su vida y su obra. VI. Repertorios bibliográficos.

Weitzdörfer, Ewald. *Die historischen Romane Ramón José Sender: Untersuchungen zum Aufbau*. Frankfurt am Main: Peter Lang,

1983. 329p. "Bibliographie," pp. 323–29. Contents: I. Primärliteratur (works of Sender). II. Sekundärliteratur (includes criticism of Sender and his works).

SENNELL, JOLES (pseud. of Pep Albanell, 1945–)
"Joles Sennell: Selected Bibliography," *Catalan Writing*, No. 4 (March 1990), 56–58. Contents: I. Fiction. II. Works by Pep Albanell. III. Works by Joles Sennell. IV. Translations. V. Awards and Citations.

SEOANE, LUIS (1910–)
Sucarrat, Francine. *Luis Seoane: Su obra poética y su importancia en la literatura gallega actual.* Sada, La Coruña: Ediciones del Castro, 1977. 200p. "Bibliografía," pp. 199–200. Contents: I. Obra literaria de Luis Seoane. A. Narrativa. B. Teatro. C. Ensayo. D. Poesía. II. Estudios sobre su poesía, contenidos en libros.

SERIS, HOMERO (1879–1969)
Beardsley, Theodore S. "Publications of Homero Serís," *Hispanic Review*, 37 (October 1969), 555–65. Contents: I. Books and Pamphlets. II. Articles and Notes. III. Reviews (by year 1919–66). IV. Unpublished and Projected Works.
Morell, Antonio Gallego. "Necrología: Homero Serís (de la Torre)," *Revista de Filología Española*, 54 (1971/1972), 165–175. "Bibliografia," pp. 167–75. Entries arranged by year, 1906–68.

SERRAHIMA, NURIA (1937–)
Galerstein, pp. 295–96.

SERRANO PLAJA, ARTURO (1909–1979)
Homenaje a Serrano Plaja. Coordinado por José Luis L. Aranguren y Antonio Sánchez-Barbudo. Madrid: Ediciones Taurus, 1985. 228p. "Bibliografía," pp. 225–26. Contents: I. Poesía (By year, 1934–1982). II. Narrativa (By year, 1942–1977). III. Ensayo (By year, 1936–1978).

SEVILLA, ALBERTO (1877–1953)
Dendle, Brian J. "Bibliografía de la obra periódistica de Alberto Sevilla Pérez," *Murgetana* (Academia Alfonso X el Sabio, Murcia), 77 (1988), 5–31.

SIJE, RAMON (pseud. of José Marín Gutiérrez, 1913–1935)
Muñoz Garrigós, José. *Vida y obra de Ramon Sijé.* Murcia: Universidad de Murcia, Caja Rural Central de Orihuela, 1987. 738p.

"Bibliografía," pp. 173–78. Includes general critical works as well as specific critical studies on Sijé.

SIMO I MONLLOR, ISABEL-CLARA (1943–)
Galerstein, p. 298.

SIMON DIAZ, JOSE (1920–)
"Publicaciones de José Simón Díaz," pp. 5–23 in *Varia bibliographica: Homenaje a José Simón Díaz* (Kassel: Reichenberger, 1988). Publications are listed by year, 1944–1987.

SOLER, BARTOLOME (1894–1975)
Román Román, Antonio. *La novelística de Bartolomé Soler*. Madrid: Colección Rocana, 1976. 211p. "Bibliografía," pp. 199–211. Contents: I. Obra de Bartolomé Soler. A. Novelas (1927–1965). B. Viajes. C. Poesía. D. Ensayo. E. Teatro (1928–1941). F. Artículos en periódicos y revistas (1928–1966). II. Artículos sobre Bartolomé Soler (por orden cronológico de aparición). A. Artículos generales. B. Viaje por América. C. Notas necrológicas. III. Crítica de las novelas (by work).

SORIA ORTEGA, ANDRES (n.d.)
"Bibliografía del profesor Andrés Soria Ortega," v. 1, pp. xvii–xxvii in *Estudios románicos dedicados al Prof. Andrés Soria Ortega en el XXV aniversario de la Cátedra de Literaturas Románicas* (Granada: Universidad de Granada, Departamento de Filología Románica, 1985). Contents: I. Libros y artículos (By year, 1943–1984). II. Reseñas (By year, 1947–1965). III. Traducciones (By year, 1954–1983). Includes 157 entries.

SORIANO, ELENA (1917–)
Alarcón, p. 62.
Galerstein, pp. 304–05.

SUAREZ DEL OTERO, CONCHA (1908–)
Galerstein, pp. 305–07.

SUNOL, CELIA (1899–)
Galerstein, pp. 307–08.

SZEL, ELISABETH (1926–)
Galerstein, pp. 308–09.

TARRAGO PLEYAN, JOSE ALFONSO (1916–1983)
Hernández Palmés, Antonio. "Bio-bibliografía de Don José Alfonso Tarragó Pleyán (1916–1983)," *Ilerda*, 44 (1983), 15–32.

TEIXIDOR, EMILI (1933–)
"Emili Teixidor: Selected Bibliography," *Catalan Writing*, No. 4 (March 1990), 69–70. Contents: I. Fiction. II. Translations. III. Awards and Citations.

TORBADO, JESUS (1943–)
"Jesús Torbado: Bibliografía," *Alonso*, p. 325. Books are listed by year, 1966–1982.

TORRE, JOSEFINA DE LA (1910–)
Galerstein, pp. 313–14.

TORRE VIVERO, CARMEN DE LA (1931–)
Galerstein, p. 315.

TORRENTE BALLESTER, GONZALO (1910–)
Becerra, Carmen. "Bibliografía de y sobre Gonzalo Torrente Ballester," pp. 81–108 in *Gonzalo Torrente Ballester: Premio de Literatura en Lengua Castellana "Miguel de Cervantes"* (Barcelona: Anthropos, Ministerio de Cultura, 1987). Annotated entries are arranged chronologically under the following headings: I. Teatro. II. Novela. III. Relatos y cuentos. IV. Ensayo y crítica. V. Periodismo. VI. Varios. VII. Diarios de trabajo. VIII. Ediciones, antologías y traducciones. IX. Prólogos. X. Artículos (journals written for). XI. Bibliografía sobre Torrente Ballester. A. Libros. B. Artículos. C. Reseñas.
______. *Gonzalo Torrente Ballester*. Madrid: Ministerio de Cultura, 1982. 274p. "Bibliografía," pp. 265–74. Contents: I. Sobre Torrente Ballester. A. Textos generales. B. Artículos y reseñas. II. Obras de Gonzalo Torrente Ballester (all are arranged chronologically). A. Textos de teatro. B. Textos narrativos. C. Textos de crítico y ensayo. D. Antologías y traducciones. E. Periodismo.
Blackwell, Frieda Hilda. *The Game of Literature: Demythification and Parody in the Novels of Gonzalo Torrente Ballester*. Valencia: Ediciones Albatros Hispanófila, 1985. 164p. (No. 36). "Bibliography," pp. 162–64. Contents: I. Primary Sources. II. Secondary Sources.
Giménez González, Alicia. *Torrente Ballester en su mundo literario*. Salamanca: Ediciones de la Universidad de Salamanca, 1984. 254p. (Acta Salmanticensia, Filosofía y Letras, 151). "Bibliog-

rafía," pp. 247–52. Contents: I. Libros. II. Artículos. III. Obras del autor (arranged chronologically under each genre). A. Narrativa. B. Relatos. C. Teatro. D. Ensayo y crítica. E. Periodismo.

Pérez, Genaro J. *La novela como burla/juego: Siete experimentos novelescos de Gonzalo Torrente Ballester.* Valencia: Albatros/Hispanófila, 1989. 107p. "Bibliografía," pp. 99–107. Contents: I. Obras de Torrente Ballester (By year, 1938–1987). II. Bibliografía selecta sobre Torrente Ballester. A. Libros. B. Artículos sobre Torrente. C. Tesis doctorales sobre Torrente Ballester (U.S. and Canada only).

Pérez, Janet. *Gonzalo Torrente Ballester.* Boston: Twayne Publishers, Inc., 1984. 188p. "Selected Bibliography," pp. 178–83. Contents: I. Primary Sources. (By year, 1935–1983). II. Secondary Sources (annotated critical works).

_____, and Stephen Miller. *Critical Studies on Gonzalo Torrente Ballester.* Boulder, Colo.: Society of Spanish and Spanish-American Studies, 1989. 196p. "Chronological Bibliography of First and Collected Editions of Creative and Critical Works by Gonzalo Torrente Ballester," pp. 195–96.

TORRES, MARIUS (1910–1942)

Prats, Margarita. *Màrius Torres: L'home i el poeta.* Barcelona: Edicions del Mall, 1986. 188p. (Llibres del Mall, Sèrie Assaig, 9). "Bibliografía consultada," pp. 181–85. Includes works by and about Màrius Torres.

TOVAR, ANTONIO (1911–1985)

Büttner, Thomas Theodor. "Bibliografía de Antonio Tovar," pp. 9–38 in *Homenaje a Antonio Tovar ofrecido por sus discípulos, colegas y amigos* (Madrid: Editorial Gredos, 1972). Titles are listed by year, 1934–71. Also included are works in press and "actividades como editor; publicaciones literarias; humores y distinciones; carrera académica."

TRENOR PALAVICINO, LEOPOLDO (1870–1937)

Pérez de Castro, J. L. "Don Leopoldo Trenor Palavicino," *Boletín del Instituto de Estudios Asturianos,* No. 108 (enero/abril de 1983), 221–24. Includes a selected bibliography, which is listed chronologically, 1895–1939.

TRIGO, FELIPE (1865–1916)

Martínez San Martín, Angel. *La narrativa de Felipe Trigo.* Madrid: C.S.I.C., Instituto "Miguel de Cervantes" de Filología Hispánica, 1983. 252p. (Anejos de *Revista de Literatura,* 41). "Bibliografía," pp. 243–52. Contents: I. Obras de Felipe Trigo. A. Novelas. B. Novelas cortas. C. Cuentos. D. Obra varia. II. Trabajos sobre Felipe Trigo y obras generales.

TROITINO, CARMEN (1918–)
Galerstein, pp. 315–16.
"Carmen Troitino," *O'Connor*, p. 175.

TUSQUETS, ESTHER (1936–)
Galerstein, pp. 316–17.

UCEDA, JULIA (1925–)
Galerstein, pp. 319–20.
"Julia Uceda," in Julia Elizabeth Cabey Riley's *Bibliografía de algunos poetas andaluces de posguerra* (Madrid: Departamento de Bibliografía de la Universidad Complutense, 1984).

UCETA, ACACIA (1927–)
CILH, p. 266. Contents: I. Poesía. II. Narrativa.
Galerstein, pp. 320–21.

UNA, OCTAVIO (1945–)
CILH, p. 82. Contents: I. Poesía. II. Ensayo.

UNAMUNO, MIGUEL DE (1864–1936)
Amézaga, Elías. "Contribución a la bibliografía de D. Miguel de Unamuno," *Revista Internacional de Estudios Vascos* (Bilbao), 32 (1987), 450–73.
Bardi, Ubaldo. "Fortuna di don Miguel de Unamuno en Italia," *Cuadernos de la Cátedra Miguel de Unamuno* (Salamanca), 14/15, 1964/65), 97–102. Includes a bibliography of *Traduzioni, saggi, altri saggi,* and *articoli su reviste*.
Cangiotti, Gualtiero. *Miguel de Unamuno e la visione chisciottesca del Mondo*. Milano: Marzorati Editore, 1985. 225p. "Bibliografia essenziale," pp. 201–17. Contents: I. Opere di Unamuno. II. Traduzioni in lingua italiana di opere di Unamuno. III. Epistolario di Unamuno (1925–1984). IV. Sussidi bibliografici. V. Opere su Unamuno. A. Libri. B. Articoli, saggi. C. Articoli e saggi in Lingua Italiana.
Chaves, Julio César. *Unamuno y América*. Prólogo de Joaquín Ruiz Jiménez. Madrid: Ediciones Cultura Hispánica, 1964. 570p. "Bibliografía americana de Unamuno," pp. 527–59. Contents: I.

Bibliografías de bibliografías. II. Libros de Unamuno. III. Obras de Unamuno. IV. Artículos y trabajos sobre Unamuno.

Correa, v. 1, pp. 40–41, 506–10. Works by and about the author.

Earle, Peter G. *Unamuno and English Literature*. New York: Hispanic Institute in the United States, 1960. 160p. Contents: I. Studies Dealing with Aspects of the Relationship between Unamuno and English Literature (p. 145). II. Index of English Authors and Works Cited by Unamuno (pp. 150–160). A. Authors. B. Works.

Foster, David William. "Adiciones y suplemento a la bibliografía de Unamuno," *La Torre*, No. 48 (octubre/diciembre de 1964), 165–72. Supplements the Onís bibliography. Same format.

Franco, Andrés. *El teatro de Unamuno*. Madrid: Insula, 1971. 347p. "Bibliografía del teatro unamuniano," pp. 327–44. Contents: I. Ediciones (por orden de publicación). II. Traducciones a otras lenguas. III. Reseñas y estudios sobre cada obra (By work). IV. Otros estudios sobre el teatro de Unamuno.

García Blanco, Manuel. "Addenda a tesis sobre Miguel de Unamuno y sus obras leídas en las universidades norteamericanas hasta febrero de 1955," *Cuadernos de la Cátedra de Miguel de Unamuno* (Salamanca), 8 (1958), 64–73. Includes not only U.S. theses, completed and in preparation, but those also from Germany, Belgium, Brazil, France, Great Britain, Holland, Italy, Peru, and Spain.

______. "Crónica unamuniana, 1937/1947," *Cuadernos de la Cátedra Miguel de Unamuno* (Salamanca), 1 (1948), 103–26. Contents: I. El hombre. Noticias para sus biografías. II. La obra. Ediciones y estudios sobre ella.

______. ______, 1948/49, in 2 (1951), 133–48.

______. ______, 1950/51 in 3 (1952), 81–104.

______. ______, 1952/53 in 4 (1953), 85–105.

______. ______, 1953/54 in 5 (1954), 185–211.

______. ______, 1954/55 in 6 (1955), 77–95.

______. ______, 1955/56 in 7 (1956), 131–47.

______. ______, 1956/57 in 8 (1958), 79–105.

______. ______, 1957/58 in 9 (1959), 117–34.

______. ______, 1958/59 in 10 (1960), 101–28.

______. ______, 1959/60 in 11 (1961), 91–109.

______. ______, 1961/62 in 12 (1962), 81–104.

______. ______, 1962/63 in 13 (1963), 95–110.

______. ______, 1963/65 in 14/15 (1964/65), 179–223. The above *crónicas* usually contained the following subject categories: I. Aportaciones biográficas. II. Epistolario. III. Unamuno y. . . . IV. La poesía. V. Novela y ensayos. VI. La filosofía. VII. El teatro.

VIII. Lenguaje y estilo. IX. Ediciones. X. Traducciones. XI. Tesis universitarias. XII. Varia.

______. *Don Miguel de Unamuno y sus poesías (Estudio y antología de poemas inéditos o no incluidos en sus libros)*. Salamanca: Universidad de Salamanca, 1954. 453p. (Acta Salmanticensia. Filosofía y Letras, VIII). "Bibliografía," pp. 425–442. Contents: I. Estudios y trabajos sobre la poesía de Unamuno. II. Ediciones y antologías. III. Traducciones a otras lenguas.

______. "Versiones italianas de las obras de Unamuno," *Quaderni Iberoamericana*, 13 (1953), 269–73. Descriptive bibliography under the following headings: I. Ensayos. II. Novelas. III. Poesías. IV. Teatro. V. Addenda.

García Morejón, Julio. *Unamuno y Portugal*. Madrid: Ediciones Cultura Hispánica, 1964. 516p. "Epistolario de Unamuno," pp. 474–76; "Obras de Unamuno (libros o referencias sobre Portugal)," pp. 477–78; "Libros portugueses en la biblioteca de Unamuno," pp. 479–82; "Estudios sobre Unamuno y su obra," pp. 483–508; and "Trabajos sobre el tema Unamuno y Portugal," pp. 509–14.

González Martín, Vicente. "Difusión de la obra de Unamuno y eco de su personalidad en Italia," *Cuadernos de la Cátedra Miguel de Unamuno*, 25/26 (1978), 92–126. "Obras de Unamuno traducidas al italiano," pp. 106–10. Contents: I. Ensayos-artículos-cartas (By year, 1905–1956). II. Narrativa (By year, 1901–1961). III. Poesía (By year, 1908–1968). IV. Prosa (By year, 1922–1964).

Gossdenovich, Leticia Feldmann. "Un primer intento de bibliografía crítica de Miguel de Unamuno." Unpublished Ph.D. dissertation, University of California/Los Angeles, 1976. 368p. Contents: I. Unamuno's Works in Chronological Order (Novels, Essays, Theatre and Poetry). II. Collections and Selections. III. Letters. IV. Short Stories (By chronological order, 1886–1934). V. Articles in *La Nación* (A list of almost 300 articles arranged in chronological order). VI. Works on Miguel de Unamuno (Criticism, tributes, doctoral dissertations, bibliographies, biographies, iconographies, translations, etc.). Annotated evaluations of the works listed in VI. VII. Appendices: A. Index of Short Stories in Thematic Order. B. Index of *Cuadernos de la Cátedra de Unamuno*, Universidad de Salamanca, 1948–1973. C. Index of Authors in Thematic Order.

Gullón, Ricardo. *Autobiografías de Unamuno*. Madrid: Editorial Gredos, 1964. 389p. "Bibliografía," pp. 357–76. Contents: I. Obras de Unamuno. II. Cartas. III. Algunos escritos referentes a Unamuno o a sus obras.

Hernández Pelayo, H. *Bibliografía crítica de Miguel de Unamuno (1888–1975).* Madrid: Ediciones José Porrúa Turanzas, S.A., 1976. 336p. Includes 5,087 items. Because of bibliographical inconsistencies, the work must be used with caution. Contents: I. Bibliografía crítica de Miguel de Unamuno (Chronological-alphabetical arrangement by year, 1888–1975; and includes books, articles, reviews, doctoral dissertations, dedicated poems, and pamphlet material). II. Indice onomástico.

Ibáñez de García Blanco, Leo. "Bibliografía unamuniana," *Cuadernos de la Cátedra Miguel de Unamuno* (Salamanca), 18 (1968), 103–111.

_____. _____. 19 (1969), 105–07.

_____. _____. 20 (1970), 133–38.

_____. _____. 21 (1971), 165–71.

_____. _____. 22 (1972), 207–13.

_____. _____. 23 (1973), 247–52.

_____. _____. 24 (1976), 259–63.

_____. _____. 25/26 (1978), 191–96.

_____. _____. 27/28 (1983), 263–65.

The above series usually contains the following subject headings within each bibliography unit. I. Estudios. II. Tesinas. III. Conferencias. IV. Traducciones. V. Ediciones. VI. Epistolarios. VII. Prensa. VIII. Libros. IX. Recensiones.

Inventario de cartas, manuscritos, papeles, fotografías, cuadros, libros especiales, objetos y recuerdos íntimos de Don Miguel de Unamuno, propiedad de sus familiares que se encuentran depositados actualmente en el Museo Unamuno de la Universidad de Salamanca. Salamanca: Universidad de Salamanca, 1980. 224p.

Kourín, Zdenek." Unamuno y Checoslovaquia," *Cuadernos de la Cátedra Miguel de Unamuno (Salamanca)*, 14/15 (1964/65), 73–76. Article includes lists of Unamuno's works published in Czech and Slovakian, and articles published in these languages on Unamuno and his work.

Lafuente, María Avelina Cecilia. *Antropología filosófica de Miguel de Unamuno.* Sevilla: Publicaciones de la Universidad de Sevilla, 1983. 253p. (Serie: Filosofía y Letras, 70). "Bibliografía," pp. 219–52. Contents: I. La obra de Unamuno (obras completas). II. Estudios sobre Unamuno. A. Obras dedicadas a Unamuno. B. Obras que traten parcialmente de Unamuno. C. Artículos sobre Unamuno.

Larson, Everette E. *Miguel de Unamuno: A Bibliography.* Washington, D.C.: Library of Congress, Hispanic Division, 1986. 38p. (Hispanic Focus, 5). A selective bibliography of Unamuno holdings in the Library of Congress, including both works by and about Unamuno. Call numbers are included.

Lottini, Otello. *Unamuno linguista*. Roma: Cadmo Editore, 1984. 295p. "Nota bibliografica," pp. 284–90. Contents: I. Unamuno: Scritti linguistici. A. Sul basco (1884–1933). B. Sulla lingua spagnola (1888–1936). C. Sulle lingue peninsulari e altre lingue (1894–1932). D. Sullo spagnolo in America Latina (1898–1935). II. Unamuno: Scritti non linguistici (1895–1953).

Malavassi V., Guillermo. "Bibliografía de Unamuno aparecida en Costa Rica," *Revista de Filosofia de la Universidad de Costa Rica* (San José), No. 10 (julio/diciembre de 1961), 219–30. Includes 159 references to works by Unamuno published in Costa Rica from 1907 to 1958. Some references, however, are incomplete bibliographically due to the compiler's inability to review copies of some of the newspapers and periodicals for which he had citations.

Onís, Federico de. "Bibliografía de Miguel de Unamuno," *La Torre*, Nos. 35/36 (julio/diciembre de 1961), 601–36. Contents: I. Ediciones. A. Colecciones y selecciones. B. Cartas. II. Traducciones (by language). III. Estudios. "No se han incluído en esta bibliografía los articulos, poesías y otras obras sueltas de Unamuno publicadas en periódicos y revistas porque son innumerables."

Palau y Claveras, Agustín. *Bibliografia de Miguel de Unamuno Jugo*. Bilbao: Imp. Industrial, 1972. 38p. This bibliography "es tirada aparte del *Manual del librero hispanoamericano*, tomo xxiv, pp. 305–338." Contents: I. Obras completas, selectas y antologías. II. Obras particulares. A. Novelas. B. Ensayos y artículos. C. Conferencias. Discursos. D. Paisaje. E. Poesía. F. Autobiografía. G. Tratado de amor de Dios. H. Epistolario. I. Teatro. J. Pajaritas de papel (Apéndice de amor y pedagogía). III. Homenaje.

Pieczara, Stefan. "La difusión de la obra de Unamuno en Polonia," *Cuadernos de la Catédra Miguel Unamuno* (Salamanca), 14/15 (1964/65), 103–18. Contains an "Ensayo de una bibliografía unamuniana en Polonia." Contents: I. Traducciones. II. Artículos críticos sobre Unamuno y su obra. III. Obras consultas.

______. "La fortuna de Miguel de Unamuno y su recepción en Polonia," *Cuadernos de la Cátedra Miguel de Unamuno*, 25/26 (1978), 161–68. "Bibliografía sobre Unamuno," pp. 165–68. The Polish language title is not included.

Sedwick, Frank. "Tesis sobre don Miguel de Unamuno y sus obras leídas en las universidades norteamericanas hasta febrero de 1955," *Cuadernos de la Cátedra Miguel de Unamuno* (Salamanca), 8 (1958), 57–63. Article originally appeared in the *Ken-*

tucky Foreign Language Quarterly, 3 (1956), 192–96. 62 titles (mostly M.A. and senior theses) are listed by university.

Unamuno, Miguel de. *Artículos olvidados sobre España y la primera Guerra Mundial*. Introducción y edición de Christopher Cobb. London: Támesis Books, 1976. 217p. (Colección Támesis; Serie B, Textos, 22). "Apéndice: Lista de publicaciones periodísticas de Unamuno desde el primero de Agosto 1914 hasta el treinta y uno de diciembre 1918," pp. lvi–lxxv. Twenty-eight journals are indexed from France, Italy, Latin America, and Spain.

_____. *Ensueño de una patria. Periodismo republicano, 1931–1936*. Valencia: Pre-Textos, 1984. 285p. "Escritos periodísticos de Unamuno, 1931–1936," pp. 41–62. Table which lists Unamuno's writings which appeared in the following newspapers: *Caras y caretas, El Adelanto, El Día Palma, El Sol, El Norte de Castilla, Ahora, El Día Gráfico, El Pueblo Gallego, El Radical, Heraldo de Aragón, La Gaceta Literaria, La Rioja, La Voz de Guizpúzcoa, La Voz de Valencia.*

_____. *La esfinge. La Venda. Fedra: Teatro*. Edición, introducción y notas de José Paulino. Madrid: Castalia, 1988. "Noticia bibliográfica," pp. 79–80. Contents: I. Manuscritos. II. Ediciones. "Bibliografía selecta," pp. 81–86. Contents: I. Estudios generales relacionados con el teatro de Unamuno. II. Bibliografía particular acerca de las obras aquí editadas (incluyendo reseñas de estreno en publicaciones periódicas). A. *La esfinge*. B. *La venda* C. *Fedra.*

_____. *Niebla*. Edición de M. J. Valdés. 2. ed. Madrid: Cátedra, 1982. 300p. "Bibliografía (documentos utilizados para la historia del texto)," pp. 59–60. "Bibliografía de ediciones, reseñas y traducciones de *Niebla*," pp. 61–65. Contents: I. Ediciones. II. Reseñas. III. Traducciones (By language). "Bibliografía escogida sobre *Niebla* y Miguel de Unamuno," pp. 66–69. Contents: I. Biografía. II. Crítica filosófica y temática. III. Narrativa. IV. Poesía. V. Teatro. VI. Bibliografía. VII. Crítica de *Niebla*.

_____. *Obras completas*. Madrid: Escelicer, 1966. 9vs. Except for volume 9, each volume contains a major "bibliografía de los escritos contenidos en este volumen." Volume 1: Paisajes and ensayos. Volume 2: Novelas. Volume 3: Nuevos ensayos. Volume 4: La raza y la lengua. Volume 5: Teatro. Volume 6: Ensayos espirituales. Meditaciones. Volume 7: Poesías. Volume 8: Autobiografía y recuerdos personales. Volume 9 which does not have a bibliography covers Unamuno's Discursos y artículos.

_____. *Poesía completa*. Edición y prólogo de Ana Suárez Miramón. Madrid: Alianza Editorial, 1987. 4vs. "Bibliografía selecta (criticism of Unamuno's poetry)," v. 1, pp. 39–42.

______. *"San Manuel Buenos, mártir" and "La novela de Don Sandalio, jugador de ajedrez."* Edited by C. A. Longhurst. Manchester, England: Manchester University Press, 1984. 104p. "A Select Bibliography," pp. liii–lv. Contains only critical literature on *San Manuel Buenos, mártir* and *La novela de Don Sandalio* (By year, 1959–1981). Each entry contains critical comments or contents descriptions.

______. *La tía tula*. Edición de Antonio Sánchez-Barbudo. Madrid: Taurus Ediciones, 1981. 179p. "Bibliografía sobre *La tía tula*," pp. 169–71. Includes translations.

______. *Vida de Don Quijote y Sancho*. Edición de Alberto Navarro. Madrid: Cátedra, 1988. 533p. (Letras Hispánicas, 279). "Bibliografía," pp. 127–30. Contents: I. Ediciones de la *Vida de Don Quijote y Sancho*. II. Traducciones (no reseñamos la de fragmentos de la obra). III. Monografías (criticism of Unamuno and *Vida de Don Quijote y Sancho*).

VALDERRAMA, PILAR (1892–1979)

Galerstein, p. 323.

VALENTE, JOSE ANGEL (1929–)

Correa, v. 2, pp. 445, 621–22. Works by and about the author.

Daydí-Tolson, Santiago. *Voces y ecos en la poesía de José Angel Valente*. Lincoln, Neb.: Society of Spanish and Spanish American Studies, 1983. 182p. "Bibliografía," pp. 175–82. Contents: I. Obras de José Angel Valente. A. Libros de poemas (arranged by year, 1955–1982). B. Libros en prosa. C. Teoría y crítica (selective, by year, 1949–1973). II. Estudios sobre la obra de José Angel Valente

Valcárcel López, Eva. *El fulgor o la palabra encarnada. Imágenes y símbolos en la poesía última de José Angel Valente*. Barcelona: PPU, 1989. 236p. (Colección Ediciones y Estudios; Estudios, 8). "Bibliografía," pp. 227–36.

Valente, José Angel. *Entrada en materia*. Edición de Jacques Ancet. Madrid: Cátedra, 1985. 210p. (Letras Hispánicas, 216). "Bibliografía," pp. 35–41. Contents: I. Obras de José Angel Valente. A. Poesía (By year, 1955–1984). B. Prosa (By year, 1971–1982). C. Ensayo (By year, 1971–1983). D. Libros con pintores. E. Traducciones. II. Sobre José Angel Valente. III. Algunas versiones de su obra (By language).

VALENTI, HELENA (1940–)
Galerstein, pp. 323–24.

VALLE-INCLAN, RAMON DEL (1866–1936)
Correa, v. 1, pp. 164, 523–26. Works by and about the author.
Díaz Migoyo, Gonzalo. *Guía de "Tirano Banderas."* Madrid: Fundamentos, 1985. 301p. "Guía bibliográfica de *Tirano Banderas*," pp. 291–301. Contents: I. Libros. II. Reseñas críticas contemporáneas (1920s; no translations, however). III. Artículos.
Doménech, Ricardo. "Contribución a la bibliografía de Valle-Inclán," *Estudios escénicos* (Cuadernos del Instituto del Teatro, Barcelona), No. 15 (julio de 1972), 10–29. Supplements and updates the José Rubia Barcia bibliography. The 350 items are arranged alphabetically by author or anonymous title. Only works about Valle-Inclán and his literary output are included.
Fressard, Jacques. "Contribution a la bibliographie de Vallé-Inclan," *Les Langues Néo-latines* (Paris), No. 207 (4e trim. 1973), 22–52. Selected bibliography of criticism concerning the work of Valle-Inclán.
Jerez Farrán, Carlos. *El expresionismo en Valle-Inclán: Una reinterpretación de su visión esperpéntica.* Sada, A Coruña: Ediciós do Castro, 1989. 279p. "Estudios sobre la obra de Valle-Inclán," pp. 269–72. "Estudios sobre el expresionismo," pp. 273–75. "Otras obras pertinentes," pp. 276–79.
Larson, Everette E. *Ramón Marí del Valle-Inclán: A Bibliography.* Washington, D.C.: Library of Congress, Hispanic Division, 1986. 15p. (Hispanic Focus, 4). A selective bibliography of the monographic holdings by and about Valle-Inclán in the Library of Congress. Call numbers are included.
Lavaud, Elaine. *Valle-Inclán du journal au roman (1888–1915).* Paris: Klincksieck, 1979. 663p. (Témoins de l'Espagne et de l'Amérique latine, 9). "Etude bibliographie des éditions et reéditions des oeuvres de Valle-Inclán (du vivant de l'auteur)," pp. 595–622. Arranged by year, 1895–1936; annotated entries. "Bibliographie: oeuvres citeés ou consultées," pp. 623–639. "Volumes ou numéros speciaux en hommage a Valle-Inclán," pp. 642–643.
Le May, Albert H. "Ramon del-Valle Inclán en las revistas *Cosmópolis y Europa*," *Revista Chilena de Literatura*, No. 31 (1988), 157–68.
Lima, Robert. *An Annotated Bibliography of Ramón del Valle-Inclán.* University Park: The Pennsylvania State University Libraries, 1972. 401p. (Bibliographical Series, No. 4). Comprehensive bibliography. Items published through mid-1972 are included.

Annotated, often with critical and explanatory comments and with details of contents, in the case of important books, of important reviews. Contents: I. Publications in Periodicals. II. First Editions. A. Aesthetics. B. Collected Stories. C. Novelettes. D. Novels. E. Plays. F. Poetry. III. Other Contemporary Editions. A. Aesthetics. B. Collected Stories. C. Novels. D. Plays. E. Poetry. F. "Opera Omnia." IV. Translations and Adaptations by Valle-Inclán. V. Book Prologues. VI. Lectures. VII. Anthologized Works. VIII. Posthumous Editions. A. Works Uniform to Those Issued by the Author. B. Collected Works. C. Selected Anthologized Works. D. Textbook Editions. E. Translations by Valle-Inclán. IX. Foreign Versions of Valle-Inclán's Works. A. Aesthetics. B. Novels. C. Plays. D. Stories. X. Studies. A. Homage Volumes. 1. Books. 2. Periodicals. B. Literature. 1. General. 2. Prose (By work). 3. Drama (By work). 4. Poetry. 5. Aesthetics. C. Life and Anecdotes. 1. General. 2. Literary and Artistic Relations. 3. The Generation of 1898. 4. Galicia. 5. America. XI. Bibliographies.

Lyon, John. *The Theatre of Valle-Inclán*. Cambridge: Cambridge University Press, 1983. 229p. "Bibliography," pp. 221–26. Contents: I. Editions of Works by Valle-Inclán Quoted in The Text. II. Articles and Reports of Lectures. III. Other Works Consulted or Cited in the Text (includes Valle-Inclán criticism).

Mainer, José-Carlos. "Libros sobre Valle Inclán," *Revista de Occidente*, No. 59 (abril de 1986), 79–92. Bibliographic essay.

Odriozola, Antonio. "Bibliografía sobre Valle-Inclán," *Insula*, No. 236/37 (julio/agosto 1966), 14.

Porrúa, María del Carmen. *La Galicia decimononica en las comedias barbáras de Valle-Inclán*. Coruña: Ediciós do Castro, 1983. 288p. "Obras sobre Valle-Inclán," pp. 279–85. The works included were basically published in the 1960s and the first half of the 1970s.

Ramón del Valle-Inclán. Edición de Ricardo Doménech. Madrid: Taurus, 1988. 451p. (El escritor y la crítica, 24). "Bibliografía selecta," pp. 438–51. Contents: I. Bibliografías. II. Ediciones. A. Compilaciones. B. Obras sueltas. C. Poesía y estética. D. Narrativa. E. Teatro. III. Estudios. A. Libros y opúsculos. B. Revistas: números monográficos. C. Artículos.

Rubia Barcia, José *A Bibliography and Iconography of Valle-Inclán (1866–1936)*. Berkeley, Los Angeles: University of California Press, 1960. 101p. (University of California Publications in Modern Philology, 59). Contents: I. Valle-Inclán's Life and Works, pp. 3–25. (Mentions in chronological order, besides his major works, all the different versions and reprints of his minor production as they are related to, and in some instances justified by, personal idiosyncrasies or certain events in his life.) II. Works on Valle-Inclán, pp. 29–59. III. Translations, pp. 56–60. IV. Iconography of Valle-Inclán. V. Appendix A: Articles by Valle-Inclán Published in *El Universal* (México, 1892), pp. 93–94.

Ruiz Fernández, Ciriaco. *El léxico del teatro de Valle-Inclán (Ensayo interpretativo)*. Salamanca: Ediciones Universidad de Salamanca, 1981. 313p. (Acta Salmanticensia, Filosofía y Letras, 130). "Bibliografía," pp. 283–93. Criticism only.

Salper de Tortella, Roberta. "Chronological List of Works by Valle-Inclán Published in *El Imparcial*," *Modern Language Notes*, 83 (1968), 287–93. Descriptive and/or critical annotations for articles that cover 1901–20.

Servera Bano, José. *Ramón del Valle-Inclán*. Madrid: Ediciones Júcar, 1983. 224p. "Bibliografía," pp. 213–19. Contents: I. Bibliografías sobre Ramón del Valle-Inclán. II. Números de revistas dedicadas a Ramón del Valle-Inclán. III. Estudios y artículos sobre Valle-Inclán.

Valle-Inclán, Ramón del. *Articulos completos y otras páginas olvidadas*. Edición de J. Serrano Alonso. Madrid: Istmo, 1987? 438p. "Cuadro sinóptico de publicaciones," pp. 53–105. Arrangement is by year, 1888–1936, and includes title, name of periodical or journal, date, and format of text.

______. *Teatro selecto. Introducción de Anthony N. Zahareas*. Madrid: Escelicer, 1969. 541p. "Bibliografía," pp. 63–79. Contents: I. Estudios generales. II. Revistas literarias dedicadas a Valle-Inclán. III. Estudios sobre el teatro. IV. Estudios sobre el esperpento. V. Estudios particulares sobre las piezas de nuestra edición. A. *Romance de lobos* y las *Comedias bárbaras*. B. *Tablado de marionetas para la educación de Príncipes*. C. *Divinas palabras*. VI. Ediciones-traducciones. VII. Cronología de las veintiuna obras teatrales de Valle-Inclán.

Valle-Inclán y su tiempo hoy: Exposición; Círculo de Bellas Artes 18 de marzo al 20 de abril. Madrid: Círculo de Bellas Artes, 1986. 163p. "Biografía y iconografía," pp. 9–17. "Bibliografía," pp. 21–37. Contents: I. Obras y ediciones de don Ramón del Valle-Inclán. A. Obras y ediciones anteriores a la *Opera Omnia*. 1. Cuentos y novelas cortas. 2. Los sonatas. 3. Obras dramáticas. 4. Obras varias. a. Otras obras narrativas. b. Poesía. c. Antologías. B. Las ediciones de la *Opera Omnia* (1913–1933). C. Números completos de publicaciones periódicas. II. Ediciones posteriores: Obras reunidas y antologías. III. Otras ediciones populares. IV. Colección Austral. V. Segunda *Opera Omnia* (1940–1958). Ed. Rua Nova. VI. Ultimas ediciones de Valle-Inclán. VII. Prólogos de Valle-Inclán. VIII. Traducciones de Valle-Inclán. IX. Números especiales de revista.

VALLVERDU, JOSEP (1923–)
"Josep Vallverdú: Selected Bibliography," *Catalan Writing*, No. 4 (March 1990), 78–80. Contents: I. Fiction. II. Translations. III. Awards and Citations.

VALVERDE, JOSE MARIA (1926–)
Correa, v. 2, pp. 341–42, 618–19. Contents: I. Libros. II. Artículos y estudios (criticism).

VAZQUEZ IGLESIAS, PURIFICACION (1918–)
Galerstein, pp. 324–26.

VAZQUEZ MONTALBAN, MANUEL (1939–)
Correa, v. 2, pp. 533–34, 624. Works by and about the author.

VENTOS I CUELELL, PALMIRA (1862–1917)
Galerstein, pp. 326–27.

VERNET I REAL, MARIA TERESA (1907–1974)
Galerstein, pp. 327–28.

VICENS, ANTONIA (1942–)
Galerstein, p. 328.

VILANOVA, ANTONIO (1923–)
Sotelo, Adolfo. "Bibliografía del profesor Antonio Vilanova," v. 1, pp. xxiii-li in *Homenaje al profesor Antonio Vilanova* (Barcelona: Departamento de Filología Española, Facultad de Filología, Universidad de Barcelona, 1989). Contents: I. Bibliografía académica (By year, 1943–1988). II. Artículos de crítica literatura (By year, 1942–1982).

VILLAESPESA, FRANCISCO (1877–1936)
"Bibliografía escogida de Francisco Villaespesa," *Las Nuevas Letras* (Almería), No. 7 (1987), 38–39.
Cortés, Eladio. *El teatro de Villaespesa: Estudio crítico*. Madrid: Edicones Atlas, 1971. 209p. "Bibliografía," unpaged. Contents: I. Obras de Francisco Villaespesa. A. Poesía. B. Teatro. C. Prosa. D. Traducciones. II. Bibliografía sobre las obras teatrales de Villaespesa. III. Bibliografía selecta sobre el teatro español.

Rosenbaum, Sidonia C. "Francisco Villaespesa: Bibliografía," *Revista Hispánica Moderna*, 3, No. 4 (julio de 1937), 278–82. Contents: I. Ediciones. A. Poesía. B. Teatro. C. Prosa. D. Traducciones. II. Estudios.

VILLALON, FERNANDO (1881–1930)

Escritos sobre Fernando Villalón. Recopilados por Jacobo Cortines y Alberto González Troyano. Sevilla: Servicio de Publicaciones del Ayuntamiento, 1982. 117p. (Compás: Biblioteca de Asuntos Poéticos, 4). "Bibliografía básica," pp. 115–117. I. Obras de Fernando Villalón. A. Libros de poesía. B. Prosa. C. Obras inéditas. D. Otras ediciones. E. Antologías en la que figura Fernando Villalón. II. Sobre Fernando Villalón.

Issorel, Jacques. *Fernando Villalón: ou la rebellion de l'automne; un poète andalou de la Génération de 1927*. Perpignan: Université de Perpignan, 1988. 732p. "Bibliographie," pp. 663–83. 306 items. Contents: I. Oeuvres de Fernando Villalón (By year, 1926–1987). II. Recensions des éditions des oeuvres du poète (By work). III. Etudes et écrits divers sur l'homme et l'oeuvre. IV. Poemes en hommage a Fernando Villalón. V. Traductions (By language).

Villalón, Fernando. *Obras: poesía y prosa*. Introducción, bibliografía, notas de Jacques Issorel. Madrid: Editorial Trieste, 1987. 363p. (Biblioteca de Autores Españoles, 38). "Cronología de Fernando Villalón: vida y obra (1881–1930)," np. "Bibliografía," pp. 41–66. Contents: I. Obras de Fernando Villalón (By year, 1926–1986). II. Reseñas de las ediciones de las obras del poeta. A. *Andalucía la baja* (1920). B. *La torida* (1928). C. *Romances del 800* (1929). D. *Poesías* (1944). E. *Taurofilia racial* (1956). F. *Poesías* (Ed. de M. Sobh, 1976). G. *Sonetos y cartas* en *Peña Labra*, Nos. 35–38 (1979–80). H. *Perfil, magia y versos* (1988). I. *Poesías inéditas* (1985). III. Estudios y escritos diversos sobre el hombre y su obra. IV. Poemas en homenaje a Fernando Villalón. V. Traducciones. A. Al árabe. B. Al francés. 298 items.

VILLALONGA, LLORENÇ (1897–)

"Llorenç Villalonga: Selected Bibliography," *Catalan Writing*, No. 2 (December 1988), 28–31. Contents: I. Chronology. II. Fiction. III. Drama. IV. Spanish Versions by the Same Author. V. Translations (By language).

Villalonga, Llorenç. *Bearn o la sala de las muñecas*. Edición de Jaime Vidal Alcover. Madrid: Ediciones Cátedra, 1985. 423p. "Bibliografía," pp. 37–42. Contents: I. Obras de Villalonga. II. Sobre Villalonga. A. Prólogo. B. Otros estudios.

_____. *Muerte de dama. La heredera de doña Obdulia o las tentaciones*. Edición de Jaime Vidal Alcover. Barcelona: Plaza & Janés, 1985. 524p. (Clásicos Plaza y Janés, 37). "Bibliografía," pp. 77–80. Contents: I. Obras de Lorenzo Villalonga. II. Narraciones cortas. III. Bibliografía mínima sobre Lorenzo Villalonga. IV. Bibliografía seleccionada sobre *Muerte de dama*. V. Bibliografía seleccionada sobre *La heredera de doña Obdulia o las tentaciones*.

_____. *Obres completes. I, Novel•la, 1*. Edició a cura de Josep A. Grimalt. Barcelona: Edicions 62, 1988. 444p. "Nota sobre l'edició," pp. 11–15. Contents: I. *Mort de dama*. A. Edicions principals. B. Traduccions. C. Sobre la present edició. II. *L'hereva de dona Obdulia o les temptacions*. A. Edicions. B. Traduccions. C. Sobre la present edició. III. *La novel•la de Palmira*. A. Edicions. B. Traduccions. C. La present edició.

VILLARTA TUNON, ANGELES (1921–)

Galerstein, p. 329.

VILLENA, LUIS ANTONIO DE (1951–)

CILH, p. 31. Contents: I. Poesía. II. Prosa. III. Ensayo. IV. Ediciones.

VINAS, CELIA (1915–1954)

Alarcón, p.71.

Galerstein, p. 330.

VINYOLI, JOAN (1914–)

Lamarca, Dolors. "Bibliografia: Joan Vinyoli," *Reduccions*, No. 20 (setembre 1983), 80–95.

Sala-Valldaura, Josep M. *Joan Vinyoli: Introducció a l'obra poètica*. Barcelona: Editorial Empúries, 1985. 126p. (Les Naus d'Empúries, Pal Major, 1) "Bibliografia," pp. 119–22. Contents: I. Obres de Joan Vinyoli. A. Poesia (By year, 1937–1985). B. Altres treballs citats. II. Sobre l'obra de Joan Vinyoli. A. Entrevistes (By year, 1980–1984). B. Articles, crítiques i ressenyes (By year, 1952–1984).

VIVANCO, LUIS FELIPE (1907–)

Correa, v. 2, pp. 149, 611. Contents: I. Libros. II. Artículos y estudios (criticism).

Vivanco, Luis Felipe. *Antología poética*. Introducción y selección de José María Valverde. Madrid: El Libro de Bolsillo, Alianza Editorial, 1976. 130p. "Nota bibliográfica," pp. 16–17. Contents: I. Poesía publicada en libros o folletos (By year, 1931–1963). II.

Algunas entregas de poesía publicadas en revistas (By year, 1929–1975).

XIRAU I PALAU, JOAQUIM (1895–1946)

Puig i Oliver, Irene de. "Aproximació bio-bibliogràfica a Joaquim Xirau i Palau," *Annals de l'Institut d'Estudis Gironins* (Gerona), 26 (1982/83), 477–521.

XIRINACS I DIAZ, OLGA (1936–)

Galerstein, pp. 331–32.

YNDURAIN, FRANCISCO (1910–)

"Bibliografía del Dr. Francisco Ynduráin (Hernández)," pp. 6–8 in *Homenaje a Francisco Yndurâin* (Zaragoza: Universidad de Zaragoza, Facultad de Filosofía y Letras, 1972). Includes articles, books and translations, 1946–72.

ZAMBRANO, MARIA (1907–1991)

Alarcón, p. 71.

Blanco Martínez, Rogelio. "María Zambrano: Una presencia en la cultura," *Insula*, No. 509 (Mayo de 1989), 19–20. A bibliography of María Zambrano's books arranged by year, 1936–1989.

Castillo, Julia. "Cronología de María Zambrano," *Insula*, No. 509 (Mayo de 1989), 18–19. Includes bibliographic information.

Galerstein, pp. 333–34.

Salinero Portero, J. "Colaboraciones de María Zambrano en *Cruz y Raya*, *Hora de España* y *Revista de Occidente* desde 1933 a 1938," *Litoral*, Nos. 124/126 (1983), 180–94. "Lista de las 27 colaboraciones de María Zambrano en las revistas citadas," pp. 193–94.

_____. "María Zambrano en algunas revistas hispanoamericanas entre 1938 y 1964," *Cuadernos Hispanoamericanos*, No. 413 (1984), 134–58. A table on pp. 134–138 lists the 23 contributions of María Zambrano to *Asomante; Cuadernos Americanos; Diógenes; El Hijo Pródigo; Luminar; Orígenes; Sur; La Torre*. The remainder of the article is devoted to an analysis of these works.

Zardoya, Concha. "María Zambrano en *Hora de España*," *Cuadernos Hispanoamericanos*, No. 413 (1984), 81–94. Descriptive analysis of nine essays that appeared in *Hora de España*, 1937–1938.

ZAMORA VICENTE, ALONSO (1916–)

Peira Soberón, Pedro, and María José Postigo de Peira. "Intento de una bibliografía de Alonso Zamora," *Papeles de Son Armadans*, Año 18, tomo 71, no. 211 (octubre de 1973), ii-xl. Contents: I. Obra literaria. A. Narraciones. B. Antologías. C. Traducciones. D. Artículos. II. Obra científica. A. Lingüística. B. Literatura. 1. Ediciones. 2 Crítica literaria. (a) trabajos de conjunto. (b) literatura española. (c) literatura hispanoamericana. (d) literatura portuguesa. (e) literaria y cine. C. Reseñas. III. Noticias diversas sobre Alonso Zamora Vicente.

Postigo Aldeamil, María Josefa. "Bibliografía de Alonso Zamora Vicente," v. 1, pp. 549–71, in *Homenaje a Alonso Zamora Vicente* (Madrid: Editorial Castalia, 1988). The 565 items are arranged by year, 1940–1986.

ZARDOYA, CONCHA (1914–)

Alarcón, p. 71.

CILH, pp. 63–64. Contents: I. Poesía. II. Biografía y crítica.

Galerstein, pp. 334–38.

Rodríguez Pequeño, Mercedes. *La poesía de Concha Zardoya (estudio temático y estilístico)*. Valladolid: Secretariado de Publicaciones, Universidad de Valladolid, 1987. 202p. (Serie Literatura, 8). "Bibliografía," pp. 195–202. Contents: I. Obra poética de Concha Zardoya (By year, 1946–87). Books only. II. Antologías que hacen referencia a su obra poética. III. Valoraciones críticas sobre su poesía. IV. Obras en prosa de Concha Zardoya (By year, 1944–1985). Books only. V. Trabajos de crítica, biográfica e historia literaria. VI. Traducciones (By year, 1945–49). Books only.

Zardoya, Concha. *Diotima*. Barcelona: Víctor Pozanco, 1981. 208p. "Obras de Concha Zardoya," pp. 203–05. Contents: I. Poesía. II. Cuentos. III. Biografía, crítica e historia literaria. IV. Ediciones con prólogo, comentarios y notas. V. Traducciones. VI. Colaboración en obra colectiva.

ZAYAS, ANTONIO DE (1871–1945)

Zayas, Antonio de. *Antología poética*. Selección e introducción de J. M. Aguirre. Exeter: University of Exeter, 1980. 73p. (Exeter

Hispanic Texts, 27). "Bibliografía," p. xxv. The books of Antonio de Zayas listed by year, 1892–1942.

ZUNZUNEGUI, JUAN ANTONIO DE (1901–)

"Bibliografía de y sobre Juan Antonio de Zunzunegui," *Anthropos*, No. 1 (1987), 51–54.

Carbonell Dasset, Delfín. "Zunzunegui: Bibliografía," *Duquesne Hispanic Review*, 6 (octubre de 1967), 37–41. Works by and about Zunzunegui.

Valencia, Antonio. "Juan Antonio Zunzunegui, novelista," *El Libro Español*, No. 95 (noviembre de 1965), 597–612. "Bibliografía de Zunzunegui," pp. 604–612. Contents: I. Novelas. II. Narraciones. A. Publicadas en España. B. Publicadas en colecciones en el extranjero. III. Antologías. IV. Traducciones. V. Tesis. Obras generales. VI. Artículos, crítica, ensayos (selected, some incomplete bibliographic entries).

ADDITIONAL BIOBIBLIOGRAPHIC SOURCES

Alarcón, Norma, and Sylvia Kossna. *Bibliography of Hispanic Women Writers (From the "MLA International Bibliography," 1922–1978.* Bloomington, Ind.: Chicano-Riqueño Studies, 1980. 86p.

Alonso, Santos. *Literatura leonesa actual: Estudio y antología de 17 escritores.* Valladolid: Consejería de Educación y Cultura, Junta de Castilla y León, 1986. 390p. (Colección de Estudios de Lengua y Literatura, 4). Includes biobibliographical information.

Amo, Julián, and Charmion Shelby. *La obra impresa de los intelectuales españoles en América, 1936–1945.* Stanford, Calif.: University Press, 1950. 146p. Bibliography is arranged alphabetically by author. The entry for each author is divided into two parts: biography and bibliography. Two appendixes give lists of Catalan and Basque intellectuals.

Aragonés Domarco, Carmen. *Contribución al Diccionario bibliográfico de Guadalajara del siglo XX.* Memoria de licenciatura dirigida por don José Simón Díaz, presentada en la Universidad Complutense de Madrid, 1973. 372p. Sixty-seven biobibliographies are arranged by author.

Ballesteros Robles, Luis. *Diccionario biográfico matritense.* Madrid: Imprenta Municipal, 1912. 702p.

Barrero Pérez, Oscar. *La novela existencial española de posguerra.* Madrid: Editorial Gredos, 1987. 306p. (Biblioteca Románica Hispánica. II. Estudios y ensayos, 356). "Referencias bibliográficas," pp. 283–94. Contents: I. Novelas analizadas. II. Estudios críticos.

Bassa, Ramón. *Llibres esitats a Mallorca (1939–1972).* Palma de Mallorca: Edit. J. Mascaró Pasarius, 1972. 322p. (Col•lecció Turmeda, 7). "Literatura," pp. 101–71. Catalan, foreign-language, and

Spanish titles are included. The following indices are included: Author, collection, editor, title, publisher, translator, and biographee.

Bellamy, Lauretta M., and Anna Carol Klemme. *List of the Plays in García Rico y Cía.'s "Colección de comedias españolas de los siglos XIX y XX."* Boulder: University of Colorado Libraries, 1956. 140p. "This list is designed to accompany a collection of 3763 plays published in Spain and a few other Hispanic countries between 1800 and 1941 and bought from García Rico y Cía., Madrid booksellers, who arranged the plays more or less alphabetically and assigned numbers to them." Bellamy's list is by author; items 3004–3735 represent criticism of plays.

Berchenko, Pablo. "Narradoras hispánicas actuales: Elementos para un índice bio-bibliográfico," *Ventanal*, 14 (1988), 217–53. Biobibliography of contemporary Spanish women narrators: "Lo que se pretende entregar es un índice de la creación literaria de las mujeres españolas, en particular, de aquéllas que cultivan la narración, y cuyas obras han aparecido en los años 80, editadas por primera vez o reeditadas, como obras individuales, o presentadas en antologías o publicaciones periódicas." (p. 217). Some French translations included. Basically, lists under each author, titles of novels, short stories, and essays. Incomplete bibliographical and biographical information, some of which is easily available from other sources. Not as complete as *Galerstein*.

Bertrand de Muñoz, Maryse. "Bibliografía de la guerra civil española," *Anales de la Literatura Española Contemporánea*, 11 (1986), 357–411; 12 (1987), 369–417. Contents: I. Fuentes bibliográficas de la creación literaria sobre la guerra civil española (bibliographic essay). II. Novela. A. Guerra presentida. B. Guerra vivida. C. Guerra recordada. D. Guerra referida. III. Narraciones, cuentos y novelas cortas. IV. Poesía. V. Romanceros y antologías. VI. Teatro. (All alphabetically arranged entries under these headings).

______. *La Guerra Civil Española en la novela*. Madrid: José Porrúa Turanzas, 1982. 2 vols. Approximately 1,000 novels are listed under four headings: "Guerra presentida" (novels about the build up to the war); "Guerra vivida" (novels about the war itself); "Guerra recordada" (novels about post-war period in which the war itself is directly evoked); and "Guerra referida" (novels in which the war is more or less explicitly in the background). Critical evaluations and summaries of the novels are included. Indexes: Novels by author's nationality; "Ciudad or región donde mayormente se desarrolla la novela"; "Grupo social al cual pertenecen los personajes"; "Ideología política de los personajes" (Not of the authors); "De temas"; "Clase de novela y por la técnica empleada"; "Año de publicación"; and "Cuadro sinóptico de indices por nacionalidad del autor y por año de publicación." Apéndice I: Novelas premiadas. Apéndice II: Novelas prologadas. Bibliografía: I. Bibliografía crítica. II. Libros de crítica. III. Artículos de crítica. IV. Bibliotecas que posen un fondo interesante sobre la Guerra Civil Española.

"Bibliografía teatral catalana, 1980–1981," *Estudis Escènics* (Quaderns de l'Institut del Teatre de la Diputació de Barcelona), 23 (1983), 135–40. Includes Catalan language and translations of foreign drama.

"Bibliography of Post Civil War Spanish Fiction—1978," *Anales de la Novela de Posguerra*, 4 (1979), 139–63. Contents: I. Bibliography. II. General. III. By Author. IV. About Authors. Creative works, critical books and essays, reviews, and general items such as documents and interviews are indexed. 268 entries.

_____ —1979," *Anales de la Narrativa Española Contemporánea*, 5 (1980), 141–63. 377 entries.

_____ —1980," *Anales de la Literatura Española Contemporánea*, 6 (1981), 241–65. 379 entries.

_____ —1981," *Anales de la Literatura Española Contemporánea*, 7 (1982), 117–35. 274 entries.

_____ —1982," *Anales de la Literatura Española Contemporánea*, 8 (1983), 163–82. 218 entries.

Biblioteca de Teatro Español Contemporáneo, Madrid. *Catálogo de obras de teatro español del siglo XX*. Madrid: Fundación Juan March, 1985? 442p. The collection was founded in 1977. The catalog includes photos and recordings.

Biblioteca "Gabriel Miro." *Bibliografía alicantina y alicantinista*. Alicante: Caja de Ahorros Alicante y Murcia, 1977. 191p. Bibliography of imprints of the Province of Alicante.

Billick, David J. "Women in Hispanic Literature: A Checklist of Doctoral Dissertations and Master's Theses, 1905–1975," *Women Studies Abstracts*, 6, No. 2 (1979), 1–11.

Supplement 1 (1976–1977): *Women Studies Abstracts*, 7, No. 2/3 (1978), 1–3.

Supplement 2 (1978–1979): *Women Studies Abstracts*, 9, No. 3 (1980), 1–4.

Supplement 3 (1980–1981): *Letras Femeninas*, 8, No. 2 (1982), 54–57. Includes general studies (covering more than one literary period) and sections on Spanish literature of the twentieth century. All entries are alphabetically arranged.

Blanco Arnejo, María D. "Repertorio bibliográfico de tesis españolas sobre literatura española contemporánea," *Anales de Literatura Española Contemporánea*, 9 (1984), 245–83. On theses completed at 16 Spanish universities, 1954–1984. 325 doctoral theses. Contents: I. General. II. General crítica. III. General narrativa. IV. General poesía. V. General teatro. VI. Autores. Covers from the "Generación del 1898."

Blaney, B. "Spanish and German Literary Relations in U.S. and Canadian Dissertations: An Annotated Bibliography (1900–1976)," *Revista de Estudios Hispánicos*, 15 (1981), 459–71. Alphabetically arranged entries.

Borràs i Feliu, Antoni. *Escriptors jesuïtes de Catalunya: bibliografia 1931–1976*. Sant Cugat de Vallès, Barcelona: Facultats de Filosofia y Teologia "Sant Francesc de Borja," 1979? 440p. (Suplements de la revista *Actualidad bibliográfica de Filosofía y Teología*, 1).

Bravo-Villasante, Carmen. *Diccionario de autores de literatura infantil*. Madrid: Escuela Española, 1985. 432p. Biobibliography.

Caballero Venzalá, Manuel. *Diccionario bio-bibliográfico del Santo Reino*. Jaén: Instituto de Estudios Giennenses, Excma. Diputación Provincial, v. 1—; 1979– . The Province of Jaén. Alphabetically arranged.

Cabey Riley, Julia Elizabeth. *Bibliografía de algunos poetas andaluces de posguerra*. Madrid: Universidad Complutense, Departamento de Bibliografía, 1984. 789p.

Calvo de Aguilar, Isabel. *Antología biográfica de escritores españolas*. Madrid: Biblioteca Nueva, 1954. 891p. Covers eighty-five women writers, with a one-page biobibliography on each and a short anthology section.

Castán Palomar, Fernando. *Aragoneses contemporáneos: Diccionario biográfico*. Zaragoza: Ediciones Herrein, 1934. 619p. Biobibliographies. Entries are by first name. "Suplemento, A-Z," pp. 557–94. "Indice de aragoneses cuyas biografías aparecen en este volumen," pp. 595–606; "Indice de los nombres de personas que se citan en este volumen," pp. 607–18.

Castañón, Luciano. *Bibliografía de Gijón*. Gijón: Ayuntamiento, 1975. 150p.

_____. "Bibliografía de novelas asturianas," *Boletín del Instituto de Estudios Asturianos*, No. 69 (enero/abril de 1970), 83–103. Alphabetically arranged by author.

Castro, José Ramón. *Autores e impresos tudelanos, siglos XV-XX. Prólogo del José Luis de Arrese*. Pamplona: Patronata José María Quadrado, Institución Príncipe de Viana, C.S.I.C., 1963. 489p. (Bibliografías locales, No. 1). Work is divided by century. Within each century, complete bibliographic entries are listed in chronological order. Pages 323–456 contain biographical sketches of a selected number of writers. Author, city, and printing/publishing indexes complete the work.

Catálogo general de la librería española, 1931–1950. Madrid: Instituto Nacional del Libro Español, 1957. 5vs. One alphabetical listing by author with complete bibliographic information; no annotations.

Catálogo general de la librería española e hispanoamericana, años 1901–1930: autores. Madrid: Cámaras Oficiales del Libro (vs. 1–3) and Instituto Nacional del Libro Español (vs. 4–5), 1932–1951. 5vs. Annotated entries by author of books, each preceded by a catalog number. Full bibliographical information is provided for each entry.

Ciudad Real, Spain (City). Biblioteca Pública. *Catálogo bibliográfico y de autores de la provincia de Ciudad Real*. Ciudad Real: C.S.I.C., Instituto de Estudios Manchiegos, 1956. 76p. Includes only works contained in the Biblioteca Pública's collection.

Compitello, Malcolm Alan. "The Novel, the Critics, and the Civil War, A Bibliographic Essay," *Anales de la Narrativa Española Contemporánea*, 4 (1979), 117–38. Contents: I. Monographs. II. Unpublished Doctoral Dissertations. III. Articles Written in Spain. IV. Articles Written Outside of Spain. V. Studies on Specific Authors.

Correa, Gustavo, ed. *Antología de la poesía española (1900–1980).* Madrid: Editorial Gredos, 1980. 2vs. (Biblioteca Romanica Hispánica, VI. Antología Hispánica, 35). "Antologías," v. 1, pp. 485–88. "Crítica y antologías de autores extranjeros e hispanoamericanos," v. 1, pp. 496–99. "Estudios monográficos sobre grupos de autores, temas, períodos y movimientos," v. 1, pp. 499–506. "Bibliografía sobre autores individuales," v. 1, pp. 506–553; v. 2, pp. 605–25.

Couceiro Freijomil, Antonio. *Diccionario bio-bibliográfico de escritores.* Santiago de Compostela: Ed. de los Bibliófilos Gallegos, 1951–54. 3 vols. Brief biographical sketches of authors of Galicia in various subject fields, with extensive bibliographies. Covers all periods.

Crespo, Antonio. *Las novelas sobre Murcia (1939–1981).* Murcia: Academia Alfonso el Sabio, 1981. 234p. (Biblioteca Murciana de Bolsillo, 66). "Notas bio-bibliográficas sobre periodistas murcianos," pp. 205–12. Alphabetically arranged.

Crespo Matellán, Salvador. *La parodia dramática en la literatura española.* Salamanca: Universidad de Salamanca, 1979. 195p. (Acta Salmanticensia, Filosofía y Letras, 107). A descriptive list of titles for the period, 1835–1970, appears on pp. 79–110. "Bibliografía," pp. 187–90.

Cuadernos de Investigación de la Literatura Hispánica, No. 7 (1986). Whole issue is devoted to modern and contemporary Spanish poetry. Biobibliographies of the poets are included.

Cuenca Benet, Francisco. *Biblioteca de autores andaluces modernos y contemporáneos.* Habana: Tip: Moderna de R. Dorrbecker, 1921. 2 vs. (Biblioteca de divulgación de la cultura andaluza contemporánea, 1–2). There are 1,071 authors listed from the seventeenth through the twentieth centuries.

______. *Teatro andaluz contemporáneo.* La Habana: Maza, Caso y Cía., 1937–40. 2 vols. Vol. 1: Autores y obras. Vol. 2: Artistas líricos y dramáticos. The biobibliographies are arranged alphabetically. Author indexes.

Cuento español de posguerra: antología. Edición de Medardo Fraile. Madrid: Cátedra, 1986. 290p. (Letras Hispánicas, 252). "Bibliografía," pp. 39–48. Critical studies mainly.

Cuesta García de Leonardo, María José. *Catálogo de la narrativa editada en el País valenciano de 1940 a 1960*. Valencia: Institució "Alfonso el Magnànim," Institució Valenciana d'Estudis i Investigació, 1986. 175p. (IAM Investigació, 11).

Delgado, Josep Francesc. "Bibliografía teatral catalina," *Estudis Escènics*, No. 26 (1985), 135–42.

Diccionari biogràfic. Barcelona: Alberti, 1966–70. 4 vols. A biographical dictionary for Catalonia. Mainly brief sketches of figures from all periods, including some living persons. There are no bibliographies. "Apèndix," v. 4, pp. 523–83.

Diccionari de la literatura catalana. Barcelona: Edicions 62, 1979. 763p. Alphabetically arranged biobibliographies.

Díez de Revenga, Javier. *Panorama crítico de la Generación de 1927*. Madrid: Editorial Castalia, 1987. 336p. "Bibliografía," pp. 279–311. Includes critical studies on the Generation of 1927 and on the following writers: Salinas, Guillén, Diego, Aleixandre, García Lorca, Dámaso Alonso, Cernuda, and Alberti.

Dölz-Blackburn, Inés. "Recent Critical Bibliography on Women in Hispanic Literature," *Discurso Literario*, 3 (1986), 331–34. Includes works on both Latin American and Spanish literature. Citations are alphabetically arranged. Covers 1970–1985.

Domínguez Lasierra, Juan. "La poesía en Aragón (fuentes generales para una historia literaria aragonesa)," *Turia* (Zaragoza), No. 9 (1988), 178–200.

Eisenberg, D. "Las publicaciones de la Editorial Séneca," *Revista de Literatura*, No. 94 (1985), 267–76. The publishing house, Editorial Séneca of Mexico City which existed from 1939–49, published many works of Spanish exiles. Contents: I. Lista de publicaciones (66 titles alphabetically arranged). II. Indice de traductores, prologuistas, editores, etc. III. Indices por series de Séneca. IV. Indice cronológico.

Falcó, José L., and José V. Selma. *Ultima poesía en Valencia (1974–1983): Estudio y antología*. Cuenca: Institució Alfons el Magnànim, 1985. 510p. (Col•lecció Politècnica, 24). "Apéndice biobibliográfico," pp. 495–501. Biobibliographies arranged chronologically by author's birth date (1932–1959).

Fernández Torres, A. *Cronología impresionista de siete años de teatro (1977–1983)," Insula*, No. 456/57 (1984), 3–4. This article gives a year-by-year breakdown of performances, prizes, and festivals.

Ferraras, Juan Ignacio. *Tendencias de la novela española actual, 1931–1969; Seguidas de un catálogo de urgencia de novelas y novelistas de la posguerra española*. París: Ediciones Hispanoamericanas, 1970. 266p. "Bibliografía," pp. 221–28. Contents: I. Bibliografía general de obras sobre la novela espñol actual. A. Libros. B. Artículos. C. Revistas. D. Cursos policopiados. II. Bibliografía general. "Catálogos de urgencia de novelistas y novelas de la postguerra española (1936–1970)," pp. 229–60. Alphabetically arranged by author and then list of novels.

Fuster, Joan. *Literatura catalana contemporánea*. Madrid: Editorial Nacional, 1975. 447p. Spanish translation of *Literatura catalana contemporània*. Barcelona: Documents de Cultura, 1972. 511p. Critical bibliographies of contemporary Catalan authors appear on pp. 393–441 by author.

Galerstein, Carolyn L., ed. *Women Writers of Spain: An Annotated Bio-Bibliographical Guide*. Non-Castilian Materials Edited by Kathleen Mc Nerney. Westport, Conn.: Greenwood Press, 1986. 389p. (Bibliographies and Indexes in Women Studies, 2). "This volume is intended to familiarize readers, however briefly, with the content and meaning of selected works by 300 women writers of Spain. Writers are entered in alphabetical order, according to the Spanish alphabet, and are provided with succinct biographical data. For each author, major literary works follow alphabetically with selective annotations." Appendix I: Authors by Birthplace. Appendix II: Authors in Catalan. Appendix III: Authors in Galician. Appendix IV: Translated Titles. Appendix V: Title Index.

Gallego Morell, Antonio. *Sesenta escritores granadinos con sus partidas de bautismo*. Granada: Caja General de Ahorros de Granada, 1970. 123p. Biobibliography.

Gallén, Enric. *El teatre a la ciutat de Barcelona durant el règim franquista (1939–1954)*. Barcelona: Editorial 62, 1986. 443p. (Monografies de teatre, 19). "Bibliografía," pp. 431–40. This work also lists plays performed and the companies that performed them.

García de Quevedo y Concellón, Eloy. *De bibliográfico burgense: Disquiciones y apuntes*. Burgos: Tip. "El Monte Carmelo," 1941.

392p. Supplements Licinio Ruiz and Julián García Sáinz de Baranda's *Escritores burgaleses* (1930). Biobibliography of writers from the Province of Burgos.

García Rámila, Ismael. *Bibliografía burgalesa*. Burgos: Institución Fernán González, Academia Burgense de Historia y Bellas Artes, 1961. 384p.

Garmendia, Pedro de: "Indice por orden alfabético de escritores vizcaínos antiguos y modernos," in *La obra de Pedro de Garmendia por Javier de Ybarra y Berge* (Bilbao: La Editorial Vizcaina, 1950), pp. 107–28.

Giralt Raventos, Emili. *La premsa clandestina i de l'exili (1936–1976): Inventari de la col•lecció del Centro de Estudios Históricos Internacionales*. Barcelona: Universidad de Barcelona, 1977. 87p.

Godoy Gallardo, Eduardo. "Indice crítico-bibliográfico del Premio Nadal, 1944–1968," *Mapocho (Santiago de Chile)*, No. 22 (1970), 109–36.

González de Mendoza Mera, Pilar. "Catálogo bibliográfico de la novela española (1960–1980)." Madrid: Universidad Complutense, Departamento de Bibliografía, 1988. 3 vols.

González Muela, Joaquín, and Juan Manuel Rozas, eds. *La generación poética de 1927*. 3a. ed. amp. Madrid: Istmo, 1987. 373p. "Bibliografía," pp. 33–78. Contents: I. Bibliografía general. A. Bibliografía, fuentes y revistas (By year, 1908–84). B. Antologías (By year, 1927–82). C. Estudios (By year, 1929–83). II. Bibliografías particulares (Arranged alphabetically; works by and about the author). Includes 785 total items.

González Rivas, Trinidad. *Escritores malagueños: Estudio bibliográfico*. Prólogo de Alfonso Canales. Málaga: Excma. Diputación Provincial, Gráficas Urania, 1971. 233p. Contents: I. Parte I: A. Bibliografía general sobre la literatura malagueña. B. Revistas literarias. C. Colecciones literarias. II. Parte II: Autores malagueños (Biobibliography). III. Parte III. Indice cronológico. IV. Parte IV: Indice topográfico. V. Parte V: Bibliografía consultada. Instituto Nacional del Libro Español.

"Guideposts to Twentieth Century Spanish Plays in English," *Estreno*, 14 (Fall 1988), 43–48.

Hugult, Damía. *Bibliografia dels escriptors de Campos (1306–1979).* Campos, Mallorca: Ajuntament de Campos, 1980. 83p. Campos, Majorca authors.

Institución "Fernando el Católico. *Biografías aragoneses.* Zaragoza: Institución "Fernando el Católico," 1967. 242p. Chronologically arranged biographies.

Instituto Nacional del Libro Español. *Quién es quién en las letras españolas.* 3.ed. Madrid: Instituto Nacional del Libro Español, Ministerio de Cultura, 1979, 479p. Biobibliographies.

Iribarren, Manuel. *Escritores navarros de ayer y de hoy.* Pamplona: Editorial Gómez, 1970. 223p. (Colección Ipar, 35). The biobibliographical entries are arranged alphabetically by author. A name index completes the work.

Kohut, K., and K. Städtler. "La investigación sobre la literatura española desde 1936 en los países de habla alemana (1974–1984)," *Iberoromania,* 24 (1986), 78–94. Indexes items by author, subject, and writer discussed.

Laurenti, Joseph L. *A Catalog of Spanish Rare Books (1701–1974) in the Library of the University of Illinois and in Selected North American Libraries.* New York: Lang, 1984. 210p.

Lindstrom, Naomi. "Feminist Criticism of Hispanic and Lusophone Literatures: Bibliographic Notes and Considerations," pp. 19–51 in *Cultural and Historical Grounding for Hispanic and Luso-Brazilian Feminist Literary Criticism* (Minneapolis: Institute for the Study of Ideologies and Literature, 1989). The article is a combination of bibliographic essay and listing of feminist sources arranged by anthologies, monographic studies, and journal articles. The entries are divided into Spanish Peninsular, Portuguese, and Latin-American headings under each section.

López de Zuazo Algar, Antonio. *Catálogo de periodistas españoles del siglo XX.* Segunda edición, muy corregida y aumentada. Tomo 1: A–F. Madrid: Fundación Universidad Empresa, 1988. 564p.

McGaha, Michael D. *The Theatre in Madrid during the Second Republic: A Checklist.* London: Grant & Cutler, 1979. 105p. Covers the period April 14, 1931–July 18, 1936. 1258 entries. Contents: I. Chronological List of plays. II. Index of Authors, Translators and

Adapters. III. Index of Titles. Information for each entry includes: Opening date; author's name; title; original performance if appropriate; name of translator and/or adapter when applicable; theatre; company (usually known by the names of the leading actors).

Manent, Albert. *Bibliografía catalana, cap a la represa (1944–1946).* Montserrat: Publicacions de l'Abadia de Montserrat, 1989. 150p. Published in Spain and abroad.

_____. *Josep María de Casacuberta i l'Editorial Barcino.* Barcelona: Associació d'Editions en Llengua Catalana, 1980. 123p. Includes a catalog of the publisher's titles, pp. 45–115.

_____. *La literatura catalana a l'exili.* Barcelona: Curial, 1976. 303p. "Apèndix: Bibliografía de les publicacions catalanes d'exili: 1939–1976," pp. 241–87. Contents: I. Llibres. II. Opuscles. III. Publicacions periòdiques, editades en català, o bilingües, a l'exili (By country).

_____. "La Societat Catalana d'Edicions (1910–1926)," v. 1, pp. 395–99 in *Miscel•lània Aramon i Serra: Estudis de llengua i literatura catalanes offerts a R. Aramon i Serra en el seu setantè aniversari* (Barcelona: Curial, 1979–80). Includes a catalog of the Societat's publications.

Manteiga, Roberto C., Carolyn Galerstein, and Kathleen McNerney, eds. *Feminine Concerns in Contemporary Spanish Fiction by Women.* Potomac: Scripta Humanistica, 1988. 183p. "Bibliography," pp. 169–79. Contents: I. Major Works by Authors Studied in Essays (By author). II. Critical Studies.

Mantero, Manuel. *Poetas españoles de posguerra.* Madrid: Espasa-Calpe, 1986. 580p. "Bibliografía," pp. 545–570. Contents: I. De los poetas. II. Otras fuentes.

Martínez Cachero, J. M. *La novela española entre 1936–1980: Historia de una aventura.* Madrid: Castalia, 1985. 639p. "Bibliografía crítica sobre la novela española entre 1936 y 1980," pp. 481–588. Contents: I. Artículos. II. Folletos y libros. 333 entries alphabetically arranged with descriptive and/or content annotations. Includes a broad subject index.

Martínez de la Fe, Juan A. "Bibliografía de escritores canarios (Tomos I a IV): Indices sistemáticos y de ordenes religiosas," *Boletín Millares Carlo*, 2 (1981), 217–72.

Martínez Morellá, Vicente. *Escritores alicantinos del siglo XX*. Alicante: Impreso en Sucesor de Such, Serra y Compañía, 1963. 108p. Biobibliography.

Mas i Vives, J. "Del realisme narrativ a la diversitat actual: dues generacions de poetes mallorquins (1960–1975)," *Randa* (Barcelona), 13 (1982), 43–136. Contains an excellent bibliography.

Mas Pérez, Mercedes. "De la poesía social y existencial a la renovación de los sesenta: una bibliografía," *Anthropos* (Barcelona), No. 106/107 (1990), 120–27. Contents: I. Autores. II. Antologías. III. Estudios (monographs). IV. Artículos publicados.

Massot i Muntaner, J. "Bibliografia de la cançó popular mallorquina," *Randa*, 12 (1982), 222–35.

Memberg, Nancy Jane Hartley. "The *Teatro por horas*: History, Dynamics and Comprehensive Bibliography of a Madrid Industry, 1867–1922 (*Género chico*; género infimo; and Early Cinema)." Unpublished Ph.D. dissertation, University of California/Santa Barbara, 1987. 1650p. Popular theatre.

Méndez Bejarano, Mario de. *Diccionario de escritores, maestros y oradores nacionales de Sevilla y su actual provincia*. Sevilla: Tip. Gironés, 1922–25. 3 vs. Contents: I. Primera parte: Maestros, escritores y oradores cristianos A-Z. II. Segunda parte: Maestros, escritores y oradores hispano-semitas A-Z. III. Indice por clasificación de los autores por materias. IV. Indice por orden alfabético de pueblos, de los autores no nacidos en la capital. V. Indice de nombres de los autores comprendidos en los apéndices. VI. Indice de nombres de los autores tratados en distintos lugares de este diccionario. Includes 3,830 biobibliographies.

Molina Damiani, Juan Manuel. "Apuntes bibliográficos para el estudio de la poesía giennense de postguerra (1913–1987)," *Boletín del Instituto de Estudios Giennenses* (Jaén), No. 132 (1987), 75–106.

Montes, María José. *La guerra española en la creación literaria (ensayo bibliográfico)*. Madrid: Universidad de Madrid, 1970. 191p. (Anejo de *Cuadernos Bibliográficos de la Guerra de España,*

1936–1939, 2). "Es un completo repertorio del eco obtenido por el hecho bélico en la literatura española de dentro y del exilio, desde los mismos días de la guerra hasta recientemente." "Repertorio bibliográfico," pp. 35–110. Contents: I. Novelas. II. Narraciones, cuentos y novelas cortas. III. Teatro. IV. Poesía. A. Libros. B. Romanceros y antologías. C. Colaboraciones en revistas. V. Literaturas extranjeras. A. Novela. B. Poesía. C. Teatro.

Newberry, Wilma. "Studies Written in English between 1960 and Early 1987 on Post-Civil War Theatre: A Selected Bibliography," pp. 225–48 in Martha T. Halsey and Phyllis Zatlin's *The Contemporary Spanish Theater: A Collection of Critical Essays* (Lanham, Md.: University Press of America, 1988). Contents: I. General Studies. II. Studies on Individual Playwrights (Selected). III. Published and Unpublished English Translations of Post-Civil War Spanish and Catalan Plays (By playwright).

O'Brien, Robert A. *Spanish Plays in English Translation: An Annotated Bibliography*. New York: Las Américas, 1963. 70p. Contents: I. The Early Drama. II. The Golden Age. III. Eighteenth and Nineteenth Centuries. IV. The Modern Period. V. Title Index. Authors and their translated works are arranged chronologically under each of the above headings.

O'Connor, Patricia W. *Dramaturgas españolas de hoy (Una introducción)*. Madrid: Editorial Fundamentos, 1988. 176p. "Indice bio-bibliográfico de los dramaturgas españolas del siglo," pp. 143–76. Includes authors' dramatic works only. Information indexed: date of publication, first performance, and/or written criticism on the play. Partially indexed in this bibliography.

Palau y Dulcet, Antonio. *Manuel del librero hispanoamericano; bibliografía general española e hispano-americana desde la invención de la imprenta hasta nuestros tiempos* . . . 2 ed. Barcelona: Palau, 1949-1977. 28 vols. Contains alphabetical listing of authors by names and titles of works. Complete bibliographical entries.

______. *Indice alfabético de títulos-materias, correciones, conexiones y adiciones del "Manual del Librero Hispanoamericano" de Antonio Palau y Dulcet*. Empúries: Palacete Palau y Dulcet; Oxford: Dolphin Book Co., 1981–87. 7 vols.

Palomo, María del Pilar. *La poesía en el siglo XX (desde 1939)*. Madrid: Taurus, 1988. 221p. (Historia crítica de la Literatura

Hispánica, 21). "La producción poética entre 1930 y 1980," pp. 16–28. Arranged by year and then by author. No publication data are given. "Bibliografía," pp. 211–21. Contents: I. Textos: Antologías. II. Estudios.

Pane, Remigio Ugo. *English Translations from the Spanish, 1484–1943: A Bibliography*. New Brunswick, N.J.: Rutgers University Press, 1944. 218p. Bibliography lists 2,682 items. Arranged alphabetically by author, individual works are entered chronologically according to publication date, except for Cervantes. Title of original work, title of translation, translator, publisher, place of publication, dates of first edition and later editions are given. Additional references and corrections are contained in Ernst Mathew's review of Pane's work, which appeared in the *Journal of English and Germanic Philology*, 44 (1945), 387–424.

Paolini, Gilbert. "A Critical-Bibliographical Essay on the Literary Relations between Italy/Spain and Italy/Spanish-America (1977–1982)," pp. 38–50 in *Papers on Romance Literary Relations Discussed by the Romance Literary Relations Group, Modern Language Association of America, Los Angeles, 1982* (San Antonio, Tex.: Department of Foreign Languages, Trinity University, 1985).

Pariente, Angel, ed. *Antología de la poesía surrealista en lengua española*. Madrid: Júcar, 1985. 466p. (Los poetas, 64/65). "Bibliografía" pp. 441–44. Contents: I. Antologías. II. Estudios ("Se relacionan antologías, artículos, ensayos, etc., que tratan de la poesía surrealista escrita en español.") "Bibliografía de los poetas incluidos en la antología," pp. 71–118. Emphasis on surrealist theme.

Peiró Arroyo, Antonio. *Bibliografía turolense: Libros impresos en la provincia de Teruel (1482–1950)*. Teruel: Instituto de Estudios Turolenses de la Excma. Diputación Provincial de Teruel, adscrito al Consejo Superior de Investigaciones Científicas, 1982. 119p.

Pérez, Janet. *Contemporary Women Writers of Spain*. Boston: Twayne Publishers, 1988. 226p. "Selected Bibliography," pp. 211–17. Contents: I. Primary Works (By author). II. Secondary Works. A. General Works on Spanish Women Writers. B. Women's Studies. C. Essays on Specific Writers.

Pérez Firmat, Gustavo. *Idle Fictions: The Hispanic Vanguard Novel, 1926–34*. Durham, N.C.: Duke University Press, 1982. 174p. "Bibliography," pp. 159–68. Contents: I. Novels (vanguard novels only are listed by author; includes reviews). II. Selected Criticism (Pertinent to the vanguard novel from the period under study).

Pérez Goyena, Antonio. *Ensayo de bibliografía navarra, desde la creación de la imprenta en Pamplona hasta el año 1910.* Pamplona: Diputación Foral de Navarra, C.S.I.C., Institución Príncipe de Viana, 1947–1964. 9 vs. There are 8,627 entries listed chronologically, 1489–1910. A name index concludes the work.

Pérez Rioja, José Antonio. *Bibliografía soriana.* Soria: Centro de Estudios Sorianos, 1975. 199p. "Literatura," pp. 141–54. Contents: I. Obras de carácter general. II. Monografías-artículos. III. Obras de creación: Soria como tema (By author). "Biografía, crítica y genealogía," pp. 53–86. Contents: I. Obras de carácter general. II. Estudios monográficos (A/Z).

______. *La literatura española en su geografía.* Madrid: Tecnos, 1980. 653p. "Bibliografía general: obras de consultadas citadas," pp. 621–28. "Indice antológico (por autores y obras de los fragmentos literarios): seleccionados y sobre las diversas regiones españolas," pp. 629–40.

Pérez-Stansfield, María Pilar. *Direcciones del teatro español de posguerra: Ruptura con el teatro burgués y radicalismo contestatario.* Madrid: José Porrúa Turanzas, 1983. 367p. "Bibliografía," pp. 325–48. Contents: I. Textos. II. Crítica. III. Bibliografía del nuevo teatro español. Number III is arranged alphabetically by playwright and includes published and unpublished plays.

Plá y Cargol, Joaquín. *Biografías de gerundenses (Gerona y sus comarcas).* Gerona: Dalmau Carles Plá, 1948. 329p.

Podol, Peter L., and Federico Pérez-Pineda, comps. "El drama español del siglo XX: Bibliografía selecta del año:
1983: *Estreno*, 11 (otoño 1985), 29–32.
1984: *Estreno*, 12 (otoño 1986), 75–78.
1985: *Estreno*, 13 (otoño 1987), 32–36.
1986: *Estreno*, 14 (Primavera 1988), 59–63, 66.
1987: *Estreno*, 15 (otoño 1989), 29–39.
Contents: I. Textos dramáticos. II. Libros de críticos. III. Artículos y crítica (By author). IV. General.

Ponce de León Freyre, Eduardo, and Florentino Zamora Lucas. *1,500 seudónimos modernos de la literatura española (1900–1942).* Madrid: Instituto Nacional del Libro Español, 1942. 126p. An alphabetical listing, with true name given, followed by reference to publications employing pseudonym. An index of authors, i.e., true names, follows the listing.

Quién es quién en poesía. V. 1: Lenguas de España. Madrid: Asociación Prometeo de Poesía, 1985. 850p. Biobibliographies.

Ramírez de Arellano, Rafael. *Ensayo de un catálogo biográfico de escritores de la provincia y diócesis de Córdoba, con descripción de sus obras*. Madrid: Tip. de la "Revista de Archivos, Bibliotecas y Museos," 1921–22. 2 vs. Volume I: Escritores nacidos en la provincia de Córdoba. Volume II: Escritores que pudieran ser cordobeses pero cuyo patria se ignora. The work's biobibliographical entries are arranged alphabetically by author. An author and anonymous title index concludes the work.

Renedo Martínez, Agustín. *Escritores palentinos (datos bio-bibliográficos)*. Madrid: Imprenta Helénica, 1919–26. 3 vols. Very complete biobibliographical entries are arranged by author.

Resnick, Margery, and Isabelle de Courtiuron. *Women Writers in Translation: Annotated Bibliography, 1945–1982*. New York: Garland, 1984. 272p. English translations of books and pamphlets listed by author. Content annotations. The work includes an author index. "Spain (since 1945)," pp. 211–26.

Rico García, Manuel. *Ensayo biográfico bibliográfico de escritores de Alicante y su provincia*. Edición a cargo de Miguel A. Auladell et al. Alicante: Instituto "Juan Gil-Albert," 1986. 542p. (Recuperación, 7). Biobibliography.

Ríos Ruiz, Manuel. *Diccionario de escritores gaditanos*. Cadiz: Instituto de Estudios Gaditanos. Diputación Provincial, 1973. 217p. An alphabetically arranged biobibliographical dictionary with an author index.

Rodergas i Calmell, Josep. *Els pseudònims usats a Catalunya. Recull de 3.800*. Barcelona: Editorial Millà, 1951. 408p. Contents: I: Pseudònims (Pseudonym first; biobibliographical information follows). II: Index d'autors i llurs pseudònims.

Rogers, Paul Patrick, comp. *The Spanish Drama Collection in the Oberlin College Library, A Descriptive Catalogue*. Oberlin, Ohio:

Oberlin College, 1940. 468p. Coverage is from the last quarter of the seventeenth century to 1924. The 7,530 items are arranged alphabetically by author. Printing, series and performance history annotations are included for almost all entries.

_____. _____. *A Supplementary Volume Containing Reference Lists.* Oberlin, Ohio: Oberlin College, 1946. 157p. Contents: I. Anonymous Plays. II. Title List. III. Composers. IV. Printers. V. List of Theaters and Printing Establishments which appear in the collection.

Rudder, Robert S. *The Literature of Spain in English Translation: A Bibliography.* New York: Ungar, 1975. 637p. Contents: I. Medieval Period. II. Renaissance. III. Golden Age. IV. Eighteenth Century. V. Nineteenth Century. VI. Twentieth Century. VI. Addenda. VII. Frequently Cited Anthologies. VIII. Index to Authors. IX. Index of Anonymous Works. Under each chronological period, arrangement is alphabetical by author and then by original Spanish work. Complete translation information is listed below the Spanish original. However, work must be used with caution due to many incomplete bibliographic citings.

Ruiz, Licinio, and Julián García Sáinz de Baranda. *Escritores burgaleses. Continuación al intento de un "Diccionario biográfico y bibliográfico de autores de la provincia de Burgos de Martínez Añibarro y Ribas."* Alcalá de Henares: Escuela de Reforma, 1930. 641p.

Ruiz Copete, Juan de Dios. *Introducción y proceso a la nueva narrativa andaluza.* Sevilla: Publicaciones de la Excma. Diputación Provincial de Sevilla, 1976. 334p. (Sessión Literatura, Serie 1ª, 6). "Indice bio-bibliográfico," pp. 285–317. Bibliography is arranged alphabetically by author. Each entry includes brief biographical information and listings of the author's *obra narrativa* and/or *otras obras.*

_____. *Poetas de Sevilla de la Generación del 27 a los "taifas" del cincuenta y tantos.* Sevilla: Editorial González Cabañas, 1971. 397p. "Indice biobibliográfico," pp. 373–84. Arranged alphabetically by author. Each entry includes brief biographical information, then listings of the author's *obra poética* and/or *otras obras.*

"Rumbos de la poesía española en los ochenta: Apéndice bibliográfico," *Anales de la Literatura Española Contemporánea,* 9 (1984), 189–96. Alphabetically arranged list of poetry published between

1980 and 1983. 1984 suplemento: *Anales de la Literatura Española Contemporánea*, 10 (1985), 175–80.

Sáinz de Robles, Federico Carlos. *Ensayo de un diccionario de la literatura, 3. ed corr. y aumentada*. Madrid: Aguilar, 1964. 3 vs. Volume 2: Spanish and Hispanic America writers. Alphabetical listing. Each entry contains biographical information, listing of works, and lists other sources for further information.

Salaün, Serge. *La poesía de la guerra de España*. Madrid: Editorial Castalia, 1985. 413p. "Bibliografía," pp. 385–91. Contents: I. Libros poéticos (1936–39) consultados. A. Ediciones españolas. B. Ediciones en catalán. C. Libros poéticos publicados fuera de España. D. Himnos y canciones. E. Teatro en verso. F. Publicado fuera de España. II. Libros poéticos (1936–39) no consultados.

Sánchez Mariana, Manuel. "Repertorios manuscritos de obras y colecciones dramáticas conservadas en la Biblioteca Nacional," pp. 233–58 in *Homenaje a Kurt y Roswitha Reichenberger* (Barcelona: PPU, 1989).

Sánchez Portero, Antonio. *Noticia y antología de poetas bilbilitanos*. Selección y notas de Antonio Sánchez Portero. Calatayud: Imp. Tipo-Línea, 1969. 420p. The volume is a biobibliography of Calatayud poets. It also contains a "bibliografía poética bilbilitana" section.

Sanz García, María del Pilar. "Contribución al diccionario bio-bibliográfico de escritores de Toledo del siglo XX." Memoria de Licenciatura, Departamento de Bibliografía, Universidad Complutense de Madrid, 1976. Published as *Autores toledanos del siglo XX (1900–1980)*. Toledo: Caja de Ahorros, 1983. 239p.

Siebenmann, Gustav. *Los estilos poéticos en España desde 1900*. Madrid: Gredos, 1973. (Biblioteca Románica Hispánica, 2: Estudios y ensayos, 183). "Bibliografía cronológica de los libros de poesía aprecidos entre 1883 y 1971," pp. 491–530. From Salvador Rueda (1857–1933) to Leopoldo María Panero (1948–).

Simón Díaz, José. *Manual de bibliografía de la literatura española*. 3ª edicion ref., corr. y aum. Madrid: Gredos, 1980. 1156p. This is a shorter version of the author's *Bibliografía de la literatura hispánica*, still in progress. Arranged by period, and then by author, the entries include references to bibliographies, editions, criticism, and biographies of the major and secondary writers. General sections refer to studies on genres, periods, and ancillary topics. Bibliography is kept up-to-date by "Información bibliográfica: Literatura castellana," published in *Revista de literatura* (Madrid).

Simón Palmer, María del Carmen. *Manuscritos dramáticos de los siglos XVIII-XX de la Biblioteca del Instituto del Teatro de Barcelona.* Madrid: C.S.I.C., 1979. 248p. (*Cuadernos Bibliográficos*, 39). Manuscripts are arranged by author or anonymous title. Name, first verse, and title indices are included.

Siracusa, Joseph, and Joseph L. Laurenti. *Relaciones literarias entre España e Italia: Ensayo de una bibliografía de literatura comparada.* Boston: G. K. Hall, 1972. 252p. Supplements as: "Literary Relations between Spain and Italy: A Bibliographic Survey of Comparative Literature," *Annali dell' Istituto Universitario Orientale, Sezione Romanze* (Napoli), 19 (1977), 127–99 and *Bulletin of Bibliography*, 40 (1983), 12–39. The book and supplements through 1980 are arranged by critic with an index of Spanish and Italian writers mentioned in the citations. The vast majority of references are unannotated.

Sito Alba, M. "Después de 1936," *Arbor*, No. 488/89 (agosto/setiembre 1986), 117–23. This bibliographic essay lists works by Italian hispanists on postwar Spanish literature.

Soldevila Durante, Ignacio. *La novela desde 1936.* Madrid: Alhambra, 1980. 482p. (Historia de la literatura española actual, 2). "Bibliografía fundamental," pp. 456–70. Contents: I. Libros: obras monográficas de alcance general (By year, 1945–78). II. Manuales. A. Panoramas generales (By year, 1966–78). B. Estudios publicados dentro de libros y revistas (By year, 1948–77). III. Estudios sobre la novela española fueron de España. IV. Estudios sobre la novela de la guerra civil. V. Estudios sobre autores reunidos en volumenes (By year, 1948–76). VI. Estudios sobre aspectos técnicos y formales de la novela (By year, 1968–77). VII. Bibliografías.

Suárez, Constantino. *Escritores y artistas asturianos; índice bio-bibliográfico.* Madrid: Sáez, 1936–59. 7 vs. Imprint varies: Vs. 4–7, Oviedo: Instituto de Estudios Asturianos; "Edición, adiciones y epílogo de José María Martínez Cachero." Comprehensive bio-bibliographies, alphabetically arranged by author. Most entries contain, in addition to biographical sketches, typical bibliographical headings such as "obras publicadas en volumen," "obras inéditas," "trabajos sin formar volumen" and "referencias a biografías." Many illustrations of writers.

Tarragó Pleyán, José Alfonso. *Indice de la bibliografía ilerdense: Ensayo recopilados de libros, folletos, hojas, artículos de publicaciones periódicas y trabajos manuscritos que tratan de la bibliografía ilerdense*. Lérida: Tip. Selecta, 1949. 78p.

Thomas, Gareth. *The Novel of the Spanish Civil War, 1936–1975*. New York: Cambridge University Press, 1990. 273p. "Bibliography," pp. 240–67. Contents: I. Bibliographical Sources. II. Background Reading. III. Novels [Selected] of the Spanish Civil War Arranged by Date of First Publication (1936–1975). IV. Novels [Selected] of the Spanish Civil War, Arranged by Title. V. Books and Articles (General Criticism). VI. Books and Articles [Selected] on Individual Authors.

Thompson, Laurence S. *A Bibliography of Spanish Plays on Microcards*. Hamden, Conn.: Shoe String Press, 1968. 490p. "This bibliography records over 6,000 Spanish, Catalonian, and Spanish-American plays from the sixteenth century to the present, all published in Microcard editions (Compiler's note: now published on microfiche) by Falls City Microcards, Louisville, Kentucky, from 1957 through 1966." The original texts are in the University of Kentucky Library, Lexington. Arrangement is alphabetical by author or by title in the case of anonymous works.

Toth, Jánosné. *Obras traducidas del español al húngaro editadas en Hungría entre 1945 y 1979. Obras traduzidas de portugues ao húngaro editadas na Hungria de 1945 a 1979*. Budapest: Asociación de Editores y Distribuidores de Libros en Hungría, 1980. 154p.

Turkevich, Ludmilla Buketoff. *Spanish Literature in Russia and in the Soviet Union, 1735–1964*. Metuchen, N.J.: Scarecrow Press, 1967. 273p. This study lists the works by Spanish authors available in Russian libraries as well as books, articles, and commentaries about the writers and their books. Arrangement is alphabetical by the names of Spanish authors, and the listings, presented chronologically, include translations and biographical and critical material.

Valdivieso, L. Teresa. "A Bibliography of Catalan Letters Studied in *Insula*," *Butlletí de la North American Catalan Society*, No. 8 (November 1980), 12–19; No. 9 (April 1981), 12–23. Contents: I. General and Miscellaneous. II. Linguistics. III. General Literature.

IV. Drama and Theater. V. Poetry. VI. Prose Fiction (By author; includes reviews and notes; original works). Includes 267 entries, partially annotated.

Vázquez i Estévez, Anna. *Catàleg de manuscrits de teatre en català de l'Institut del Teatre*. Barcelona: Generalitat de Catalunya, Department de Cultura i Mitjans de Comunicació, 1981. 420p. "Comprèn els manuscrits en llengua catalana, des del segle XVII fins ara, que se conservan al fons de la Biblioteca i Museu de l'Institut del Teatre de la Diputació de Barcelona." The catalog includes 2,351 pieces.

Vilches de Frutos, María Francisco. "La generación del nuevo romanticismo: Estudio bibliográfico y crítico (1924–1939)." Unpublished Ph.D. dissertation, Universidad Complutense de Madrid, 1984. 514p. "Ensayo en el que se delimitan los autores que integraron este movimiento . . . , se analizan sus principios estéticos, se explican sus relaciones con los escritores de la 'Deshumanización del arte' y se exponen sus constantes temáticas y estilísticas. Una bibliografía exhaustiva basada principalmente en el estudio de las publicaciones periódicas de la época completa el trabajo."

Woodbridge, Hensley C. "Bibliografía de catálogos de la literatura española en bibliotecas de los Estados Unidos," pp. 659–65 in *Varia Bibliographica: Homenaje a José Simón Díaz* (Kassel: Reichenberger, 1988).

_____. *Spanish and Spanish-American Literature: An Annotated Bibliography to Selected Bibliographies*. New York: The Modern Language Association of America, 1983. 74p. "Spanish Literature," pp. 3–33. Contents: I. Current Bibliographies (Items 1–8). II. Manuals (Items 9–11). III. General Bibliographies (Items 12–14). IV. Twentieth Century (Items 69–73). A. Second Republic (Item 74). B. Franco and Post-Franco Period 1939– (Items 75–93). V. Women Authors (Items 94–95). VI. Translations (Items 99–106). VII. National Bibliography (Items 128–134).

_____. "Spanish Fiction in English Translation: A Bibliography for 1944–1955," *Kentucky Foreign Language Quarterly*, 3 (1956), 197–205. "It is our aim to present notes on translations into English since 1943 of Spanish novels and short stories. Our listing will be by chronological periods rather than alphabetical by author. Our annotations on the writers of the Golden Age will be fuller than on those of today." Contents: I. Fifteenth-Seventeenth Centuries. II. Nineteenth and Twentieth Centuries.

______, and John Dagenais. "A Bibliography of Catalan Belles-Lettres in English Translation," *Scripta Mediterranea*, 4 (1983), 41–70. "Material is arranged alphabetically by the Catalan spelling of the author's name. . . . The most complete entry will include the English title of the translation, the name of the translator, if a book, the place of publication, publisher, date, pagination and the title in Catalan. If an item appears in a journal, the entry will include the title of the journal, volume, complete pagination and date. Under each author, his or her separately published works are listed first, followed by material published in journals, followed by brief excerpts of the author' works." A works-in-progress or press section is included for items after 1982.